Are We On Track To
End Hunger?

HUNGER REPORT 2004

*14th Annual Report on the
State of World Hunger*

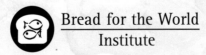

Associate Publisher
International Fund for
Agricultural Development

Bread for the World
Institute

50 F Street, NW, Suite 500
Washington, D.C. 20001
USA

Bread for the World Institute

HD
9000.5
.H815
2004

©2004 by Bread for the World Institute
50 F Street NW, Suite 500
Washington, DC 20001
Telephone: (202) 639-9400   Fax: (202) 639-9401
E-mail: institute@bread.org
Web site: www.bread.org

Printer: HBP, Hagerstown, MD.

Cover photos: Background: IFAD/R. Grossman, Africa: IFAD/A. Conti, Asia: IFAD/A. Hossain,
Latin America: IFAD/G. Bizzarri, North America: USDA photo by Ken Hammond.

Manufactured in the United States of America
First Edition Published in April 2004
ISBN 1-884361-13-7

Table of Contents

Foreword

Thirty years ago, one-third of the world's population was hungry. At the World Food Summit of 1974, the world's leaders agreed that it was possible to end world hunger if they could muster the political will. Bread for the World, a Christian citizens' movement, was organized that year to build U.S. political will to end hunger.

The world has made progress against hunger since then. The proportion of the world's people who are hungry has been reduced to one-sixth. Despite the population explosion, fewer people are hungry now than in 1974. Dramatically fewer children die of preventable causes. Nature-induced famines are a thing of the past.

But progress has been much slower than it could have been. Scandalously, the United States has made little progress against hunger and food insecurity in the last three decades. And hunger now is on the rise in the United States and around the world. A sluggish global economy and an international upsurge in violence are pushing millions of struggling people into hunger and poverty.

Are we on track to end hunger? The answer is a resounding, No. Yet we now know better then ever what to do to end hunger. There is no reason – save politics – that 842 million men, women and children are hungry. Even in a time of economic difficulty and conflict, the world – and certainly the United States – could still be making progress against hunger. What's mainly missing is a stronger commitment.

The report finds that the most direct way to reduce hunger in the United States is to improve and expand the national nutrition programs. The most direct way for the United States to help reduce world hunger is to improve and expand development assistance – the kind of assistance that helps poor countries cope with AIDS or helps subsistence farmers raise their productivity.

A large majority of Americans now favor effective initiatives to reduce hunger. According to recent polls, 94 percent of U.S. voters say it is important to pay for anti-hunger programs in the United States, even in times of budget deficit and economic hardship. Sixty-four percent say the United States has a moral obligation to lead the battle against hunger worldwide.

In this election year, 2004, we urge citizens to vote and work for candidates who are serious about justice for hungry and poor people. This year's U.S. elections are important to hungry people everywhere.

This year is also the 30th anniversary celebration of Bread for the World. For three decades, Bread for the World's grassroots network of concerned citizens and churches has persistently urged their representatives in Washington, D.C., to do their part to reduce hunger. Almost every year, Bread for the World has won significant changes in laws and structures that affect hungry people. We dedicate this anniversary volume to Bread for the World's members.

Yet no one organization can by itself build the political will needed to end hunger. So we also salute our partners – church bodies, charities, a wide array of concerned organizations, and those political leaders who work with us against hunger. We are this year launching the Alliance to End Hunger, a very broad coalition of U.S. institutions committed to building the public will to end hunger.

We also look to God to come to the rescue of hungry people. Ending hunger within the next decade or two remains a very real possibility. That is our prayer.

David Beckmann

Rev. David Beckmann

Rick Reinhard

Introduction

IFAD/A. Conti

Hunger is both unassuming and unpretentious. Perhaps that is why the world does not seem appalled and outraged that it is falling so far behind in the fight against hunger.

Across the world today, at least 842 million people are hungry. That means that for every six people who have enough food to eat, one man, woman or child does not. For Rosalba Garcia Ogarrio, a widow and mother of six who lives in Santa Maria Matagallinas, Mexico, it means, "We seldom have money to buy milk and other nutritious foods. And sometimes I have very little to give to my children," she says.

The first half of the 1990s saw hunger cut by 37 million people, putting the world about one-fifth closer to reaching its goal of cutting hunger in half by 2015. But the world economy since has slowed, and adverse weather and conflicts in Africa and the Middle East have undermined progress for millions more. Now the number of hungry people is rising at a rate of 4.5 million per year. We've lost half of the earlier gains won.

Worse yet, if international communities continue with the attitude of "business as usual," according to the Food and Agriculture Organization of the United Nations (FAO), the number of hungry people worldwide will not be halved until at least 2050.

In the United States, too, hunger and food insecurity are on the rise. Census-based data from the U.S. Department of Agriculture (USDA) show that hunger declined slightly in the late 1990s, but has been increasing since 1999. As of 2002, nearly 35 million people – including 13 million children – live in homes that struggle to put food on the table. Since 1999, the number of children living in homes at risk of hunger has increased by more than 1 million.

Are we on track to end hunger? No. But dramatic progress against hunger still is tantalizingly feasible. Bread for the World Institute's 14th annual report on the state of world hunger explores what has gone wrong and how we can get back on track. It finds that the world community essentially knows what steps must be taken to end hunger: policies that promote economic development generally, coupled with targeted programs to help hungry people feed their families and boost their incomes.

The most direct way for the U.S. government to help reduce hunger in the United States is to improve and expand the federal nutrition programs. Internationally, the government should improve and expand development assistance to help poor people in developing countries.

Hunger in urban areas often is related to a family's inability to buy food. Women living in urban areas tend to work farther from home and often spend more time shopping and preparing food for their families.

But knowing what needs to be done is different from doing it. When we look at why hundreds of millions of men, women and children continue to be without enough food every day, we see that hunger does not have to be a fact of life. Hunger is not an insurmountable food-shortage problem. Hunger is a political problem, and more than anything, an end to hunger will require people and their leaders to demand change.

This year, 2004, is a crucial election year in the United States. We will be choosing leaders who will make important decisions. Instead of debating more tax cuts for the wealthy, U.S. leaders should be working to improve and expand development assistance to poor countries and federal assistance for hungry people in the United States.

It's Been 30 Years

It's been 30 years since the World Food Summit of 1974, when world leaders first committed themselves to end hunger in a decade. Even then, experts agreed that the main obstacle would be political.

Bread for the World also began 30 years ago, inspired in part by the World Food Summit. Rev. Arthur Simon and a group of Protestant and Catholic leaders in New York developed plans for a nationwide Christian citizens' movement against hunger. Their first national outreach in 1974 launched an organization that has won legislative victories for hungry people year after year and now mobilizes about 250,000 letters to Congress annually.

Bread for the World:
30 Years of Seeking Justice, Ending Hunger

Over the last 30 years, the proportion of people in developing countries who are undernourished has declined from about one-third to one-sixth, and the number of hungry people in the world has declined. Based on U.S. poverty data, the percentage of people in the United States who are hungry or food insecure is about the same today as 30 years ago.

Rick Reinhard

1970s

Political Climate

- Nixon, Ford and Carter presidencies
- Leaders gather for the World Food Conference sponsored by the United Nations (1974)
- Bread for the World, some church bodies and other groups organize around hunger (1974)
- U.S. Presidential Commission on World Hunger (1979)

Domestic Win

- U.S. national nutrition safety net expands (food stamps, Special Supplemental Nutrition Program for Women, Infants and Children (WIC) and child nutrition programs)

International Wins

- Congress adopts Bread for the World's Right to Food Resolution (1975)
- Congress creates a farmer-owned grain reserve to aid in international food crises (1977)
- Bread for the World helps secure U.S. support for a new U.N. institution, the International Fund for Agricultural Development

1980s

Political Climate

- Reagan and George H.W. Bush presidencies
- House of Representative Select Committee on Hunger established (1984)

Domestic Loss

- Deep cuts made in U.S. anti-poverty programs (1981)

International Loss

- Cold War priorities distort much development assistance

Domestic Win

- Bread for the World helps build strong bipartisan support for WIC

International Wins

- Congress passes hunger and global security legislation reforming development and food aid (1980)
- Congress requires USAID to target development aid to people living in absolute poverty (1982)
- Congress establishes Child Survival Fund

1. EVERYONE HAS THE RIGHT TO A STANDARD OF LIVING ADEQUATE FOR THE HEALTH AND WELL-BEING OF HIMSELF AND OF HIS FAMILY, INCLUDING FOOD, CLOTHING, HOUSING AND MEDICAL CARE AND NECESSARY SOCIAL SERVICES, AND THE RIGHT TO SECURITY IN THE EVENT OF UNEMPLOYMENT, SICKNESS, DISABILITY, WIDOWHOOD, OLD AGE OR OTHER LACK OF LIVELIHOOD IN CIRCUMSTANCES BEYOND HIS CONTROL.

UN/DPI Photo / Artwork by Brazilian artist Octavio Roth. © Octavio Roth

1990s

Political Climate

- Bush and Clinton presidencies
- U.S. anti-hunger groups agree on Medford Declaration strategy (1992)
- Decade of international conferences:
  World Food Summit: 2015 goal to cut hunger in half set (1996)

Domestic Losses

- Bread for the World's Harvest of Peace campaign tries to shift Cold War funds to human needs (1990)
- U.S. welfare reform made law, cutting $60 billion from nutrition and other programs to help low-income people

International Loss

- Development assistance declines

Domestic Wins

- Every Fifth Child Act helps win nearly $2 billion in increased federal aid to poor mothers and children (1994)
- The U.S. government launches national nutrition monitoring system (1995)

International Wins

- President Bush signs Horn of Africa Recovery and Food Security Act (1992)
- Bread for the World secures commitments to include poor people in World Bank decision making (1997)
- President Clinton signs Africa: Seeds of Hope Act (1998)
- Jubilee Campaign wins $1 billion in international debt relief, leveraging $60 billion in debt forgiveness for the world's poorest countries (1999-2000)

UN/DPI Photo

UN/DPI Photo

New Millennium

Political Climate

- George W. Bush presidency
- International community agrees to comprehensive development strategy and goals – Millennium Development Goals – including cutting hunger in half by 2015
- U.S. anti-hunger groups issue Millennium Declaration to End Hunger in America
- Bread for the World Institute convenes Alliance to End Hunger (2001)

Domestic Win

- Congress restores food stamp benefits for legal immigrants (2002)

International Wins

- Congress passes Africa: Hunger to Harvest resolution and increases annual appropriations for African development by $700 million (2001 and 2002)
- Congress launches Millennium Challenge Account and approves a 33 percent increase in poverty-focused international assistance (2003)

Over the next 30 years, the world's population is expected to grow by 2 billion people. Feeding this growing population and reducing hunger will require increased investment in sustainable rural development and agriculture.

Progress was made. Between the mid-1970s and mid-1990s, the proportion of hungry people in developing countries dropped from about one-third to one-sixth. Despite the population explosion, even the number of hungry people in the world declined slightly. But when the leaders of the world gathered again for the 1996 World Food Summit, they set a more modest goal. Instead of renewing their commitment to end hunger, the nations of the world agreed to cut hunger in half by 2015. That would reduce the number of hungry people in developing countries from about 800 million in 1995 to about 400 million in 2015. But since, the number of hungry people in the world in fact has grown.

The United States Also Is Behind

Subsequently, the U.S. government officially adopted a goal of cutting domestic hunger and food insecurity in half by 2010. However, this goal never has received the high-level political attention it needs. While the United States made some progress against hunger in the late 1990s, for three consecutive years now, food insecurity and hunger have increased. Poverty also is on the rise.

People are considered food insecure and at risk of hunger in the United States when they do not always know where their next meal will come from, or have to cut back on the types and amount of food they eat because they do not have enough money. According to USDA's 2002 food security survey, nearly 35 million Americans live in homes at risk of hunger — about 2 million more than the year before.

Today the U.S. government has less than seven years to fulfill its promise and reduce by approximately 20 million the number of people living in homes at risk of hunger.

This failure to move forward against hunger is incomprehensible. The global economy is producing more than ever before. The United States is wealthier than it ever has been. Yet hunger continues. The world produces food enough for everyone. But inequities at international, national and even family levels prevent millions of people from growing, buying and/or consuming enough food to sustain healthy lives.

The vast majority of poor and hungry people work hard to provide for themselves and their families. They're not looking for a handout. They're seeking dignity and justice for themselves and their children. But this task is nearly impossible for people who are hungry and living in extreme poverty.

A Better Understanding of Hunger . . .

Fortunately, much has been learned about who is hungry, why people are hungry and how they cope. Chapter 1 details many of these specifics and reviews the different ways researchers have and continue to define and measure hunger. Data tables at the end of the report also provide specific information about hunger and poverty around the world and in the United States.

Although much has been learned about hunger and how to measure it and track related trends, gaps remain in our understanding of hunger at its various levels — international, national, community, household and individual — and how they interact.

FIGURE I.1
Number of Undernourished People, 1999-2001 (millions)

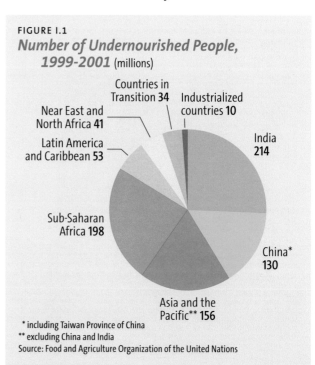

Countries in Transition 34
Industrialized countries 10
Near East and North Africa 41
Latin America and Caribbean 53
India 214
Sub-Saharan Africa 198
China* 130
Asia and the Pacific** 156

* including Taiwan Province of China
** excluding China and India
Source: Food and Agriculture Organization of the United Nations

In the United States, efforts to define and measure hunger culminated in the 1990s with the emergence of USDA's food security measure. Bread for the World played an important role in establishing this measure (see related story, p. 108) Since 1995, USDA has conducted national surveys to count the number of U.S. citizens suffering from food insecurity and hunger.

The 2002 survey shows that the number of hungry and food insecure people in the United States is rising. Chapter 2 takes a closer look at these numbers, noting which U.S. regions and groups of people are suffering the most. The annual collection of official data allows the United States to better gauge its success against hunger and helps citizens hold U.S. leaders accountable.

Even more challenging is measuring the extent of hunger among and within developing countries. Chapter 3 looks at the strengths and weaknesses of the FAO's undernourishment measure. Although researchers have limited information about specific populations and household-level hunger, we know that most of the hungry people in the world live in rural areas. And women, children and the elderly tend to be more vulnerable to hunger than men.

We also know that poverty is directly linked to hunger and that poor populations are at greater risk of going hungry. But not all poor people go hungry, and not all poor countries face food insecurity. As researchers work to understand why, better data and measurements are needed.

... and Poverty

Hunger is part of a dynamic and complex poverty cycle. Hunger can be both a symptom and cause of poverty based on the choices families are forced to make when they do not have enough food and money to make ends meet. In Portland, Ore., a mother may be forced to pay rent and utilities to keep her family off the streets, even if it means skipping meals for a week or two and making due with an emergency food ration from the local food pantry. In Ghana, after a mother cooks the traditional meal of cornmeal and sauce, she

may be forced to serve the handful of carrots and onions to her husband and eldest son because it's harvest time and they need their energy for work in the fields, even if it means her three younger children – the youngest recently weaned – will eat only leftover scraps of cornmeal, lacking both nutrients and calories.

Hunger is one of the most basic threats to human survival. It imperils life, health and our ability to work and think clearly. Yet when people are pushed to poverty's edge, food often is the first thing sacrificed in an effort to hold families and lives together.

Although some countries still struggle with acute food shortages, many more countries grapple with providing people with the jobs they need so they can earn the income necessary to buy their families food.

In the United States, nearly 35 million people – including 13 million children – lived in homes that struggled to put food on the table at some point in 2002.

Margaret W. Nea

Lessons Learned

As seen in Chapter 4, the U.S. government has a crucial role to play in ensuring that no one in the United States is forced to skip meals or go hungry. The U.S. nutrition programs are fairly effective at helping to guard against hunger and move people toward self-sufficiency – but these programs could be improved and expanded. For example, food stamps help buffer people against hunger during a job loss or if they have a low-paying job. Yet barely half of people who are eligible for food stamps actually use them. Cultural and systemic barriers are keeping many people out of this important program. If we are to win the fight against hunger in the United States, we must think more creatively – and inclusively – about how to address some of these problems.

While many charities have expanded their services to help feed hungry Americans, they cannot meet the need alone. Food banks and church pantries cannot provide enough food to the people who come to them and do not reach many of the people who need help, especially in sparsely populated rural areas.

Moreover, if the goal is to help people gain self-sufficiency and climb out of poverty, food is only one of many needs. A single mother in the United States earning twice the minimum wage ($10.30/hour) and

Assessing Progress Toward Ending Hunger in the United States

By Peter Eisinger

Millions of Americans still experience real hunger in the early years of the 21st century, and many millions more live on its very edge, making it from one month to the next only by visiting local emergency food pantries, borrowing from friends and relatives, skipping meals, or even scavenging in the waste bins behind supermarkets.

Such deprivation remains a surprisingly stubborn problem in an otherwise affluent society, so accustomed to agricultural abundance that households, restaurants, food processors and farmers throw away more than a quarter of our food stock every year. Hunger in the United States became a public issue in the 1960s, and the federal government responded with several major policy initiatives, including, among others, the Food Stamp Program (1964); School Breakfasts (1966); the Special Supplemental Nutrition Program for Women, Infants and Children (WIC) (1974); and The Emergency Food Assistance Program (TEFAP) (1983), which provides food to local emergency food providers.

Federal funding for these and other food assistance programs is more than $44 billion annually. In any given year, about one in six Americans is served by one or more of these programs. In addition to these public programs, private religious and secular charitable organizations operate thousands of emergency soup kitchens and food pantries, distributing billions of pounds of food to perhaps as many as 23 million people annually.[1]

Gauging the success of these substantial public and private food assistance programs in reducing hunger has not been a simple task. Although most of these initiatives trace their beginnings back to the 1960s and 1970s, we have only agreed on how to measure and track hunger since 1995. In that year, the U.S. Census Bureau began including in its annual Current Population Survey a series of questions designed to ascertain the prevalence of "food insecurity" among the American public.

"Food insecurity" is a term that encompasses varying degrees of food deprivation caused primarily by lack of money, ranging from being uncertain about the ability to regularly acquire enough food to lead an active and healthy life through conventional means (such as the grocery store or home gardens or food stamp benefits) to being unable to acquire enough food so that one must actually reduce consumption and go hungry. The importance of this concept was (1) that it permitted government analysts and nutritionists to measure the sort of food deprivation found in America rather than the more severe war- or drought-induced malnutrition and starvation typically found in less developed nations; and (2) it permitted the measurement over time of varying degrees of food deprivation.

The short trendline of data on food insecurity in the United States shows scant progress to date. In 1995, the baseline year, 10.3 percent of all households, containing 30.4 million people, were said to suffer some degree of food insecurity.[2] Nearly a third of this total or about 11 million people lived in households that were deemed "food insecure with hunger." Since the Census Bureau gauges the food security status of households rather than individuals, it is not clear that all 11 million people in those households were actually hungry at some point.

While food banks, church pantries and other charities play a critical role in helping to feed hungry people in the United States, they cannot meet the need alone.

After falling slightly during the economic boom of the late 1990s, the rate of overall household food insecurity actually had risen slightly by 2002 from its original baseline to 11.1 percent of all households.[3] The percentage of food insecure households that experienced hunger, however, improved slightly from 3.9 percent of all U.S. households in 1995 to 3.5 percent by 2002. The number of people living in households with hunger had dropped in this seven-year span from 11 million to 9.3 million, of whom less than 1 percent were children. Since parents will go to great lengths to shield their children from the pain of hunger, most of the children in these severely deprived households did eat regularly while their parents or guardians missed meals. But in some households, even this stratagem was not sufficient: the U.S. Department of Agriculture (USDA) estimates that just more than half a million children (567,000) actually went hungry at some time in the year.

Food insecurity is related to poverty, which helps to explain why food insecurity rates rise and fall with the economy. The relationship is not perfect, however: two-thirds of all poor households in 2002 were actually classified as "food secure." Conversely, nearly 10 percent of the households whose earnings were twice the national poverty standard were food insecure.[4] Food insecurity, then, is not related simply to a household's income. Differences in housing costs or medical burdens may account for the differences in food security of two households with similar incomes. Even a household with income well above the poverty line that experiences a temporary setback, such as job loss, death or divorce, easily can fall into the food insecure category if it has no reserve resources. Many households in dire circumstances enroll in federal food assistance programs. If these sources provide sufficient food each month to go along with what the household can afford through its own resources, then the household will be classified as "food secure."

But herein lie two vexing problems: Many food insecure households fail to take advantage of public food assistance, and those that do often find that help inadequate. The USDA's Economic Research Service estimated that in 2002 nearly three-fourths of food insecure households were not enrolled in the Food Stamp Program. Many food insecure households – perhaps four out of five – do not even avail themselves of food from nonprofit food pantries or emergency kitchens.[5] Many factors help to explain why such large numbers of people in food insecure households do not take advantage of ready assistance: pride, lack of information, failure to meet eligibility standards, lack of access, and lack of mobility are among the most important. Even those who do receive aid, however, often find that the food stamps do not assure consistent food supplies. A family with small children receives as much food stamp aid as a family with growing teenagers. In any case, the typical food stamp benefit per person per meal is only around 80 cents.

To make dramatic progress toward reducing food insecurity, which the United States has pledged to cut to half its 1995 level by 2010, we cannot rely on the nonprofit charitable sector. While it fills a crucial gap, it is too small to meet the demand. Instead food stamp benefits must be increased; WIC must be funded as an entitlement program; eligibility restrictions that still remain from the 1996 welfare reform must be eliminated (some were eliminated in the 2002 Farm Bill); and federal summer food programs for children must be substantially expanded.

One hopeful sign is that there is substantial public support for expanded federal programs. A 2003 poll found strong bipartisan support for expanding federal aid of children's food programs and a broad desire among politicians to make hunger abatement a high priority.[6] The fund of political support exists; it simply remains to be tapped.

Dr. Peter Eisinger is a professor of urban politics and economic development policy at Wayne State University who also wrote the 1998 book *Toward an End to Hunger in America*.

[1] Estimates of the number of emergency food providers vary. America's Second Harvest, the nation's largest charitable food organization, estimates that 94,000 soup kitchens, pantries and shelters provide free food to needy people. A recent U.S. Department of Agriculture survey suggests the number is lower, around 38,000.

[2] Mark Nord and Margaret Andrews, "Food Security Is Improving in the United States." Agriculture Information Bulletin Number 765-7, Economic Research Service (ERS), U.S. Department of Agriculture (USDA), April 2001.

[3] Mark Nord, et al., *Household Food Security in the United States, 2002.* ERS, USDA (Washington, DC: USDA) October 2003

[4] Mark Nord and Margaret Andrews, "Reducing Food Insecurity in the United States: Assessing Progress Toward a National Objective." Food Assistance and Nutrition Research Report Number 26-2, ERS, USDA, May 2002.

[5] Nord, *Household Food Security in the United States, 2002.*

[6] America's Second Harvest, "New Bipartisan Poll Finds Hunger is a Powerful Political Issue: Anti-hunger Programs Have Strong Support." Press release, June 5, 2003.

paying $800 a month for housing will have $165 a week (after taxes) for food, clothing, transportation, school supplies and health care for herself and two children. It's not enough. And research shows that often a mother will skip a meal or two a week so her children can eat. In more dire circumstances, she and her family may have to skip one or more meals a week.

To end hunger, the United States must make it possible for everyone to receive a livable income. That requires better education and job opportunities, assistance that helps low-wage workers support their families, and a social safety net for people who cannot work, such as the disabled or elderly.

Similarly, nutrition and agriculture assistance are important for helping hungry people in developing countries, but broad efforts to reduce poverty also are needed. Nutrition assistance is necessary in emergencies and among vulnerable groups, notably pregnant women and small children. But nutrition assistance cannot reach all the undernourished people in developing countries. Most of them live in rural areas, so improving agriculture allows them to grow more food and earn a living. Agriculture and rural development efforts should focus on arid, mountainous and other difficult terrains, where hunger and severe poverty are concentrated. Broader efforts to reduce poverty – better education and health care, economic growth, and improved governance – also are important to fighting world hunger.

Widespread hunger impairs the economic performance not only of individuals and families, but also countries. Policies to eradicate hunger go hand in hand with those to reduce poverty.

Making Progress in the New Millennium By Pursuing the MDGs

By Eveline Herfkens

In September 2000, nearly 200 heads of state and government gathered at the U.N. Millennium Summit and firmly committed their countries—rich and poor—to a set of time-bound and measurable goals to combat poverty in all its forms by 2015. Among these countries was the United States. Here, President Bush signed the Millennium Declaration and reaffirmed the commitment of his country "to bring hope and opportunity to the world's poorest people." He called for a new compact for development "defined by greater accountability for rich and poor nations alike" and proposed the Millennium Challenge Account (MCA) devoted to projects in developing nations that govern justly, invest in their people and encourage economic freedom.

The MCA is a welcome and groundbreaking initiative that if fully funded by Congress will focus aid on growth and poverty reduction and provide the largest boost in U.S. development assistance since the Marshall Plan, with a $5 billion annual increase in foreign assistance levels. Today the United States ranks at the absolute bottom of all 22 rich countries when it comes to development assistance. Despite this ranking, polls indicate that most Americans believe that 17 percent of the overall budget goes to foreign aid when in fact the United States spends less than 1 percent on official development assistance. This disconnect underscores the need for continued efforts to address the enormous disparity between American public attitudes on foreign aid and actual government policy.

To that end, Bread for the World is playing a leading advocacy role on a number of issues, including incredible work on debt relief, hunger and the MCA. I am particularly impressed by Bread for the World's efforts to mobilize Americans to call members of Congress and urge them to approve $1.3 billion for the MCA, without taking money from existing development assistance or HIV/AIDS initiatives. By advocating for the compatibility of the MCA and Millennium Development Goals (MDGs), Bread for the World and others will help hold their government accountable to its pledges.

The central and most important component of the MDGs is the partnership for development—expressed in Goal 8. It explicitly recognizes that eradicating worldwide poverty can be achieved only through a global partnership for development and through increased action by developing countries. Terms for this unprecedented compact based on mutual accountability between rich and poor countries were further advanced in the Monterrey Consensus that emerged from the International Conference on Financing for Development, at the Johannesburg Summit and at the recent G-8 meeting in France.

Developing country leaders are tasked with the responsibility to steer their country's own progress; they pledge to good governance, greater accountability and efficient use of resources and sustained social, political and economic reform. To that end, developing countries are primarily responsible for achieving the first seven goals while the rich countries promise to provide more aid, deliver more meaningful debt relief and increase access to trade for poor countries that demonstrate good faith efforts to meet their pledges.

It is of critical importance for developed countries to deliver on Goal 8 well in advance of 2015, if poor countries are to have any chance of realizing the first seven goals. Reforms of the policies in industrialized countries – specifically on aid, debt and trade – will directly provide the resources to strengthen the capacity of developing country governments to implement pro-poor policies needed to achieve the MDGs.

Three-quarters of the world's poor – about 900 million people – live in rural areas, most of them as small farmers. The agriculture sector – employing well over half the rural population – can potentially be a key engine for economic growth in many poor countries. But industrialized country agricultural policies, specifically those of the United States and European Union, are destroying the markets on which developing countries most depend. Bread for the World continues to be on the forefront of educating Americans about the negative impact of agricultural subsidies on the poorest countries. Rich countries, to varying degrees, grant large agricultural subsidies to their domestic food producers, totaling $311 billion a year – more than the income of

Margaret W. Nea

Most farmers in Africa are women, who balance their farm activities with a range of other responsibilities related to feeding the family, such as collecting wood for fuel, fetching water and cooking.

half the world's population. These subsidies depress world prices, lead to worldwide overproduction, hinder poor farmers' access to rich consumer markets, flood domestic poor country markets with low-cost foreign surplus, undermine incentives for local production and impoverish millions of smallholder farmers and their communities in the developing world.

Despite these obstacles, the past 30 years have seen some improvements in the developing world. Life expectancy has increased from 43 years to 51 years; literacy increased by nearly one half; and the share of people suffering from extreme poverty fell from 30 percent to 20 percent in the 1990s, largely the result of progress in China and India. But still, a staggering 1.2 billion people – one in every six on earth – live on less than $1 a day, and the majority live in sub-Saharan Africa.

That so many countries around the world will fall far short of the MDGs in the 12 years to 2015 points to an urgent need to change course. Achieving the goals requires national ownership and action by individual governments and communities worldwide. The goals are achievable – we have the resources, technology and know-how – but reaching them will require additional political will.

To this end, I have been asked by U.N. Secretary-General Kofi Annan to lead efforts in a global campaign to generate support and political will for the MDGs. Rich and poor country leaders need to sustain the political will demonstrated by their pledges and this will only be possible when citizens and electorates demand from their politicians needed action and reform.

It is time to move from rhetoric to action, from goals set to goals met. Otherwise the legacy of this generation will be another series of broken promises, with disastrous consequences for the world's poorest and most vulnerable citizens. In short, it was U.S Treasury Secretary John Snow who said, "Developed and developing countries, together with the international financial institutions, must redouble their efforts toward achieving these goals."

The MDGs are the ultimate bottom-up, grassroots and pocket-book development agenda, firmly focused on the bread and butter of political life everywhere. It is only with groups like Bread for the World holding governments accountable and sustaining the political will necessary that we have a chance to achieve the 2015 deadline.

Eveline Herfkens is the U.N. Secretary-General's executive coordinator of the Millennium Development Goals Campaign.

Supporting agriculture, rural development and nutrition are especially important to reducing hunger. But other social and economic factors are crucial as well, such as ensuring that all boys and girls worldwide complete a full course of primary schooling.

Fortunately, as described in Chapter 5, the international community – including the United States – has adopted a new framework for designing and implementing development programs. This framework, called the Millennium Development Goals (MDGs), is a set of eight measurable, achievable international goals that put the target of reducing hunger within the context of poverty and other social issues. This integrated approach makes sense. Agriculture, rural development and nutrition are especially important to reducing hunger. But other aspects of social and economic development also are crucial.

As a group, developing countries have agreed they need to improve governance and focus on reducing poverty, hunger and disease. The industrialized countries, as a group, have agreed to increase development assistance and, in other ways, support progress toward the MDGs. Yet development assistance declined in the 1990s. In sub-Saharan Africa, where one in three people is malnourished and about half the people lives on less than $1 a day, assistance levels dropped by nearly a third.

While no one knows exactly how much it will cost to reduce hunger, it certainly will require more development assistance than is being provided. The FAO estimates that cutting hunger in half by 2015 would require an additional $8 billion a year in international assistance for agriculture and nutrition. The U.S. share would probably be less than $2 billion.

The World Bank estimates that meeting all the MDGs would require an additional $50 billion in annual funding for development assistance – with the United States contributing about a fourth of that amount. The U.N. Development Program says that this figure is conservative and is developing a new estimate.

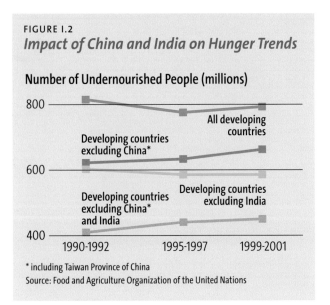

FIGURE I.2

Impact of China and India on Hunger Trends

Number of Undernourished People (millions)

800

All developing
countries

Developing countries
excluding China*

600

Developing countries
excluding China*
and India

Developing countries
excluding India

400

1990-1992   1995-1997   1999-2001

* including Taiwan Province of China
Source: Food and Agriculture Organization of the United Nations

Aid also can be made more effective, mainly by targeting more of it to help the people most in need. The industrialized countries also should help in other ways, mainly by reforming agriculture policies and changing trade rules to provide more opportunities for poor people in developing countries.

We Can Do Better

Ending hunger is both a credible and achievable goal that has been a priority for many individuals and organizations over many years. We know we can end hunger today if we just garner the leadership and political will of people to do so. Because hunger remains primarily a political problem, Chapter 6 explores how politics has helped and hurt efforts to reduce hunger and poverty, and Chapter 7 suggests ways in which people can get involved to make hunger a political priority.

A few positive signs are emerging on the political front. Internationally, a handful of countries are making serious efforts to end hunger. In Brazil, Luiz Inácio Lula da Silva won the presidency on a hunger platform, promising to eradicate hunger before his term's end. In the United States, polls continue to show that a large majority of likely voters support effective efforts to reduce hunger domestically and worldwide.

Who Is Responsible?

The United States exerts more influence in the world than any other nation, yet is one of the least forthcoming of the industrialized countries in its politics and policies toward poor and hungry people within its borders and worldwide. If the world is to end widespread hunger, U.S. politics and policies must change.

If you are reading this report, you already have demonstrated exceptional interest in ending hunger.

Getting back on track to end hunger depends largely on what you and other people do to build the needed political commitment. Nearly three in four likely voters say that the issue of hunger is important to them in deciding how they vote. More than half of U.S. voters say the government is not spending enough to fight hunger. Many Americans are concerned that guaranteed social programs are wasteful or create dependency. But four out of five potential voters respond favorably to proposals that would both reform and expand anti-hunger programs.

Yet ending hunger is not anywhere near the top of the president's or Congress' to-do list. Instead, programs that help low-income families remain at or near the top of the list for funding cuts when budgets get tight. On the international front, the United States gives less in development assistance – as a share of gross domestic product – than any other rich country.

More Than Words

Ultimately, any decision to place food on the table rests with each of us. And this responsibility extends to poor and hungry people as well, though their task is not as easy. People often are so burdened by hunger and poverty, they do not have the time or energy to participate, much less organize and petition governments for change. In the United States, less than half of low-income voters typically turn out for presidential elections.

Margaret W. Nea

In addition to cutting hunger in half by 2015, the Millennium Development Goals call for reducing by two-thirds the mortality rate of children younger than age 5.

Hunger is growing at a rate of 4.5 million people each year. According to the Food and Agriculture Organization of the United Nations, if the world continues with "business as usual," hunger will not be halved until at least 2050.

Hungry and poor people rarely even speak about their experience. Few hungry people will tell a stranger, "I am hungry." And fewer still can describe the way hunger erodes the quality of their daily lives. For them, words and language are not a useful, powerful means for changing or even expressing their lives. Urgency is what moves them from one meal to the next, one rent payment to the next, one harvest to the next.

Still, the words are there for those who would see them. They are in the look of a hungry child's listless stare or his mother's anxious glance as she searches for firewood, not to cook with, but to sell. The words are in a little girl standing near furniture piled on the sidewalk after her family has been evicted, or a husband and wife who barely see each other because both work opposite shifts so someone is always home to take care of the children.

Academics, politicians and even advocates are the ones anxious to assign words to the experience, to bring order to the confusion and anguish of poverty and hunger. They are the ones eager to complete hunger's language with definitions and technical terms. But in doing so, we risk oversimplifying the murky interplay among personal dilemma, tragedy and responsibility. We risk obscuring the urgency of change.

People have become so absorbed in sorting out others' mistakes and rearranging the blame for why "they," and not "us" are limited by hunger and poverty that the public has lost site of the cruel hand of fate that most often decides who lives certain lives, who suffers certain atrocities while other people wake every morning healthy and whole.

For Rosalba, the widow and mother of six who lives in Santa Maria Matagallinas, Mexico, there is no blame. She may not always be able to feed her children, but she blames no one. She knows that her dreams of studying to become a secretary so she can provide a better life for her children are unlikely. Still she blames no one.

"We don't have any grandiose expectations for our future," Rosalba says. "We simply want our government to do more to improve our lives, perhaps by creating more jobs."

Rosalba, like most poor and hungry people, knows what she and her family needs. She's willing to work hard to secure it. But alone she cannot change the economic and political structures working against her. We must join Rosalba in her struggle, make her daily realities are own, and demand – person to person, community to community, nation to nation – an end to hunger.

CHAPTER 1

Hunger
Basics

IFAD/G. Bizzarri

Hunger is difficult to define and difficult to see, and for these reason, can be difficult to understand. It doesn't help that hunger is a word that is thrown around casually today, and oftentimes has nothing to do with food. An athlete hungers for a championship. A child hungers for affection, or an employee hungers for a promotion. These words and images can trivialize the very real impact hunger has on people's lives.

Most people recall a time when they skipped a meal or worked late and were reminded of that fact by their stomach's unpleasant rumblings. This temporary, fleeting sensation is what many people think of when they hear the word "hunger." Most people know from personal experience that even mild hunger is disagreeable and can make them grumpy and unable to concentrate. But when academics, politicians and advocates talk about helping people, they are talking about more severe and sustained hunger.

At its most basic, hunger is the lack of enough food to live a healthy and productive life. It is involuntary and for many people persists over time. "There is no way to get used to hunger," says Adilesi Faisoni, who lives in Malawi where for many people finding enough to eat can be a daily struggle.[1] "All the time something is moving in your stomach," she says. "You feel the emptiness. You feel your intestines moving. They are too empty, and they are searching for something to fill up on."

At its most extreme, hunger claims lives. Adilesi lost both her husband and daughter to hunger in 2003. Her elderly husband, Robert Mkulumimba, and adult daughter, Mdati Robert, died within a month of each other because they were unable to subsist on pumpkin leaves and wild vegetables – the family's only nourishment during the months of December to March when Malawi suffers a food shortage every year.

"There is no way to get used to hunger," says Adilesi Faisoni, who lives in Malawi where for many people finding enough to eat can be a daily struggle. "All the time something is moving in your stomach. You feel the emptiness."

In between these most basic and extreme forms, hunger wears away at varying degrees people's health, productivity, sense of hope and overall well-being. A lack of food can cause confusion, slow thinking, sap energy, stunt growth, hinder fetal development and contribute to mental retardation. Socially, the lack of food erodes relationships and feeds shame. Economically, the constant securing of food consumes people's time and energy, leaving little more for escaping poverty.

Celia Escudero-Espadas

Reducing world hunger not only will require improved agriculture and food systems, but also improvements in poverty, education, health, water and the empowerment of poor people, especially women.

High Costs

People and communities living with hunger pay the highest price, but hunger's costs eventually cheat everyone. Poor nutrition and calorie deficiencies cause nearly one in three people to die prematurely or have disabilities, according to the World Health Organization (WHO).[2] The toll is even higher for children. Every year, 6 million children younger than 5 die of malnutrition and hunger-related causes, according to the Food and Agriculture Organization of the United Nations (FAO).[3] Other studies report more than half of childhood deaths resulting from malnutrition.

The direct economic cost associated with this lost potential is hard to comprehend, much less measure. The FAO estimates that cutting the number of hungry people in half by 2015 would yield more than $120 billion.[4] This figure reflects the economic impact of longer, healthier and more productive lives. It also reflects the inherent injustice of a food system that provides more than enough for some people, leaving others with less. Such injustice can breed instability and discontent, factors made more poignant after the terrorist attacks of Sept. 11, 2001.

More than a queasy, unpleasant feeling or a distant problem that affects only poor, developing countries, hunger is an economic and political problem that in some way touches everyone.

Hunger, Poverty in Oaxaca, Mexico Are the Rule, Not the Exception

During a trip to an indigenous community in the southern mountains of Oaxaca, Mexico, Rev. Octavio Hernádez Miranda, associate pastor of the Iglesia Nacional Presbiteriana San Pablo in Oaxaca City, took time to chat with Rosalba Garcia Ogarrio and her family to gather their impressions about how poverty affects their lives. According to the Fundaci's Comunitaria Oaxaca, 70 percent of the state's 3.5 million residents live in poverty and a full third of the population suffers from extreme poverty (living on less than $1 a day). Oaxaca is Mexico's second-poorest state, with extreme poverty prevalent primarily in indigenous communities.

My name is Rosalba Garcia Ogarrio, a widow and mother of six. I live in Santa Maria Matagallinas, one of several poor communities nestled in the southern Sierras of Oaxaca. Our village is a three-hour drive from the City of Oaxaca. We are of Zapotec origin, like most families who live in our village and nearby communities.[1]

Our family struggles to make ends meet, but we are the rule not the exception. We seldom have money to buy milk and other nutritious foods, and sometimes I have very little food to give to my children. All I can give them on those occasions is a type of cinnamon tea to fill their stomachs.[2]

But we do not face this type of hunger every day. More often than not, we are able to put together a meal of tortillas and beans, and occasionally we may have eggs from the four chickens we own.

I know that this lack of nutrition is the reason why my children have become so vulnerable to chicken pox and other diseases. But the only place I can take my children when they get sick is the government health center, which is a 30-minute walk from our village.

When my husband died 16 months ago, I was left as head of my household. Many families in my village and nearby villages are headed by a mother.[3]

At least my neighbors hold the hope of seeing their husbands and often receive letters and money from the United States. I am not so lucky. My husband, the driver for the only public bus in our community, was murdered early last year in a revenge killing. My youngest child, Antonio Abisaid, was only 2 months old when his father died.

In a sense I am lucky that my grown children are able to help out in many ways. My eldest daughter, Marilu, who is 18, left our village to work as a maid for a rich family in Oaxaca City. We supplement the money that Marilu brings us with a few pesos that other families in the village give me for helping with the tedious work of separating the corn kernels from the cobs to make corn meal. More often than not, my neighbors pay me in corn because they have no money. We also receive about $20 once every two months through a government program called Oportunidades, and sometimes my late husband's brother will send us a bit of money from California.

With my husband's death, my 14-year-old son, Alvaro, was left with all the responsibilities of being the man of the house. He dropped out of middle school three months ago so he could devote his full attention to cultivating our corn and bean crops on the 1-hectare plot (2.47 acres) left by his father. This is an important job because we rely on these basic staples to put food on our table. Since we lack water for irrigation, we

These three children live in Santa Maria Matagallinas, about a three-hour drive from Oaxaca. The city of Oaxaca is Mexico's second poorest, with one of the highest number of indigenous people. According to the Ministry of Health, in this area more than two of every five children between the ages of 6 and 9 are malnourished.

often have to pray for a normal rainy season. Sometimes drought is not the problem but too much rain, especially during the hurricane season.

With Marilu gone six days a week, I rely on Celiflora, 16, Narceralia, 12, and Arilda, 8, to help with the chores around the house when they are not in school. They take care of the chickens, wash the clothes in the river, and carry water back from the community well (which is a 15-minute walk from the house). Celiflora will complete high school soon, but her options are limited. Most probably she will go to Oaxaca City to work as a maid like her sister Marilu.

Our house is humble like the rest of the dwellings in our village. We live in a small single-room house roughly 3 meters by 4 meters (9 feet by 13 feet), with tin walls and a tin roof that are held together by wooden posts. We do all our cooking outside in a griddle called a comal.

Believe it or not, we are fortunate to have electricity in our dwelling, although obviously we do not have running water. Every third day we wash our clothes and bathe in the river, which is 30 minutes away.

Our home lacks basic plumbing. We have a septic tank in the back, which we use as bathroom (and is also enclosed by tin and wooden posts).

We don't have any grandiose expectations for our future. We simply want our government to do more to improve our lives, perhaps by creating more jobs. Our mayor could also be very helpful in pushing to obtain more resources for the needy in our community.

I would some day like to take some personal steps to improve my life, including the opportunity to study and train to become a secretary.

Carlos Navarro, a former Bread for the World board member and currently editor/writer of the weekly online newsletter SourceMex at the Latin America Data Base (University of New México), contributed to the research included in the narrative.

[1] According to the government's statistics agency, Instituto Nacional de Estadistica Geografia e Informatica (INEGI), more than 68 percent of the population of Mexico is of indigenous origin, with the Zapotecs and Mixtecs as the two major groups.

[2] According to the Oaxaca Health Ministry, 42 percent of the children in the state who are between ages 6 and 9 are malnourished.

[3] More women head households in Mexico because seven men out of every 10 from rural Oaxaca leave their communities to try to find employment in the United States. They can find no jobs in Oaxaca and few jobs elsewhere in the country, according to INEGI.

Difficult to Define

The first step in solving any problem is to define it. As the global community has gained a better understanding of hunger, distinctions have developed to explain various aspects of the problem. Hunger has social, economic and political facets, each with corresponding causes and consequences. Together, these dimensions reveal a sequence of events and pattern of increasing vulnerability that can lead to ever more severe degrees of hunger and poverty.

Food is one of the most basic human needs. Because it sustains life, the stress and anxiety of not knowing where the next meal comes from creates a sense of vulnerability, insecurity. Indeed, the term "food security" has become a common way to talk about hunger-related issues. The FAO defines food security as people having at all times "physical and economic access to sufficient, safe and nutritious food to meet their dietary needs and food preferences for an active and healthy life."[5]

The comfort of knowing where the next meal comes from plays a large part in defining people's sense of worth and well-being. Poor people in Kaoseng, Thailand, describe being poor as "find in morning, eat in evening" because they "buy food day by day."[6] A group of men in Dobile Yirkpong, Ghana, describe the connection between hunger and well-being this way: "Food is life and . . . no hungry man can claim to have a good life."[7]

Celia Escudero-Espadas

Approximately 60 percent of deaths of children younger than 5 are associated with undernutrition (e.g., pneumonia, diarrhea, malaria, measles and HIV/AIDS). This means that every minute about 11 children younger than 5 are dying of hunger-related causes.

Key Hunger Terms

Key Terms	Definition
Hunger	A condition in which people do not get enough food to provide the nutrients (carbohydrates, fats, proteins, vitamins, minerals and water) for active and healthy lives.
Malnutrition	A condition resulting from inadequate consumption (undernutrition) or excessive consumption of one or more nutrients that can impair physical and mental health, and cause or be the consequence of infectious disease.
Undernutrition	A condition resulting from inadequate consumption of calories, protein and/or nutrients to meet the basic physical requirements for an active and healthy life.
Food Insecurity	A condition of uncertain availability of or ability to acquire safe, nutritious food in a socially acceptable way.
Food Security	Assured access for every person to enough nutritious food to sustain an active and healthy life, including: food availability (adequate food supply); food access (people can get to food); and appropriate food use (the body's absorption of essential nutrients).

The connection between hunger and poverty are strong worldwide, and the causes and effects of both are intricately linked. Poverty leaves people financially strapped and often unable to buy food, which both causes and perpetuates hunger. Meanwhile hunger and poor nutrition increase people's chances of becoming sick and less productive, undermining their ability to work, leading them into deeper poverty. Poor people also usually lack assets, increasing the risk of becoming hungry. Without assets, people are less able to withstand temporary economic shocks, such as poor weather that undermines a harvest or a debilitating illness that prevents a family breadwinner from working. Moreover, because people trapped in poverty spend more of their time, energy and income on securing food, they are less able to save and invest in ways that allow them to rise above poverty. These hunger and poverty cycles overlap and build on each other, severely limiting people's lives and opportunities.

Difficult to Measure

Hunger in many ways is the severest form of poverty. Because people must eat to survive, they will sacrifice many needs – clothes, shelter, transportation – before they surrender to hunger. Though poverty and hunger are not direct measures of the other, they are closely related. Shifts and trends in poverty often foretell similar changes in hunger. The past few years have seen poverty rise both worldwide and within the United States. Not surprisingly, hunger also has been on the rise.

The most widely accepted measure of world hunger is the FAO undernourishment measure, which considers the amount of food available per person in a country as well as the extent to which he or she is able to access that food. Using a calculation based on population, income, food distribution and the total amount of food calories available in a country, the FAO determines how many people consume less than 1,800 calories per day – its measure for undernourishment. Take Mozambique. With a population of 18.3 million and a per person calorie supply of 1,950, one could conclude that the country is food secure and everyone has enough to eat. But the FAO considers the fact that two-thirds of the population lives in poverty and likely cannot afford everything it needs. Using what the FAO knows about income distribution, it determines food distribution patterns as well. For Mozambique, FAO concludes that about half the population consumes less than 1,800 calories per day, giving the country an undernourishment count of 9.7 million people.

Many rural communities in developing countries face serious water shortages, both for drinking and agriculture. In Africa, where only 4 percent of cropland is irrigated, small-scale irrigation and rainwater harvesting projects can increase agriculture productivity greatly.

FIGURE 1.1
The Rate of Hunger Is Highest in Africa, But the Number of Hungry People Is Highest in India

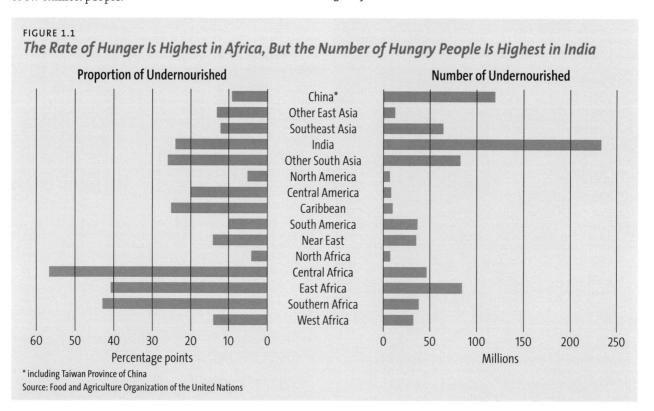

* including Taiwan Province of China

Source: Food and Agriculture Organization of the United Nations

Worldwide, the most recent FAO estimates put the number of hungry people at 842 million. Most hungry people (798 million) live in developing countries; 34 million hungry people live in transitional countries, and 10 million live in industrialized countries.

The FAO publishes these results every year, though the data reflect two-year intervals at two-year lags. For example, the most recent 2003 report compares data gathered between 1999 and 2001. Unfortunately, the time lag creates delays in assessing the impact of sudden changes in populations experiencing or at-risk of hunger. As such, it has been only since the 2003 report that the world community as seen evidence that hunger has been increasing since 1998. Moreover, the 1999-2001 data may not yet fully reflect the food shortages and famines occurring today in North Korea and Southern Africa.

Because FAO data depend largely on national food availability and not the quantity of food reaching and being consumed by people, some researchers are calling for improved methods. Lisa Smith, a researcher at the International Food Policy Research Institute, notes that the FAO measure fails to adequately reflect poverty's strong influence on food security. "For most countries, the biggest food security challenge is not assuring adequate food availability," she says, "but assuring people have access to food."[8]

Understanding Food Availability, Access and Use

Fighting hunger is not just about supplying countries in need with food or the money to buy food, but also ensuring that hungry people have access to this food and can use it to nourish their bodies. As such, researchers, policymakers and advocates think of hunger and food security in terms of food availability, access and use. It may be useful to think of these concepts as forming a "food security tripod" – if any one leg is missing, then the whole collapses.

Food Availability

"Availability" refers to communities and countries having enough food. In parts of the world, some countries do not produce enough food to feed their people,

and they are too poor to buy food from other countries. These food-deficit countries have food availability problems. The most common examples are countries embroiled in famine or war. But food shortages can occur for other reasons as well, including poor crop years or even bad weather that washes out roads from farms to marketplaces.

In most of these cases, emergency food aid programs, such as those run through the U.N. World Food Program, assist with the purchase and delivery of food.

Access

"Access" refers to the ability of a household to physically acquire food. Most people must buy food. If they do not have access to enough money or the markets where food is sold, then they have food access problems. For the 1.2 billion people who live on less than $1 a day, access to even cheap food can be difficult.[9] Other access barriers range from poor infrastructure and lack of transportation to illness and family structure. For example, HIV/AIDS or malaria may incapacitate a family's breadwinner, leaving him or her with no money to buy food. A family's car may breakdown or a family may not be able to afford gas one week, leaving no way to travel to a market or town.

Within a household, certain family members often are more vulnerable to hunger than others. In some cultures, the men eat first, then the women and finally the children. Because of limited food availability, the younger children, especially girls, may be fed meals that have been picked over by those with a higher status, putting them at greater risk for undernutrition and hunger.

Celia Escudero-Espadas

Hunger and poverty are intricately linked. Families must balance the costs of basic needs such as food, clothing, shelter and transportation to survive. And when budgets get tight, families often first cut back on the amount or quality of food they eat.

Hunger Seasons

Food availability and access often are interrelated, especially in rural communities. Rural people primarily rely on agriculture for both food supply and income, and its seasonality and unpredictability greatly impact whether they experience food shortages. Many rural farming families do not produce enough food to meet their needs throughout an entire year. And even when

Hunger Hotspots Threaten Lives of Millions in 2003

By Margaret Zeigler

Despite an abundance of food in the world during 2003, more than 840 million men, women and children faced chronic hunger. Included among these 840 million hungry people are those many millions impacted by war, extreme drought and economic shocks that have combined to create hunger hotspots or zones of acute crisis requiring outside humanitarian assistance.

The most severe humanitarian emergencies during 2003 occurred in countries across the world, in which millions of people required food aid, health and shelter services, and protection from violence and war (see Table 1.1, p. 23). Hunger hotspots facing the world today remain in Eastern Africa (the Horn of Africa), Southern Africa, North Korea, Afghanistan and Iraq, with significant regions of hunger in Central America as well. But it is the Iraq crisis that has dominated the media and has excluded other hotspots from public view. The international community has been preoccupied with Iraq and has done relatively little to provide aid and help negotiate peace in trouble spots such as the Democratic Republic of the Congo. This is one reason why world hunger now is increasing.

Iraq: History's Largest Food Pipeline

One of the largest emergency food operations in history was established after the United States and allied coalition forces entered Iraq in March 2003. For the U.N. World Food Program (WFP), the operation to supply food in Iraq was the largest in its history, requiring $1.3 billion to support a public food distribution system for some 27 million people from March 2003 through September 2003. WFP had operated a public food distribution system entitled "Oil for Food" during the economic sanctions against Iraq in the 1990s. After the fall of the Baathist regime in March 2003, the public distribution system was re-established during the late spring and early summer months of 2003, reaching nearly 60 percent of the total population of 27 million Iraqis by the summer. WFP operated this system with the assistance of Iraqi nationals and international donors to bring flour, cooking oil and other food products into the country.

During 2003, the humanitarian community feared that the large costs of assistance and attention focused on Iraq would divert resources from other crises. Historically, levels of response to U.N. humanitarian appeals have registered an average of 33 percent, and this same level appears to have held true in 2003, despite the focus on Iraq.[1] But the trend to only partially fund U.N. appeals continues, as does the trend to rely on food aid over other forms of assistance. Donors continue to be generous with food aid, but tend to supply less of the cash needed for improvements in water and health sectors.

Africa: Region of Crisis and Hope

Africa contains a cluster of hunger hotspots, with some 40 million men, women and children facing food emergencies in 2003. The largest hunger hotspot is centered in the Horn of Africa, consisting of Ethiopia, Eritrea and parts of Somalia, with more than 16 million people requiring emergency food aid and other humanitarian assistance during 2003 and into 2004. Most of Ethiopia's and Eritrea's farmers rely on rain for

Mothers are sitting with their children in a therapeutic feeding center in the Coban Hospital of northern Guatemala. The children here suffer severe malnourishment and related illnesses.

irrigation, and the lengthening cycles of drought prevent opportunity for recovery. Four successive years of drought have weakened the production systems of farmers in Ethiopia and Eritrea. A continuing lack of support for agriculture and little opportunity for rural farmers to move products to markets has resulted in plummeting production and reliance on imported food assistance. The 1998 border war between Ethiopia and Eritrea also displaced millions of people, including women who lost their husbands in the war. Large tracts of land now are unproductive due to landmines leftover from the conflict.

International donors have mobilized food aid for the Horn of Africa, but a multi-year response is required, including much more than simple food aid. Nutritious foods are needed to provide therapeutic feeding to infants and small children particularly impacted by acute hunger. Measles vaccinations also will be required to prevent outbreaks that typically occur during periods of hunger and drought. Especially needed are longer-term agricultural support programs, including improved seed varieties that are drought tolerant, the dissemination of simple irrigation technologies, and fertilizer and better pest-control methods. The governments of Ethiopia and Eritrea must put agriculture at the center of their development agenda in order to reverse the long-term trend of hunger in their countries.

The second largest hunger hotspot in Africa is centered on the five Southern African nations of Malawi, Mozambique, Swaziland, Zambia and Zimbabwe. Almost 12 million people relied on emergency food assistance during 2003, and despite a massive mobilization of food aid, the region will remain prone to food shortages into 2004. This particular hunger hotspot has been complicated by the HIV/AIDS epidemic, in which some 30 percent of the adult population is infected and unable to work in agriculture and other productive activities. The political crisis in Zimbabwe, a former food-producing nation in Southern Africa, also has created fears of growing regional instability. The governing party of President Mugabe continues to use emergency food aid as a political tool of intimidation and coercion against the opposition.

Other acute food crises in Africa include Angola, Cote d'Ivoire, Democratic Republic of the Congo, Central African Republic, Liberia, Sierra Leone and Sudan. Most of these hunger hotspots resulted from internal conflict and drought, with lack of access by aid workers complicating the relief efforts (see related story, p. 22).

Hope in Africa – Sudan and Sierra Leone

Despite the grim situation in many African countries, progress has been made in two nations that are emerging from civil war. For more than 20 years, Sudan has suffered the ravages of famine caused by a civil war between the northern Khartoum government forces and rebel Sudan People's Liberation Army (SPLA) in the south. During December 2003, these two warring factions held a final round of peace negotiations in Kenya, with a strong likelihood of an imminent peace accord to be finalized in 2004. If a negotiated settlement occurs, an end to over 20 years of war and famine may result, providing new opportunity for millions of people in the south of Sudan.

Former Sen. John Danforth (R-MO), who is now President Bush's special envoy to Sudan, has helped with these negotiations. His success demonstrates what a little attention from the powerful U.S. government sometimes can do to bring wavering partners together in conflict-ridden countries.

In another sign of hope, the people of Sierra Leone are progressing along a path of increasing stability and reconstruction in the wake of the horrific internal conflict of the past decade. The major development banks and other international donors invested in Sierra Leone during 2003, particularly in agriculture, water and sanitation, and education programs. Instability from neighboring Liberia continues to threaten the hard-won progress in Sierra Leone, but for now, hope is beginning to take root for a future free from war and famine.

Hunger Hotspots in Asia

The two largest hunger hotspots in Asia remain in the Democratic People's Republic of Korea (North Korea) and Afghanistan. In North Korea, a series of natural disasters such as floods and drought have contributed to famine that may have claimed more than 2 million lives during the mid-1990s. With the collapse of the partnership between North Korea and Russia after the Cold War, a near total economic collapse has resulted in at least 6.5 million of the country's 22 million inhabitants becoming dependent on international food aid. Despite being unable to grow enough food for its people, the government of North Korea has proclaimed a policy of self-sufficiency or "juche." The dire situation for the people of North Korea continued in 2003 amid a geo-political struggle between the United States and the Pyongyang

regime over the development and possession of nuclear weapons material. Allowing the WFP the necessary access to monitor the food aid has been one of the biggest challenges to the humanitarian aid agencies and donors contributing food aid. The Pyongyang regime refuses to grant full and unlimited access to all parts of the country, which causes donors such as the United States and the European Union to worry about diversion of food aid to the military or government officials.

At the time of the printing of this report, the WFP was expected to cut off food aid to 3 million North Koreans due to lack of donations.[2] The agency has received only 60 percent of the food needed in 2003 for its goal of feeding 6.5 million North Koreans.

In Afghanistan some 6 million of a total population of 27 million were at risk of starvation in 2003. Most of these people were returnees from camps in Pakistan, rural laborers and women-headed households. A four-year drought between 1999 and 2002 greatly weakened the economy and population, and the 20-year war between the Taliban and the Northern Alliance and then the U.S. invasion have destabilized this mountainous nation in Central Asia. Food aid will be required at least through 2005 for a large number of these 6 million most vulnerable people in Afghanistan. Continuing attacks on aid workers and the fledgling government forces by Taliban and Al Qaeda forces present a serious threat to future food security in Afghanistan during 2004.

> *In Afghanistan some 6 million of a total population of 27 million were at risk of starvation in 2003 ... Food aid will be required at least through 2005 for a large number of these 6 million most vulnerable people in Afghanistan.*

Central America – Hunger Hotspots Close to Home

Food insecurity in Guatemala, El Salvador, Honduras and Nicaragua has been triggered by Hurricane Mitch in 1998, earthquakes, drought, and most recently, by the collapse of coffee prices on the world market that have put hundreds of thousands of regional coffee farmers out of work.

Since 1998, more than 9 million people in this region have been severely impacted by hunger and poverty. Yet little attention has been given to this hunger hotspot because the crisis is not the result of a dramatic civil war and nor linked with the war on terrorism. This silent emergency is impacting children younger than 5, particularly in Guatemala, where nearly half of these children are malnourished. Food assistance is targeting pregnant and nursing mothers and children younger than 5, as well as temporary assistance to those rural families affected by drought and the coffee crisis.

Dr. Margaret M. Zeigler is deputy director of the Congressional Hunger Center in Washington, D.C.

---

[1] U.N. Consolidated Appeals Process: Mid-Year Review 2003, www.reliefweb.int.

[2] "U.N. Warns on N. Korea Food," CNN.com, Feb. 26, 2004,
    http://edition.cnn.com/2004/WORLD/asiapcf/02/25/nkorea.food/.

Aid Workers Become Targets on the Frontline

The past year saw an unthinkable experience become reality as humanitarian aid workers became vulnerable targets of war.

The deterioration of security in Baghdad, Iraq, culminating in the Aug. 19, 2003, attack on the U.N. compound, has prevented humanitarian aid workers from fully implementing food and health assistance programs. The killing of 22 U.N. and international humanitarian staff in the Baghdad attack took a particularly grim toll, as the U.N. Administrator Sergio Viera de Mello, one of the world's foremost experts in tackling the complicated efforts of effective nation-building, lost his life that day. Security concerns now are hampering food aid and reconstruction operations worldwide.

In Afghanistan, humanitarian aid workers and reconstruction experts are the new "soft targets" of the reconstituted Taliban and Al Qaeda forces. In Colombia, aid workers and development experts are kidnapped for ransom in the ongoing civil war, and in Somalia, three international aid workers were gunned down with impunity in their homes and places of work during October 2003.

Aid workers are devising new strategies to adapt to these security threats, but remain vulnerable targets in the frontline battle against hunger, war and poverty.

The people of Lesotho, Malawi, Mozambique, Swaziland, Zambia and Zimbabwe are struggling to cope with a food crisis, poverty and HIV/AIDS. In some countries, up to a third of the adult population is infected with HIV.

BFWI Photo/R. Almeida

they do, many families must sell the bulk of their harvest for money to pay for other necessities, leaving them without enough food. Frequently, such communities define and measure their own food security by how many months they have enough to eat. The lean months often are referred to as a "hunger season."

Use

How food is used – meaning how it is prepared and how well the body can absorb its nutrition – also is important to food security. Unsafe water, lack of sanitation or severe disease could impede the full benefit of having enough to eat. If a family in Ethiopia receives rice from the U.S. Agency for International Development but has no water for cooking, the rice is virtually useless. If children have diarrhea, even if they are eating well, they will not be able to fully absorb the nutrients they need.

Hunger Measure's Limits

Hunger also is not defined or measured solely by time or scale. It is both chronic and temporary and can be considered at many levels: worldwide, country-specific, within a region or community, and among a family or individual. These various ways of looking at hunger greatly impact how it is measured and assessed, and what interventions are pursued.

Consider chronic hunger. People who experience chronic hunger do not face immediate starvation. Rather, these people experience a prolonged, consistent lack of food and nutrition that slowly erodes their health and well-being. A husband and wife in Kotiyagoda Village in Sri Lanka describe how their seasonal employment makes it difficult for them to always know where the next meal is coming from. "Money is short when there is no sugarcane to be cut," they say. "This situation prevails for six months of the year. At such times, we do not purchase any food. We borrow from relations. In return, we do whatever work they have. During this period, we have only two meals a day, or one meal or none at all."[10] When there is sugarcane to cut, this couple works and essentially is food secure. But for at least half of the year, they have little to no work and are food insecure. Because this periodic food insecurity recurs persistently, they are considered chronically hungry.

Temporary hunger, on the other hand, is food insecurity that has a beginning and end. Often it includes people who face temporary food shortages because of job loss or a change in family structure, such as a death or divorce. Such people may face food insecurity or hunger for a few days, month or even a year, but eventually they are able to get back on their feet. Hunger crisis situations, such as devastating weather and war, also can be temporary, though potentially severe and life-threatening (see related story, p. 20).

In cases of temporary hunger, a lack of food most often is the culprit, and direct interventions such as food stamps and food aid can be used to meet the need. Whereas chronic hunger most often is related to poverty, and people need longer-term economic and social help to reach a point where they can earn a living that keeps them from periodically going hungry. Together, these different approaches to solutions – short-term and long-term – help people today so they can help themselves tomorrow.

Unfortunately, while efforts are being made to distinguish between chronic and temporary hunger, no definitive method currently exists. The FAO measure estimates the number of people chronically undernourished to be 842 million. Whereas, the U.N. Millennium Project Task Force on Hunger recently projected that about 60 million people are victims of extreme events, which include natural disasters, and these people could be considered temporarily hungry.[11] However, these two measures are based on different criteria and do not necessarily complement each other.

The FAO measure also fails to distinguish hunger levels among households, communities and nations. Again, such differences are important when assessing the true nature of the problem and how best to solve it.

TABLE 1.1

Millions of People Face Severe Humanitarian Crises

Country	Number Affected in 2003
Iraq	27 million
Ethiopia and Eritrea	16.7 million
Southern Africa Region	14.4 million
North Korea	6.4 million
Afghanistan	4.1 million
Angola	3.7 million
Cote d'Ivoire	3 million
Indonesia	3 million
Sudan	2.8 million
Dem. Rep. Of Congo	2.6 million
Central African Republic	2.2 million
Occupied Palestinian Territory	1.5 million
Sierra Leone	1.3 million
Chechnya	1.2 million
Tajikistan	1 million
Central America	600,000

Source: U.N. Consolidated Appeals, 2003

Margaret W. Nea

Impressive progress has been made against child hunger in many parts of the world. Thailand reduced the prevalence of underweight children younger than 6 from more than 50 percent in 1982 to 10 percent in 1996 – about 3 percentage points per year. In five other countries – Indonesia, Malaysia, Pakistan, Tanzania and Zimbabwe – the decline was at about 1 percentage point per year.

Researchers are continuing to refine current measures and pursue new ones. Current alternatives to the FAO undernourishment measure include surveying dietary diversity, 24-hour food recall surveys, anthropometrical measurements of children, and indirect measures such as asset ownership and household size. However, many of these methods are expensive, time-consuming and impractical for areas disrupted by conflicts or other disasters. Moreover, none of these methods has the broad recognition and acceptability of the FAO measure. For now, the FAO measure is the best way to assess the prevalence of hunger. And the FAO is working to improve its data and make the undernourishment measure as accurate as possible.[12]

Difficult to See

While undernourishment is the official and most widely accepted hunger measure, many people still think of hunger in terms of wasting and starvation that most often result from famine. Wasting is the term used to described severe malnutrition from a chronic lack of calories, resulting in people with stick-thin arms and legs, and when combined with a lack of dietary protein, extended bellies. Most often wasting results in starvation.

These most extreme forms of hunger remain a problem even today. In Southern Africa, more than 10 million people reportedly died from the severe drought and food shortages that have plagued this region for the past two years.[13] In North Korea, experts estimate that up to 3 million people may have died from starvation since 1995.[14]

But for the most part, severe malnutrition and starvation no longer terrorize people the way they once did. This is one of the great accomplishments of the past century. That said, the less obvious forms of malnutrition that result from overall poor nutrition and specific nutrient deficiencies – often referred to as "hidden hunger" – are more common than many people realize.

Malnutrition, when linguistically broken down, means "bad nutrition." It can mean both undernutrition – a lack of calories or specific nutrients and minerals – and overnutrition – too many calories or too much of specific nutrients and minerals. In addition, someone can be overweight or obese from too many calories over time, while also suffering temporary calorie shortages and chronic deficiencies of important vitamins and minerals. Because of these complexities, it is important to distinguish between calorie and nutrient deficiencies.

Even if people have enough food to meet caloric needs, it may not be enough to keep them from hunger. The absence of a diet rich in vitamins and minerals weakens people's immune systems, among other problems, making them more susceptible to disease and infection and ultimately death. An estimated 2 billion

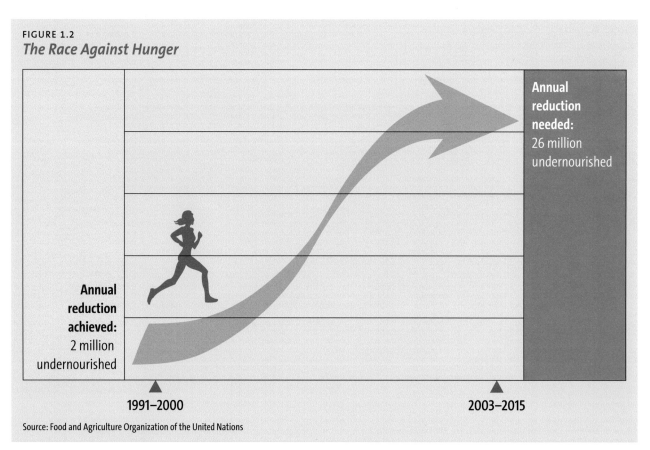

FIGURE 1.2
The Race Against Hunger

Annual reduction needed: 26 million undernourished

Annual reduction achieved: 2 million undernourished

1991–2000

2003–2015

Source: Food and Agriculture Organization of the United Nations

Poor people typically spend between 60 percent and 90 percent of their household consumption budget on acquiring food, according to the U.N. Hunger Task Force.

people do not get enough of the micronutrients – vitamins and minerals – they need for proper growth and development.[15] Because many of these people do get enough calories and protein, micronutrient deficiency often is called hidden hunger. The most common deficiencies are in vitamin A, iodine and iron.

More than 2 million children each year suffer severe visual problems, with more than a quarter million becoming blind from a lack of vitamin A. Insufficient iodine is responsible for 20 million people worldwide living with mental handicaps. Among adults, iron-deficiency anemia reduces work productivity by between 10 percent and 15 percent.[16] Hidden hunger thus represents a huge loss of potential and an unaffordable drain on the human capital of those afflicted.

As anti-hunger advocates work to assure people enough food calories, they also must remember that people need nutrient-rich foods as well. Poor families in Zambia framed the need for quality foods and a varied diet this way: The poor "eat kapenta [dried fish] occasionally," while the rich "eat meat and chicken occasionally and kapenta frequently."[17]

Obesity: Rising Nutrition Problem

The issues of proper nutrition are growing in importance as people worldwide become wealthier and have greater access to foods, especially calorie-dense foods. With more income people not only are shielded from

too few calories, they also can buy a wider variety of foods, better ensuring a balanced diet. Unfortunately, as incomes have risen worldwide, so have rates of overweight and obesity, even in some of the poorest countries. The health problems associated with being overweight and obese are numerous, expensive and life-threatening. Nowhere is this more evident than in industrialized countries like the United States where overweight and obesity affect nearly half of the population.[18]

Because overweight and obesity are the result of consuming too many calories, people assume that people who are obese or overweight cannot be hungry. But that is not the case. A person is considered food secure if they have access to enough food at all times to lead a healthy life. Even an overweight or obese person can struggle with temporary hunger, or be faced with chronic malnourishment as they receive enough – more than enough calories – but lack important nutrients. In fact, people who struggle with hunger are especially vulnerable to some causes of obesity, such as poor knowledge of nutrition.

Difficult to Understand

Some 50 years ago, the United Nations in the Universal Declaration of Human Rights declared that all people in all places have a right to food:

> "Everyone has the right to a standard of living adequate for the well-being of himself and his family, including food, clothing, housing and medical care and necessary social services, and the right to security in the event of unemployment, sickness, disability, widowhood, old age or other lack of livelihood in circumstances beyond his control."[19]

Based on this right, the world community promised 30 years ago to end hunger by 2000. And great progress was made. Whereas one in three people were hungry in 1974, that proportion has dropped to one in six.

But ultimately the 2000 goal was not reached. Instead, the world made a new – more feasible goal – to cut hunger in half by 2015. Yet it is not clear whether that goal will be reached either (see Figure 1.2). The world produces enough food to feed everyone. And much has been learned about who is hungry, why they are hungry and what to do about it. Yet hunger has not gained the political attention necessary to ensure its end.

For the 842 million people who are hungry, this failure can be difficult to understand.

Daniel Martin, former project assistant at Bread for the World Institute, contributed to this chapter.

CHAPTER 2

Hunger in the United States

USDA Photo/Ken Hammond

It's Tuesday morning, and 32-year-old Natalie peers into the window of the local food pantry on the way to her mother's house. "I know the pantry's not normally open today," she says, but she had seen a few people gathered there earlier and hoped that a surprise food shipment had come in.

"Sometimes we're lucky and an extra truck stops here," she says. But most times, the local pantry in Shelby, Miss., is not open. It has two food drops a month, and within an hour of a truck arriving, a line of people already has formed down the block.

Natalie explains how she's been out of work now for almost two years, after a manufacturing plant that had employed nearly half the town closed its doors. Her mother watches her two children most days while she registers with temporary placement agencies 45 miles away. She's had on-and-off employment, but nothing that's turned into a permanent, full-time stint.

"It's hard," she says of trying to keep up with the rent and other bills. She calls herself lucky because most of the town is in the same plight, so people are more understanding if she has to pay the rent a bit late. "I worry a lot," she says. "Sometimes I cry. But what are you going to do? I have to keep on for my children."[1]

Natalie is just one of the nearly 35 million people in the United States who lives in a household that has difficulty at times during the year putting enough food on the table. To advocates, she is one of millions of Americans fighting hunger. To researchers, she is part of a household that is food insecure.

The word "hunger" conjures images of people severely malnourished and perhaps starving, as still happens in some parts of the world. But this type of extreme hunger or calorie deficiency is rare in the United States, with the exception of a few vulnerable populations such as people who are homeless.

Using the Food and Agriculture Organization of the United Nations' (FAO) undernourishment measure, an estimated 2.75 percent of the U.S. population has inadequate calorie intake, as compared to countries like Somalia and Burundi, which have rates over 65 percent. Protein-energy malnutrition also is rare in the United States, with about 400 deaths per year, usually cases of child abuse and neglect or debilitating illness.[2]

This makes sense given that the United States is both the world's largest exporter and importer of food. A shortage of food is not the problem. But despite this abundance, what this measure fails to reflect is the struggle some people in the United States face in providing themselves and their families adequate food

BFWI Photo/S. Bunch

Food pantries and soup kitchens, such as this one in Jackson, Miss., help feed more than 13 million people every month, according to the U.S. Department of Agriculture.

at all times – a struggle that has worsened over the past few years.

Hunger has been on the rise in the United States three years in a row. Poverty also is on the rise. The government has promised to cut U.S. hunger and food insecurity in half by 2010.[3] But it now has less than seven years to fulfill this promise and reduce by about 20 million the number of people living in homes at risk of hunger.[4]

Measuring U.S. Hunger

The effort to measure U.S. hunger began more than 30 years ago, when reporters and elected officials first found extreme forms of hunger among America's poor farmers and other rural populations, especially in Appalachia, the Mississippi Delta and on Native American reservations. The first attempts to measure hunger were based on definitions of malnutrition, similar to what was being used in developing countries.

But as the national debate evolved, it became clear that hunger in the United States was more of an economic issue; it more often was about people not always having enough money to buy food. In 1990 Congress passed the National Nutrition Monitoring and Related Research Act, which required a plan to be developed for measuring food security.[5] In 1995 the U.S. Department of Agriculture (USDA) crafted a set of questions to measure food security, which has become part of the Current Population Survey.

One Indiana Family Finds Even Government Help Falls Short of Need

By Melvin Durai

A well-stocked fridge and tidy home may not show it, but these are worrisome times for Larry Dye and Miriam Delgado. Without permanent jobs, the Lafayette, Ind., couple have had to resort to various means – even donating blood plasma – to provide for themselves and three children: their 17-month-old daughter, Chastity; and Larry's two nieces, Kelly, 6, and Jessica, 3.

"I'm not really concerned about myself," says Larry, 21, who is taking care of his nieces temporarily while their divorced parents sort out personal problems. "I'm worried about the kids. Their needs come before mine."

Snacking on orange Jello and bagels, the children look well-fed and healthy, thanks in large part to the $240 in food stamps the family receives monthly.

"If it wasn't for food stamps, we'd have it really hard," Larry says.

The food stamps provide all the necessities, but don't stretch as far as the couple would like. "Most of the time, it becomes very tight," Larry says. "It's just having this many kids – they're always hungry."

They try to save money by buying most of their groceries at Aldi, a discount food store. "I like going there, because it's a lot cheaper," says Miriam, 19.

During her pregnancy and her daughter's first year, Miriam received vouchers from WIC, about $25 a month to buy nutritious food for herself and formula for the baby.

She also has visited local food pantries – during a month when she didn't receive food stamps because she had missed an appointment to renew them. "I didn't have transportation to get to the office," she says.

Both she and Larry have held a variety of blue-collar jobs, most assigned by a temporary-placement agency and paying only minimum wage. Miriam has been a factory worker and receptionist; Larry a roofer, janitor and car washer, among other jobs.

"We make a little money here and there, enough for gas and diapers," Miriam says.

About once a month, Larry receives a $25 check for donating plasma, money that helps buy diapers and wipes. "I don't like doing it that much," he says, "because it wears me out."

Larry Dye, Miriam Delgado and their three children (left to right) – Chastity, 17 months; Jessica, 3; and Kelly, 6 – sit outside their home in Lafayette, Ind. Even with the help of food stamps, the family finds it difficult to buy all the food they need every month.

Miriam Delgado feeds her 17-month-old daughter, Chastity, a Jello cup that the girls made the previous day.

Though their expenses rose after Chastity's birth, they weren't all that comfortable about seeking food stamps. "We felt kind of odd about it," Larry says. "It was our first kid. We wanted to do everything right."

"I felt weird, because I've never really asked for help before," says Miriam. Her parents are financially secure and give her money whenever she asks. "But I usually don't like to call them up and say, 'Hey, I need some money,'" she says.

Despite her misgivings about seeking help, she was forced to turn to Medicaid during her pregnancy and delivery. "I knew I couldn't afford the medical bills," she says.

While she and Chastity are covered by Medicaid, Larry lacks insurance of any kind. "If I did, I'd get my teeth taken care of," he says of his two cavities.

They live in government-subsidized housing, paying only $25 a month for their small townhouse, which looks ragged outside but clean and homey inside. On a wire cart beside their circular-glass dining table sit two loaves of bread and a bag of bagels. The refrigerator door displays the children's alphabet magnets and crayon drawings. Inside, among the milk and eggs, are cups of Jello and a cake, which Miriam and the girls made the previous day, along with Kool Aid and frozen Popsicles.

"They were having a blast," Miriam says. "They get so happy when we do things like that."

***

Melvin Durai is a freelance writer who lives in Lafayette, Ind.

This survey contains a series of 18 questions to gauge the food security status of a household (10 questions for households without children) for the past 12 months (see Figure 2.3).[6] The first question is subjective, asking whether the household ever worried about having enough food to last the month. The other questions are objective and deal with economic realities of food situations in the house, such as having enough money to eat balanced meals. Essentially, the survey is designed to distinguish between people who consistently have access to enough food (food secure), people who are unable to count on regular, adequate, nutritious meals (food insecure), and people who suffer the physical distress of sometimes not having enough to eat because they can't afford enough food (food insecure with hunger).

USDA defines food security as, at a minimum, the "ready availability of nutritionally adequate and safe foods and the assured ability to acquire acceptable foods in socially acceptable ways."[7] While the food security survey is a starting point to understanding the depth and degree of hunger, some critics question whether it captures the full extent of food insecurity in the United States.

America's Second Harvest, the nation's largest organization of emergency food providers, interviewed people using its facilities throughout the country and compiled the findings in a report titled, Hunger in America 2001.[8] Based on person-to-person interviews with 32,000 clients and 24,000 questionnaires completed by agency staff, America's Second Harvest determined that it serves an estimated 23.3 million people annually. In any given week, its facilities assist approximately 7 million people.

These findings contrast with USDA's most recent survey, which found only 3.3 million households reporting that they received food from an emergency source, such as a church, food bank or food pantry.[9] This discrepancy is important because people seeking emergency food assistance essentially are food insecure. The different totals have raised important questions that have researchers looking at possible ways to further improve USDA's food security measure (see related story, p. 32).

Already, the USDA has followed up with additional research to better understand how food insecure families use emergency services and whether the services complement national food assistance programs. In July 2003, USDA released a study, "The Emergency Food Assistance System – Findings From the Client Survey," which found 13.6 million people used emergency food services in a typical 2001 month. Of these, three out of four people were determined to be food insecure.[10]

Additional research is needed to ensure that people are not being missed by the official food security measure. For example, migrant farm workers may seek emergency services, but are not captured in the federal survey. Similarly, nearly all military personnel are excluded from the Current Population Survey and therefore excluded from national food security statistics.

What The Numbers Say

According to USDA's most recent survey, nearly 35 million people lived in households that were food insecure at some time during 2002 – a jump of 1.26 million people. Some 9.3 million people lived in households in which one or more persons were hungry at times during the year because they lacked sufficient money and other resources for food.[11]

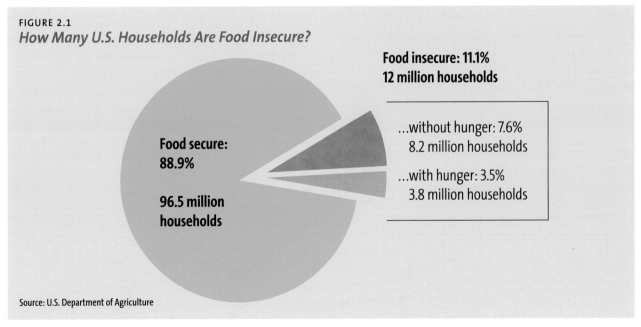

FIGURE 2.1
How Many U.S. Households Are Food Insecure?

Food secure:
88.9%

96.5 million
households

Food insecure: 11.1%
12 million households

...without hunger: 7.6%
8.2 million households

...with hunger: 3.5%
3.8 million households

Source: U.S. Department of Agriculture

FIGURE 2.2
High Poverty Counties: Counties with Poverty Rates 20% or Higher in 1999

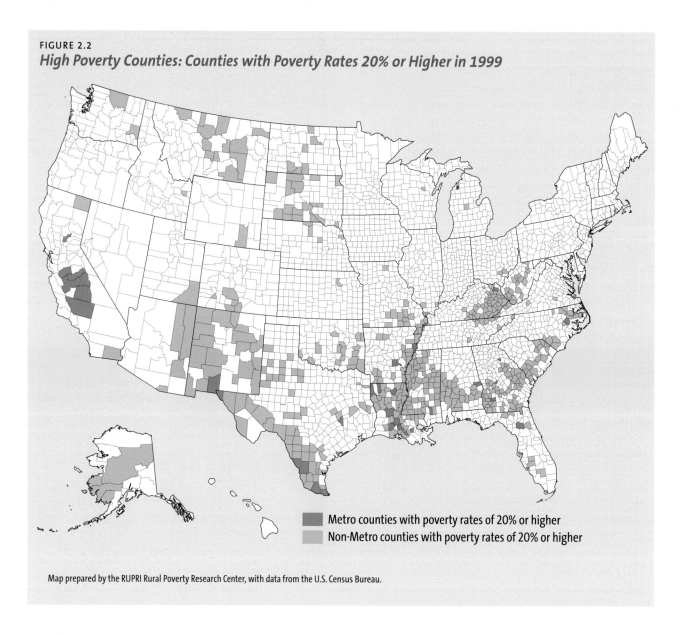

Metro counties with poverty rates of 20% or higher
Non-Metro counties with poverty rates of 20% or higher

Map prepared by the RUPRI Rural Poverty Research Center, with data from the U.S. Census Bureau.

People who discount that hunger exists in the United States point to these numbers and the food security survey and say that because being considered "food insecure" can mean that a family only had to cut back on what they ate once in a year, most of this measure likely includes people who had just that experience. The food security approach is designed to register occasional or episodic occurrences. And the survey finds that only one in every five food insecure households experience such conditions frequently or chronically.

However, when looking at the more severe experience of food insecurity with hunger, two of every three households experience it on a recurring basis. On average, these households must cut back on what they eat or skip meals eight-to-nine months of the year.[12]

Where Is Hunger?

Broadly speaking, food insecurity and hunger are more prevalent in regions that also have higher poverty rates. While the national food insecurity rate is 11.1 percent, it is highest in the South (12.4 percent) and West (12.1 percent), with the Midwest and Northeast under the national average at 9.6 percent and 9.2 percent, respectively.[13] Food insecurity with hunger follows a similar pattern.

It would make sense that where there is more food insecurity, there would be more hunger. However, that is not always the case. In 2002 Utah had the highest food insecurity rate at 15.2 percent, followed by Mississippi and Texas, both at 14.8 percent. But Oklahoma and Oregon had the highest food insecurity with hunger rates, at 5.1 percent and 5 percent, respectively.

Other states that have high rates of food insecurity and hunger include Arizona and New Mexico, while some of the lowest rates are found in Delaware, Massachusetts and New Hampshire – all with food insecurity rates below 7 percent.

While greater numbers of people living in urban areas face food insecurity and hunger (9.6 million households), the rates for food insecurity and hunger are slightly higher in rural areas.[14] The food insecurity rate in metropolitan areas is 11 percent while in rural areas it is 11.6 percent, representing 2.4 million households. However, the rates are highest for people living in central cities: 14.4 percent.[15]

Pockets of Hunger

The national survey's strength is highlighting some of the general populations that are at risk for food insecurity, but other evidence shows pockets of hunger throughout America as well. These pockets are areas or regions of the country that are experiencing substantially higher rates of food insecurity and hunger than the rest of the nation. These pockets include, but are not limited to, Native American reservations, some parts of Appalachia, the Mississippi Delta and among farm workers mostly in California and the Southwest-border states of New Mexico and Texas.

While 11.1 percent of U.S households are food insecure, the rate is 22.2 percent in Native American households – twice the general population. Poverty here is not only widespread, but also severe. Five of the top 10 counties for extreme child poverty (below 50 percent of poverty line) are located in South Dakota and contain largely Native Americans.[16] There, hunger was almost three times higher, with 8.6 percent of Native American households experiencing hunger compared to 3.3 percent nationally. With poverty and unemployment rates two-to-three times higher than the national average as well, Native American communities struggle with health and nutrition problems.[17]

Native Americans also face problems with obesity. Because of poverty and lower quality food selection, many Native Americans are forced to buy cheap food that is higher in fat and has much lower nutritional quality than other foods. And because money may run out at the end of the month, as happens in many food insecure households, families can fall into a cycle of eating more food at the beginning of a month to compensate for skimping at the end of the previous month.[18]

Appalachia also continues to struggle with food insecurity and hunger. The Appalachian region of Kentucky "was significantly more food insecure than other regions" of the state, researchers found in 1999.[19]

Migrant farm workers are another sub-population that suffers from nutrition problems: 61 percent of

People who are hungry or food insecure most often are poor or facing economic hardship. Recent hikes in housing and health care costs coupled with high unemployment over the past few years make it even harder for low-income families to cover basic household needs, such as food.

all farm workers live in poverty, with two-thirds of foreign-born farm workers falling below the poverty line.[20] According to the California Research Bureau, "Farm workers suffer a higher incidence of malnutrition than any other sub-population in the country."[21] Infant mortality rates among migrant farm worker families are more than twice that of the overall population, and their children suffer from deficiencies of vitamin A, calcium and iron at higher rates than most children. The U.S. Department of Education found that more than two in five migrant farm worker families suffered from seasonal food shortages.[22]

The Mississippi Delta has been plagued with poverty and hunger for decades. With poverty a major factor influencing food security, the counties that line the Delta in both Louisiana and Mississippi are among the nation's highest in childhood poverty. The Lower Mississippi Delta, including counties in Arkansas, Louisiana and Mississippi, has food insecurity rates (21.1 percent) and hunger rates (6.5 percent) more than twice the national average.[23] According to the Lower Mississippi Delta Nutrition Intervention Research Initiative's 2002 annual report, "Nutrition-related chronic diseases in the [Lower Mississippi Delta] are among the nation's highest," and the area "is underserved by food and nutrition and other health professionals."[24] In some of these counties, more than 30 percent of children live in extreme poverty or below half the poverty line (see Figure 2.2).[25]

Better Understanding the Pluses, Minuses of the U.S. Food Security Measure

The Current Population Survey (CPS) contains a series of 18 questions used by the U.S. Department of Agriculture (USDA) to gauge the food security status of a household for the past 12 months (10 questions for households without children).

The first question is subjective, asking whether the household ever worried about having enough food to last the month. The other questions are objective and deal with economic realities of food situations in the house, such as having enough money to eat balanced meals or if anyone in the house had to skip a meal or cut back on how much they normally would eat due to lack of money for food. Households that answered affirmatively (Yes, I have had to skip a meal because of lack of food) to three or more questions are considered food insecure.

Survey Weaknesses

The survey is conducted by phone and based on a list of people with addresses. This means that people without phones or addresses, such as the homeless and seasonal migrant workers, are not surveyed. Some researchers also have expressed concern that when interviewed, a small number of people may not be willing to admit to running out of food.

In addition to the 11.1 percent of households classified as food insecure, a significant number of households responded affirmatively to one or two of the 18 survey questions. While not technically food insecure (which requires three indications of food insecurity), the food security of these households may have been tenuous at times. Some may be on the brink, perhaps a medical crisis or job loss away, from becoming food insecure. If these households were added to the official totals, food insecurity rates would jump to 37.5 percent of households with children and 14.3 percent of households without children.[1]

By confirming even one food insecurity indicator, families affirm that they lacked "assured ability to acquire acceptable foods in socially acceptable ways," a condition that the Life Sciences Research Office includes in its definition of food insecurity. Consequently, USDA is examining this group further to better understand its food security situation.

Celia Escudero-Espadas

Early research indicates that the lack of school meal programs during the summer contributes to higher food insecurity rates for low-income families with children.

FIGURE 2.3
How is Food Security Measured? Questions in the Food Security Scale

Worried food would run out   *Food Secure*
Food bought didn't last

Couldn't afford to eat balanced meals
Relied on a few kinds of low-cost food for children
Adult cut size of meals or skipped meals   *Food Insecure*
Couldn't feed the children a balanced meal
Respondent ate less than felt they should

Adult cut or skipped meals, 3 or more months
Children were not eating enough
Respondent hungry but didn't eat   *Food Insecure*
Respondent lost weight   *with Hunger*
Cut size of child's meals

Adult did not eat for whole day
Child hungry but couldn't afford more food   *Food Insecure*
Adult did not eat for whole day, 3 or more months   *with Hunger*
Child skipped meal   *(Severe)*
Child skipped meals, 3 or more months

Source: Mark Nord, ERS, U.S. Department of Agriculture

While the CPS supplemental survey has been used since 1995, it has been used in different months in different years (April 1995; September 1996; April 1997; August 1998; April 1999 and September 2000). Starting in 2001, it has been administered in December every year.[2]

It would seem that when asked about the past year, it should not matter when people are surveyed – spring or fall. But food insecurity rates were higher when surveyed in the fall than in the spring, by a little more than 1 percent. (Hunger was higher by 0.6 percent.) One explanation could be that people recall recent events more easily than those further in the past.

Another explanation is that people have different household costs, depending on the season. In a recent paper, USDA's Economic Research Service (ERS) attributes some of the seasonal fluctuation in food security numbers to families' higher costs of cooling residences during summer months, especially among low-income elderly households.[3] In fact many households face high utility bills at both temperature extremes. Some experience a "heat or eat" dilemma in the winter, and even more go without food when they face "cool or eat" in the summer. Tentative evidence also suggests that the lack of school meal programs during the summer contributes to food insecurity among low-income households with children.

The complexity of the food security measure also can be a disadvantage. In educating people about hunger in the United States or reporting on the country's progress against hunger, one has to explain what "hunger" and "food insecurity" mean and how they are measured. That said, the complexity of the measure does reflect the reality that people experience hunger at various degrees, which also is important.

Positive Steps

Having an official, nationwide annual survey of hunger and food insecurity has been a major step forward on the road to ending hunger in the United States. Moreover, these annual surveys are beginning to show revealing trends, such as the impact of utility costs on household budgets. Over time, such analysis will deepen and strengthen our understanding of U.S. hunger.

A significant improvement has been USDA's efforts to standardize data collection and reporting. Still, the agency needs to improve how it releases and publicizes this information. The 2003 report on household food security was published without advance notice or fanfare, and at a time designed to minimize press coverage – late in the afternoon on Halloween Friday.

By setting a predetermined date for the report's release, hunger advocacy groups and the media could do more to make the nation aware of the United States' progress to cut hunger in half.

---

[1] Though classified food secure, 11 percent of households with children and 6.2 percent of households without children reported affirmatively to at least one indicator of food insecurity; Mark Nord, et al., *Household Food Security in the United States, 2002*. ERS, USDA (Washington, DC: USDA) October 2003, 39.

[2] Barbara Cohen, Mark Nord, Robert Lerner, James Parry and Kenneth Yang, *Household Food Security in the United States, 1998 and 1999: Technical Report*. ERS, USDA, E-FAN 02-010 (Washington, DC: USDA) June 2002. Found at http://www.ers.usda.gov/publications/efan02010/efan02010fm.pdf.

[3] Mark Nord, "Keeping Warm, Keeping Cool, Keeping Food on the Table: Seasonal Food Insecurity and Costs of Heating and Cooling," Unpublished conference presentation, July 7, 2003; Mark Nord and Kathleen Romig, "Hunger in the Summer: Seasonal Food Insecurity and the National School Lunch and Summer Food Service Programs," Unpublished conference presentation, Nov. 5, 2003.

Who Is Hungry?

Race

While most hungry and food insecure people in the United States are white, minorities are more likely to become food insecure or hungry.

In 2002 less than one in 10 white households experienced food insecurity, yet more than one in five Black or Hispanic households was considered food insecure.[26] Similar race-based income patterns were found as well. In 2002 the median white family earned $46,900, whereas Hispanic families earned only $33,103 and Black families only $29,026.[27]

Though food insecurity can be found across all incomes, it is more prevalent among people closer to the poverty line. Of those households that are food insecure, more than two-thirds are at or below 130 percent of the poverty line. Only 5.1 percent are above 185 percent of the poverty line.[28]

Age

When children and the elderly have to go without food, they are especially vulnerable to health problems. Fortunately, they are most shielded from hunger. Whereas 11.1 percent of all households are food insecure, only 6 percent of households with elderly are. And while 3.5 percent of households experience hunger,

only 1.5 percent of households with elderly do.[29] As with other age groups, both food insecurity and hunger are more common among Black and Hispanic elderly than among white elderly.

According to the USDA's Economic Research Service (ERS), irregular income – especially sudden drops in income – most contribute to higher food insecurity rates. The elderly have more wealth on average than other age groups. And for those who do not, the United States assists with programs like Social Security, Medicaid and Medicare. These income-boosting measures likely explain the higher food security rates among the elderly.[30]

Still, service providers and news reports often relay anecdotal evidence that hunger among the elderly may be more prevalent than official reports indicate. In its 2001 survey, America's Second Harvest found that 11 percent of its clients were elderly. Research also has found that elderly who live alone are more likely to be food insecure or hungry.[31]

Moreover, despite qualifying for food stamps, few elderly apply for them. According to ERS, "For the elderly who seek food assistance, community food programs largely substitute for, rather than supplement, the Food Stamp Program."[32] Increasing food stamp participation among the elderly could drastically cut this group's food insecurity and hunger rates.

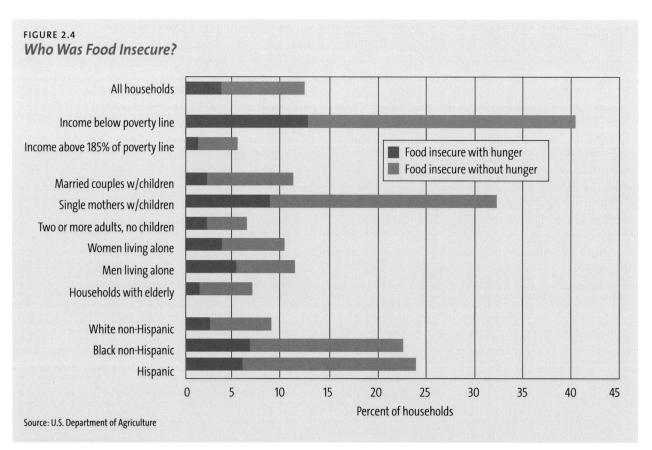

FIGURE 2.4
Who Was Food Insecure?

Legend:
- Food insecure with hunger
- Food insecure without hunger

Categories (Percent of households):
- All households
- Income below poverty line
- Income above 185% of poverty line
- Married couples w/children
- Single mothers w/children
- Two or more adults, no children
- Women living alone
- Men living alone
- Households with elderly
- White non-Hispanic
- Black non-Hispanic
- Hispanic

X-axis: Percent of households — 0, 5, 10, 15, 20, 25, 30, 35, 40, 45

Source: U.S. Department of Agriculture

Children are most protected from hunger in the United States. In food insecure families, adults cut back on their own meals — and even skip meals — before they reduce the amount of food they feed their children. Still, more than half a million children went hungry at some point during 2002.

On the other end of the age spectrum, research shows that adults in food insecure households usually protect children from hunger, even if it means they forego food. While the elderly have the advantage of stable income to insulate them from hunger, children are protected from hunger by caring parents and guardians. More than 13 million children lived in food insecure households in 2002, yet only 567,000 experienced hunger.[33] In other words, more than 90 percent of children in food insecure households were protected from hunger. Still, nearly all children living in food insecure households suffer some nutritional deprivation, sometimes with lasting consequences.

Children also are helped through various government programs. Low-income children have access to free and reduced-price school lunch and breakfast, at least while school is in session. Unfortunately, the summer months leave many of these children without direct food assistance. In July 2001 the number of children served lunch through the Summer Food Service Program was 2.1 million per day — about 8 percent of the number who received free or reduced-price meals during the school year.[34]

Young children also are aided through the Special Supplemental Nutrition Program for Women, Infants and Children (WIC). WIC is available to pregnant or nursing mothers and parents of children up to age 5. WIC provides vouchers for certain food products that contain nutrients that poor mothers and children often lack, such as milk. Since its inception in the 1970s, WIC has become one of the nation's most popular and effective nutrition programs. In 2003 more than 7.5 million women participated in WIC.[35]

Family Structure

Single-parent households — especially single-mother households — are most at risk for food insecurity. Whereas 16.5 percent of households with children experience food insecurity, nearly one in three (32 percent) households headed by a single mother do. Children in single-mother households are 50 percent more likely than those in single-father households to experience hunger, and three times as likely as children in two-parent households. Over half (57 percent) of children who experience hunger live in homes with single mothers.[36]

Both Black and Hispanic households with children are more than twice as likely to experience food insecurity (26.5 percent and 27.9 percent, respectively) than their white counterparts (11.9 percent). These households also are three-to-four times as likely to experience

FIGURE 2.5
How Many Households with Children Are Hungry?

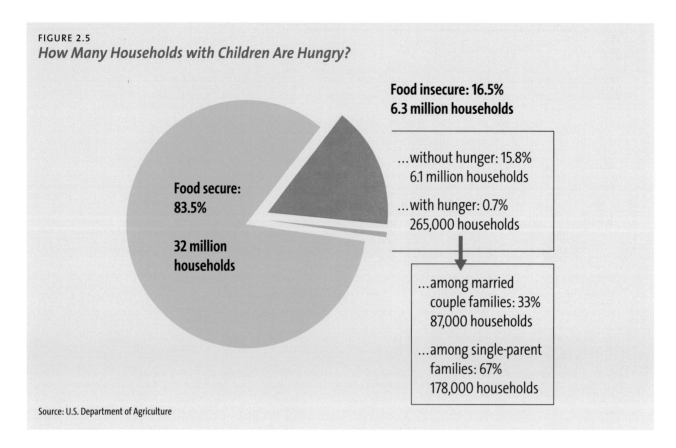

Food insecure: 16.5%
6.3 million households

Food secure:
83.5%

32 million
households

...without hunger: 15.8%
6.1 million households

...with hunger: 0.7%
265,000 households

...among married
couple families: 33%
87,000 households

...among single-parent
families: 67%
178,000 households

Source: U.S. Department of Agriculture

hunger among children (1.2 percent and 1.5 percent, respectively) than white households with children (0.4 percent).[37]

In contrast, childless households are much more likely to be food secure, with only 8.1 percent being food insecure and 3.3 percent being food insecure with hunger.[38] Men living alone experience more food insecurity and hunger than women living alone, which is surprising considering men typically earn more money than women.[39]

How People Cope

Food insecurity and hunger in the United States are closely linked to being poor or experiencing periodic financial hardships. Often, hunger is not just about whether a family has enough money to buy healthy food, but whether they have enough to pay rent and utilities, child care and transportation, and if someone gets sick, medical expenses.

The economic slump of the past few years has led to higher unemployment and increasing financial pressures for families. Such pressures are only exacerbated by skyrocketing health care and housing costs. Health insurers keep raising rates, and employers are passing along greater shares of these hikes to employees. Greater numbers of people have no insurance or are declining to be insured. Meanwhile, as federal and state budgets shrink, states are reducing such social services as Medicaid.

Many families, including middle-class families, are one medical crisis away from poverty. According to a recent study, one-half of all personal bankruptcy claims filed in 2000 were due to "the crushing burden of medical expenses."[40] The America's Second Harvest survey found that 30 percent of people using emergency food services did so after choosing to pay health care expenses over food.

Families also are paying more for housing. The continuing escalation of housing costs, especially rents in urban areas, increasingly are burdening families' budgets. Housing experts, including those at the U.S. Department of Housing and Urban Development (HUD), use the term "fair market rent" – rent that does not exceed 30 percent of a household's income – to determine housing that is affordable.[41] Using this measure, three in four households that qualify for the Food Stamp Program are paying more in rent than they can afford. More than one in two food stamp households spend more than half of their income on housing.[42]

Unable to afford market rents and often unable to qualify for limited housing assistance, many families are being forced to live in cramped and substandard housing. Increasing numbers of families also are becoming homeless. Inadequate, crowded or costly housing can pose serious problems to children's physical, psychological or material well-being.[43] Between 1978 and 1999, the percentage of families with children paying more than

FIGURE 2.6

What Does Food Security Really Mean?

Worry, stretch, juggle   **Food Secure**

Reduce quality and variety of diet   **Food Insecure**

Reduce food intake of adults   **Hunger**

Reduce food intake of children   **Severe Hunger**

Source: Mark Nord, ERS, U.S. Department of Agriculture

half of their income for housing almost doubled, rising from 6 percent to 11 percent.[44] Among very low-income renters – those with incomes at or below half the median family income in an area – nearly 30 percent of families with children experience these severe housing problems.[45]

Utility bills also compete with grocery bills. People who live in poorer neighborhoods often have older, more dilapidated homes or apartments, making it more difficult to keep them warm in the winter and cool in the summer. America's Second Harvest found that 45 percent of its clients were forced to choose between food and utilities.[46] The "heat or eat" conundrum is not a predicament that people in this wealthy country should face. Yet these are the types of decisions people are making everyday.

When Natalie thinks about providing a future for her two children, she knows that she likely will have to leave her hometown of Shelby, Miss. The thought scares her. "My family is here," she says. "And with them around, I know I'll always have someone to turn to. But in the city – I wouldn't know anyone."

But if she stays in Shelby she'll have to continue relying on the local food bank and other people for help. Neither is a choice she willfully would make.

Dorothy Grady, a registered nurse and nutritionist, fights hunger in Shelby, Miss., by teaching older women and children how to grow vegetables in local gardens and raise small animals for food.

CHAPTER

3
Hunger in Developing Countries

IFAD/G. Bizzarri

For 842 million people in the world, hunger is a battle with no end in sight. The impact of this constant struggle on their daily lives is profound. The leading cause of human mortality and morbidity in the world today is malnutrition.[1]

Overall, world hunger has declined in the past 30 years, dropping from 37 percent to 17 percent.[2] During this time, however, the world population also increased by half, making it easier to reduce the proportion of hunger, but harder to reduce the total number of hungry people. Still, the number of hungry people in developing countries declined by nearly 19 million in the past decade, with the largest decrease in China.

Much of the progress to date is due to economic gains and higher income growth in some developing countries, particularly Asian countries, coupled with investments in health, education and rural development. Global food production has increased, and food prices have remained low because of new crop varieties and increased fertilizer use.

But if China's success is excluded, the number of people considered hungry actually has increased in the past decade, with the largest concentration remaining in sub-Saharan Africa. While the first half of the 1990s saw the number of hungry people in developing countries decline by 37 million, the second half of the decade has seen the number creep up again by 18 million.[3] The global economic slump that began in Asia in 1997 and in North America and Europe in 2000, adverse weather, and escalating conflicts in the Middle East and central Africa are among the causes.[4]

The global community has set the goal of reducing hunger by half by 2015 – little more than a decade away.[5] But unless the world gives higher priority to hunger-alleviating efforts, this goal will not be reached until 2050.[6] Current efforts to reduce hunger must be accelerated.

Measuring Global Hunger

The U.N. Food and Agriculture Organization's (FAO) annual assessment of undernourishment is the most widely accepted indicator of hunger. One of its major shortcomings is that it has been unable to illuminate how hunger is distributed within countries, so-called hunger hotspots. National estimates of hunger are helpful in assessing a country's general progress over time, but are not useful in targeting those areas where hunger and undernutrition are most severe. FAO is committed to improving how it measures hunger,[7] and in December 2003, FAO released its first maps that show the distribution of chronic undernutrition within countries.[8]

BFWI Photo/E. Byers

Almost three of every four people who are undernourished in the world live in rural areas, and most of them rely on agriculture as a way to make a living.

In a similar effort, the Hunger Task Force of the U.N. Millennium Project has identified eight hunger hotspots in Africa, based on both the number and proportion of underweight children under 5 (see related story, p. 44). Newly available data draw attention to a number of geographical areas where child undernutrition is concentrated. These areas often are within countries, but sometimes extend regionally across two or three countries. The Hunger Task Force analyzes hotspots according to types of farming, ecological conditions and national economic conditions. By more precisely identifying areas prone to hunger, governments and donors can better allocate development assistance, food aid and other resources.[9]

Several countries also are improving their data collection efforts and broadening how they measure undernutrition, food insecurity and micronutrient deficiencies. For example, more countries are assessing children's physical growth to monitor hunger, using such methods as height-to-weight ratios and mid-arm circumference measures.[10] Unfortunately, because of resource constraints, most countries only take these anthropometric measurements once. To best highlight populations suffering or at risk of hunger, these measurements need to be taken much more frequently.[11]

Togo's 'Untapped Potential': Alex's Story

By Briana Collier

The Togolese economy has been trapped in recession for more than a decade. In fact, many of the country's most important industries, such as tourism, have been in steep decline since the 1970s. The United States and the European Union have cancelled all development assistance to Togo due to political instability and repression of opposition groups by the authoritarian regime in power. Togo also has been excluded from the most recent regional trade deal, the African Growth and Opportunity Act (AGOA). As a result, almost all the active trade projects in Togo are small, private and work from the ground up. These local efforts to encourage small enterprise development among the private sector work quite effectively. However, they face the challenges of combating a long tradition of nepotism and interacting with a generation of young people unfamiliar with many business practices and skills.

One man, Alex Fiakowodoua, shares the story of his struggle.

Alex Fiakowodoua lives and works in Kpalime, Togo, a modest city in a small, narrow country that sits along the belt of the West African seacoast. Alex is 25 years old, intelligent and hardworking. Yet like most Togolese, he earns barely enough money to get by. He has few possessions. He lives in a simple room with no electricity or running water, and sleeps on a straw mat. He eats inexpensive staple foods from street stalls and often skips meals.

Yet Alex does not complain. Most of his peers and relatives struggle in the same way. They too know how it feels to be hungry. Although Kpalime is located in the country's southern, forested region which gets lots of rainfall and regularly yields abundant crops, the average person can afford to buy only the inexpensive starch foods and little to none of the more nutritious meats and vegetables. The annual 2001 per capita income in Togo was $270, equal in purchasing power to $1,620 in the United States.[1]

Alex Fiakowodoua lives and works in Kpalime, Togo. Togo has a population of 4.5 million people, of which one in four are undernourished.

Most Togolese have difficulty not only buying food, but also paying for school. Despite his hardship, Alex worries about his lack of food much less than his lack of education. He will tell you he wishes every day that he could finish high school. Although he was determined to graduate, Alex could not cover his school fees and stopped attending classes two years shy of earning a diploma. Now the few jobs that pay well in Togo are out of his reach.

For many people in Togo and across the developing world, such dreams of a better life are similarly beyond reach. Lack of infrastructure and weak economies contribute to millions of people living day to day to feed themselves instead of working toward a better future. Like Alex, many Togolese children leave secondary and even primary school before graduating to work. Only 50 percent of male and 22 percent of female would-be students in Togo are enrolled in secondary school. Moreover, of all primary school entrants, only 52 percent reach grade 5.[2] As a result, the Togolese experience low literacy levels and lack employment skills, perpetuating slow economic growth and high unemployment. In this way, poorly funded and neglected school systems feed a cycle of low productivity and hinder developing nations from catching up to the more developed countries.

For Alex, not gaining his diploma was not for lack of trying. He grew up with his father, his father's second wife and her five children in a small house in a village north of Kpalime called Kpele Dafo. Because his father was able to work only sporadically, money was stretched to provide for all the children. Food was the first priority, seldom leaving enough money to cover school fees and supplies. In fact, Alex began school three years late, when he was 8, because his father could not afford the fees. More than once, Alex also started the year late and had to work hard in his lessons to catch up with the other students.

Alex's mother and father divorced when Alex was young. His mother followed job opportunities to Burkina Faso, the neighboring country to the north. Without his mother to protect and provide for him, Alex often was left to fend for himself at mealtime. His father's second wife did not always feed him and took whatever opportunities she had to redirect her husband's income toward her own children. Alex says he understands that she did not act purely out of spite. Resources were tight and pencils for one child meant no pencils for another.

When Alex reached his teens, he left his father's house to live with an aunt, and later to the house of a friend. As is customary when joining a household, Alex assumed a share of the housekeeping duties. He also had to work to pay for school. So in addition to preparing meals, washing dishes, cleaning the house and studying, he picked up odd jobs after school hauling cement bags and cutting wood.

When asked about Togo's future, Alex asserts that the Togolese must take the lead in helping their country grow and develop. "We have to do most of the work, and it all starts with educating people," he says. "Togolese need to be better educated so that they can take charge of their own lives and make things better for their families."

Alex Fiakowodoua (far left) works with Peace Corps volunteer, Jess Collier, (inside left), on ways to strengthen Alex's nonprofit organization, which uses community development and organizing to improve employment prospects and access to education for youth in Togo.

Alex tried to adjust to his new workload. The first year that he lived on his own he failed his exams and had to repeat a grade. The next year he adapted by working fewer hours and closer to home (in his neighbors' fields harvesting crops) and he spent more time studying. He was able to earn a primary education certificate and passed into secondary school, but money again became tight. Alex's father invited him back to the house, and he returned. His mother started sending whatever money she could scrape together to help feed him while he stayed in school. Alex completed another two grades this way.

But the day came when he learned that his mother had been struggling to find work and was considering prostituting herself in order to continue sending him money for school. That was the point when Alex finally gave up his fight for an education. He says simply, "That was the end of the line."

At 18, he quit school and has not reenrolled since. Without a diploma, Alex's employment options are limited. He cannot work as a public employee, at the post office or for the telephone company, for example. Most of the businesses in the formal market in Togo are recently privatized companies that provide infrastructure services such as electricity. They only hire employees with a high school education, often requiring professional training as well.

Through his hardships and experiences, Alex has formed his own ideas on how to improve employment prospects and access to education in Togo. In 2000 he put those ideas to work by starting a nonprofit organization called l'Association sans Frontiere des Jeunes pour la

Promotion de l'Education et du Tourisme[3] (AFJEPET) that focuses on community development and organizing. He based one of his first projects in his home village of Kpele Dafo. There, Alex built an education center with a library where he hosts seminars for villagers on such diverse topics as forming agricultural cooperatives, developing tourism projects, promoting literacy, the legal responsibilities of marriage and family management. The center offers a holistic approach to education, while Alex's other projects focus specifically on teaching people the skills they need to save more money and start, grow and manage small businesses. For these projects, AFJEPET works closely with local and international microcreditors to help people secure needed credit. AFJEPET also collaborates with volunteers from the U.S. Peace Corps' small business development program.

When asked about Togo's future, Alex asserts that the Togolese must take the lead in helping their country grow and develop. "We have to do most of the work, and it all starts with educating people," he says. "Togolese need to be better educated so that they can take charge of their own lives and make things better for their families." He also believes that international support is critical if Togo is to ever truly join the international community and global economy.

"We also have so much to give," he says. "There is so much untapped potential here in Togo. The developed world and the developing world, we really both need each other."

Briana Collier is a project assistant at Bread for the World Institute, who visited Togo in December 2003, where she met Alex Fiakowodoua and learned of the work he was doing with l'Association sans Frontiere des Jeunes pour la Promotion de l'Education et du Tourisme.

[1] World Bank, *2003 World Development Indicators*. Table 1.1 (Washington, DC: World Bank Group) 16.
[2] UNICEF, *The State of the World's Children 2003*. Table 4 (New York, NY: UNICEF) 29.
[3] Association without Borders of Young People for the Promotion of Education and Tourism.

What the Numbers Say

The FAO estimates that 842 million people around the world were undernourished in 1999-2001. The majority of these people (798 million) lived in developing countries. In the last decade, the developing world experienced a modest overall reduction in the number of hungry people, but mainly because of gains in a few large countries. Between 1990-1992 and 1999-2001, China reduced the number of undernourished people by 58 million.[12] Ghana, Indonesia, Peru, Thailand and Vietnam all achieved reductions of 3 million or more, helping to offset an increase of 76 million undernourished people in 46 other countries where progress stalled.[13]

Seventeen countries that lowered the number of hungry people in the first half of the 1990s saw the number of undernourished begin to climb again in the second half. Between 1995 and 2001, the number of hungry people in the developing world has risen by an average of 4.5 million per year. During the past decade, 26 countries have seen increases in hunger, and only 19 countries were able to make progress against hunger throughout the 1990s.[14]

Where Is Hunger?

Sub-Saharan Africa continues to have the highest rate of undernourishment. This region also suffered the largest increase in the number of undernourished people between 1998 and 2001. The greatest setbacks occurred in Central Africa, where chronic warfare in the Democratic Republic of Congo helped to triple the number of undernourished people, from 12.1 million in 1992 to 38.3 million in 2001.[15] East and Southern Africa

also are suffering, each struggling with undernourishment rates greater than 40 percent. West Africa is the continent's only bright spot, and success there is threatened by the region's growing instability due to civil wars and conflicts.

While Africa possesses the highest concentration of hunger, South Asia is home to the most hungry people. India alone accounts for nearly one-fourth – 214 million – of the world's hungry people. Encouragingly, levels of undernourishment in every South American country except Venezuela either fell or stayed the same during the 1990s. In Southeast Asia, only Cambodia and

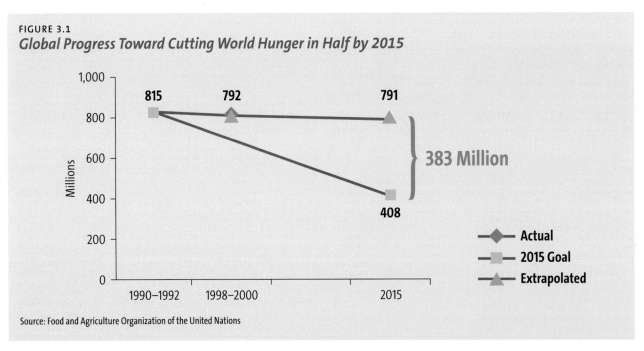

FIGURE 3.1
Global Progress Toward Cutting World Hunger in Half by 2015

Source: Food and Agriculture Organization of the United Nations

the Philippines registered increases in the number of hungry people.

Central America, however, is faring poorly. Only Costa Rica avoided an increase in hunger. Progress also has faltered in the Near East, where hunger has risen in six of 11 countries. In Afghanistan, more than two out of every three people are undernourished.

East Asia also is faltering, with the exception of China and South Korea. In sharp contrast, North Korea has almost 4 million more hungry people today than 10 years ago. Its hunger rates have nearly doubled, from 18 percent to 34 percent.[16]

If the world is to achieve the goal of cutting world hunger in half by 2015, then it must accelerate annual reduction in the number of hungry people to 26 million per year – more than 12 times the current pace.[17]

Who Is Hungry?

Almost three of every four food insecure families live in rural areas, where agriculture and natural resources play a crucial role in how people earn a living. Yet the degree of this dependence varies, based on specific occupations. To better identify such differences, the U.N. Hunger Task Force has identified two broad ways to categorize hungry people.[18] First, it groups people by how they obtain food and make a living.

Second, it considers the special nutritional needs some people may have. Using the first method, the Hunger Task Force identifies four basic groups and the portion of food insecure households they comprise:

- Food insecure farm households (approximately 50 percent);

- Food insecure rural landless households (approximately 22 percent);

- Food insecure herders, fishers and forest-dependent households (approximately 8 percent); and

- Food insecure urban households (approximately 20 percent).[19]

Women and children are more prone to hunger because they have special nutrient needs. Undernourished mothers tend to give birth to underweight babies, which puts the children at a nutritional disadvantage from the start.

BFW/Photo/K. Burge

Farmers

About half of undernourished people in developing countries live in low-income farm households that depend on agriculture for food and income. Two-thirds of these households live in fragile marginal lands that are deteriorating due to soil erosion, soil-fertility decline and deforestation. As population increases and land productivity declines further, the prevalence of hunger and poverty among this group likely will increase. Even in more favorable climates, farmers are finding less arable land available, threatening their ability to provide enough food and income for their families. In both cases, continued improvements in agriculture productivity are needed to ensure economic development and this group's overall well-being.

Rural Landless People

The number of rural landless people in developing countries is estimated at about 180 million and rising fast.[20] These people are mostly farm workers who rely on income from agricultural wage labor to purchase food and meet other needs. As agricultural productivity and rural incomes decline, their economic prospects worsen. Lack of alternative employment in rural areas exacerbates this situation and can leave people susceptible to exploitation by employers and others. Rural landless people, especially the poorest, often depend on wild foods to supplement their diets, gathering from common forests or savannahs.[21] Because landless people often are uneducated and unskilled, many ultimately migrate to nearby cities in search of work, swelling the population of unemployed people there.

Herders, Fishers and Forest-dwellers

Herders, fishers and forest-dwellers – people dependent on natural resources for their livelihoods – also are facing an uncertain future with declining quality and quantity of available natural resources in many developing countries. From the Amazon Basin to the equatorial forests of Central and West Africa, these people are

U.N. Hunger Task Force Looks Anew at World Hunger

The U.N. Millennium Project Task Force on Hunger is one of 10 groups assigned to identify policies and programs that will help countries meet the Millennium Development Goals. Toward the first goal of eradicating extreme poverty and hunger, the Hunger Task Force is devising a new method for assessing hunger "hotspots."[1] By identifying hotspots, such as these proposed for Africa, policy makers will be able to better target policy interventions.

To create the proposed hunger hotspot map for Africa, researchers considered various underweight measures for children younger than 5. The first map identifies geographic areas (subnational) where the number of underweight children exceeds 100,000. The second map highlights the prevalence of underweight children, using rates that exceed 20 percent. To reflect concentration differences, a third map was developed based on population density. Together, these three maps allow researchers to rank geographical areas based on the severity of underweight among children younger than 5.

To select the eight hotspots for further analysis by the Hunger Task Force, these areas then were filtered through five additional criteria related to farming systems, ecological zones and social conditions. These comparisons help researchers begin to understand why a forest zone may have more underweight children (greater number) than savanna areas, and why some farming systems have a higher prevalence of underweight children.

---

[1] Hotspot in this instance refers to areas where hunger is entrenched and intractable, as opposed to hunger crisis areas.

FIGURE 3.2
Population Density of Malnourished Children

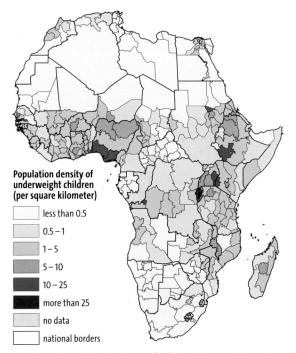

Population density of underweight children (per square kilometer)
- less than 0.5
- 0.5 – 1
- 1 – 5
- 5 – 10
- 10 – 25
- more than 25
- no data
- national borders

Sources: UNICEF, Demographic and Health Surveys (DHS), National Human Development Reports (nHDR), African Nutrition Database Initiative (ANDI), Gridded Population of the World (GPW) v. 3 alpha. Data for 96% of countries are from 1995 or later. All data are from 1992 or later.

FIGURE 3.3
Prevalence of Child Malnutrition

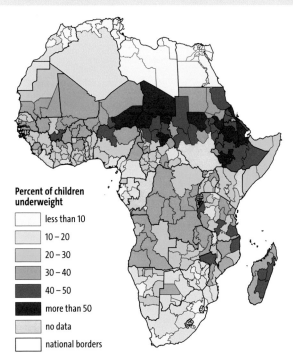

Percent of children underweight
- less than 10
- 10 – 20
- 20 – 30
- 30 – 40
- 40 – 50
- more than 50
- no data
- national borders

Sources: UNICEF, Demographic and Health Surveys (DHS), National Human Development Reports (nHDR), African Nutrition Database Initiative (ANDI). Data for 96% of countries are from 1995 or later. All data are from 1992 or later.

FIGURE 3.4
Population of Malnourished Children by Survey Unit

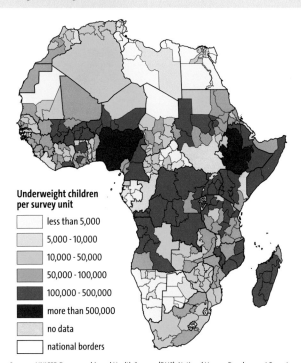

Underweight children per survey unit
- less than 5,000
- 5,000 - 10,000
- 10,000 - 50,000
- 50,000 - 100,000
- 100,000 - 500,000
- more than 500,000
- no data
- national borders

Sources: UNICEF, Demographic and Health Surveys (DHS), National Human Development Reports (nHDR), African Nutrition Database Initiative (ANDI), Gridded Population of the World (GPW) v. 3 alpha. Data for 96% of countries are from 1995 or later. All data are from 1992 or later.

FIGURE 3.5
Proposed Hunger Hotspots

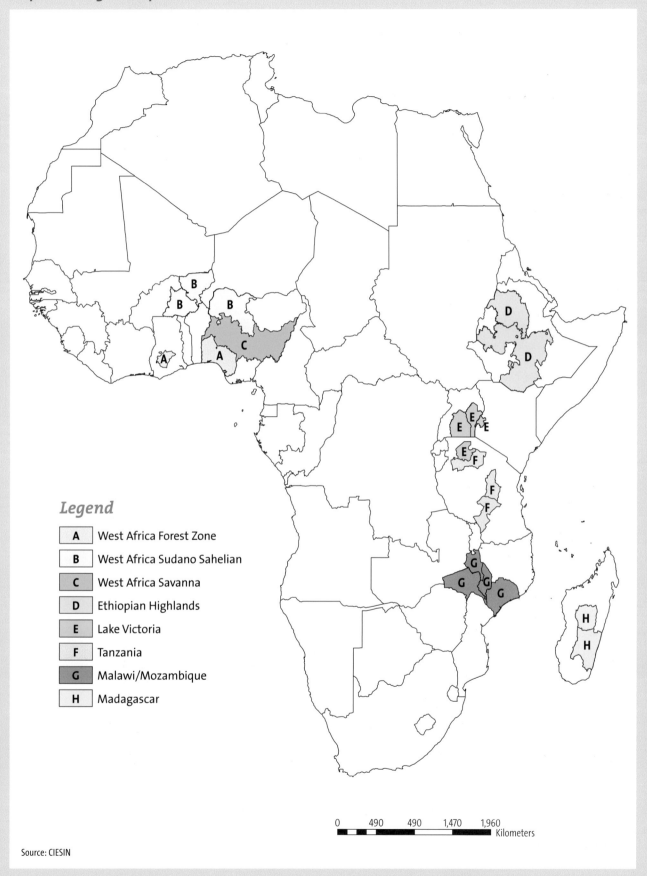

Legend

A	West Africa Forest Zone
B	West Africa Sudano Sahelian
C	West Africa Savanna
D	Ethiopian Highlands
E	Lake Victoria
F	Tanzania
G	Malawi/Mozambique
H	Madagascar

0   490   490   1,470   1,960
Kilometers

Source: CIESIN

Putting Nutrition First Yields Healthy People and Economies

By Isaac Akinyele

Sub-Saharan African countries that seek to develop economically and socially first must ensure that their people are healthy. Yet the governments and institutions seeking such change continue to ignore the erosive force of hunger and poverty, which robs countless people of promise and opportunity.

Today one in three Africans is malnourished, and about half of the continent's 700 million people live on less than $1 a day. Moreover, the Food and Agriculture Organization of the United Nations (FAO) reports that the depth of hunger is greatest in sub-Saharan Africa, where 16 of the region's 40 countries are experiencing undernourishment rates of 35 percent or higher.

Chronic hunger not only increases people's susceptibility to disease, it leaves children listless and unable to concentrate in school, mothers more likely to give birth to underweight babies and adults lacking the energy to think and work productively. These costs are high. In 1990 per capita gross domestic product (GDP) in sub-Saharan Africa was $800. If the region had eradicated undernourishment by that point, the FAO calculates that its GDP could have reached up to $3,000.

Unfortunately, most sub-Saharan African governments have failed to recognize the link between socioeconomic development and proper nutrition. The result: untold suffering, death and economic loss related to hunger and malnutrition.

Good Nutrition for Life

Adequate nutrition is needed throughout a person's life, but especially during critical development periods such as pregnancy, early childhood (birth through age 5), children's school age years, and early adolescence through young adulthood.

Hunger and malnutrition during any life stage can lead to serious development and health problems, ranging from intrauterine brain damage and growth failure to an increased risk of developing diet-related diseases later in life. But proper maternal nutrition during pregnancy and while breastfeeding is especially important because irreversible malnutrition-related development problems can occur during this time.

Research shows that malnourished mothers tend to give birth to malnourished babies, promoting intergenerational problems. Half of all underweight babies are born to mothers who were malnourished at conception and have low-weight gain during pregnancy. Low birth-weight babies are at greater risk of morbidity and mortality, stunting, and poor neurological development. As adults, they experience lower work capacity and are at higher risk of chronic disease.

Costs of Hidden Hunger

While proper caloric intake is necessary to guard against hunger, proper nutrition also is needed to guard against "hidden hunger" or micronutrient deficiencies, such as a lack of vitamin A, iron or iodine. While such deficiencies can cause irreversible damage like blindness, they also cause overall physical weakness and greater susceptibility to illness, creating a vicious cycle of malnutrition and infection. In 2002 more than 90 percent of deaths from infectious diseases worldwide

Poor people often are not able to buy enough of the most nutritious foods, putting them at risk for poor nutrition. In this way, pursuing policies that help reduce poverty also can help fight hunger.

were caused by only a handful of diseases: diarrhea, HIV/AIDS, lower respiratory infections, malaria, measles and tuberculosis. In sub-Saharan Africa, infectious diseases are the leading cause of death.

Vitamin A Deficiencies

Vitamin A deficiency (VAD) often is associated with protein-energy malnutrition, which principally affects preschool children. VAD is the leading cause of preventable visual impairment and blindness. Between 250,000 children and 500,000 children with VAD become blind every year, and about half of them die within a year of becoming blind.

VAD also significantly increases the risk of severe illness and death from common childhood infections, particularly diarrhea and measles. In communities where VAD exists, children are 23 percent more likely to die and 50 percent more likely to suffer acute measles. Among women, VAD not only causes ocular lesions, but also may contribute to maternal mortality and problems during pregnancy and with lactation.

Iron Deficiencies

Iron deficiencies profoundly impact human health and development. In infants and young children, iron deficiencies can lead to impaired psychomotor development, coordination and scholastic achievement as well as decreased physical activity. In pregnant women, iron deficiency increases the risk of maternal and fetal mortality and morbidity, as well as intrauterine growth retardation. In all adults, iron deficiency can cause fatigue, which diminishes productivity.

It is estimated that half of all anemia is caused by dietary iron deficiency, although in many cases blood loss from malaria and parasites such as hookworm and schistosoma also are contributing factors. The groups most affected by anaemia are adolescent girls, women of childbearing age and preschool children.

Iodine Deficiency

Iodine deficiency disorder (IDD) most often occurs among people living in flood-prone areas, where heavy rains wash away iodine in the soil. This deficiency may lead not only to a visible goiter, but also impaired physical and mental development. The more severe IDD consequences include cretinism, mental retardation, deaf-mutism, squint, spastic diplegia (spastic paralysis of the lower limbs), coordination abnormalities, impaired learning capacity and dwarfism. A 1990 World Health Organization report estimated that some 26 million people suffered from brain damage associated with IDD.

Iodine deficiency also affects reproductive functions, leading to increased rates of stillbirths, congenital anomalies, low birth weights, and infant and young child mortality.

Helping Fight Poverty

Most people suffer micronutrient malnutrition because they do not have enough vitamin- and mineral-rich foods in their diets, a situation often aggravated by the body's impaired absorption or use of food nutrients because of an infection and/or parasitic infestation. Food fortification – adding nutrients to staple foods – is a tried-and-true way of battling nutrient deficiencies as seen with salt iodization. Adding vitamin and mineral supplements to people's diets is another successful – though expensive – means for improving nutrition. However, the ultimate long-term solution to hunger and malnutrition is dietary diversification. Because poor diets most often stem from poverty itself – inability to purchase enough of the most nutritious foods – poverty reduction efforts must be tied to any nutrition intervention in poor countries.

Conversely, by addressing hunger and malnutrition, poor countries are best able to tackle poverty. By integrating food security and proper nutrition in economic and social policy, countries benefit from healthier, more intelligent, better educated and more productive citizens, who in turn help create sustainable economic progress in their countries.

Dr. Isaac Olaoluwa Akinyele is president of Food Basket Foundation International and a professor of the Department of Human Nutrition at the University of Ibadan, Nigeria.

experiencing greater rates of hunger and poverty. Agricultural encroachment and the loss of rights to use and manage forests pose significant dangers to forest-dependent people. Pastoralists are facing harder times securing sufficient pasture and water for their animals, and fishermen endure longer periods without a sustaining catch. Better environmental management would greatly benefit these populations.[22]

Urban People

Rising rural migration rates coupled with limited urban employment and worsening urban poverty is fueling greater hunger in urban areas. Approximately 25 percent of poverty in sub-Saharan Africa is urban, and nearly one-fifth of all underweight children live in urban areas.[23] Though the majority of undernourished people in developing countries live in rural communities, academics predict that by 2015 more than one in three people could be living in urban areas.

Families in cities buy almost all of their food, so a steady income source is vital to guarding against hunger. Yet many urban poor people depend on temporary jobs, which provide unsteady income. Poorer people also tend to live on the outskirts of a city, often in slums, far from food markets and without proper infrastructure, such as roads, water and sanitation facilities. Women who work far from home also have less time to buy and prepare food. In many urban centers, drinking water is scarce, and disease outbreaks are rising. Schools and health centers lack resources and are short-staffed.

The split between rural and urban hunger varies greatly among countries. In Brazil, Mauritania and the Philippines, between 40 percent and 60 percent of hungry people live in urban areas. In China, Bangladesh,

Celia Escudero-Espadas

Poor people living in urban areas presently account for about 160 million of the undernourished population, and those numbers are expected to increase rapidly. Efforts to improve employment opportunities are most important to addressing urban hunger.

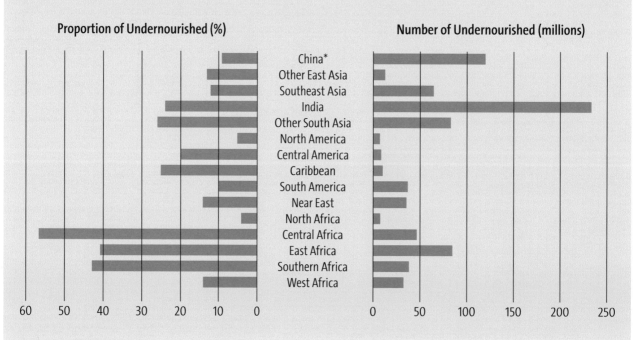

FIGURE 3.6
Number and Proportion of Undernourished People

Proportion of Undernourished (%)

Number of Undernourished (millions)

China*
Other East Asia
Southeast Asia
India
Other South Asia
North America
Central America
Caribbean
South America
Near East
North Africa
Central Africa
East Africa
Southern Africa
West Africa

60 50 40 30 20 10 0

0 50 100 150 200 250

* including Taiwan Province of China

Source: Food and Agriculture Organization of the United Nations

FIGURE 3.7
Changes in Numbers of Undernourished People

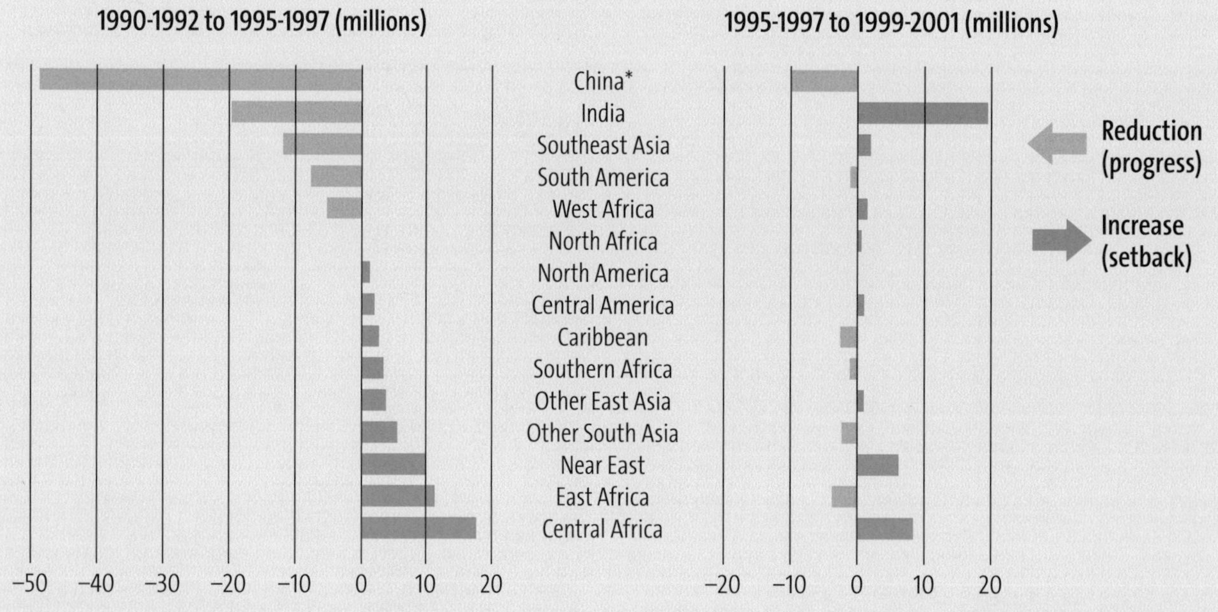

1990-1992 to 1995-1997 (millions)

1995-1997 to 1999-2001 (millions)

China*
India
Southeast Asia
South America
West Africa
North Africa
North America
Central America
Caribbean
Southern Africa
Other East Asia
Other South Asia
Near East
East Africa
Central Africa

−50 −40 −30 −20 −10 0 10 20

−20 −10 0 10 20

← Reduction (progress)

→ Increase (setback)

* including Taiwan Province of China

Source: Food and Agriculture Organization of the United Nations

At least 60 million food insecure families depend on natural resources for their food and livelihoods, according to the U.N. Hunger Task Force. To help these herders, fishers and forest-dependent people, efforts must be made to protect and better manage the natural resources while also improving poor people's long-term access to the resources.

Malawi and Tanzania, less than 20 percent of hungry people are urban.[24] Labor-intensive manufacturing is creating new jobs for low-income people in urban areas. But improving economic opportunities in rural areas also will help urban areas by moderating the pace of migration to cities.

Who Is More Prone to Hunger?

Certain people also are more prone to hunger because of special nutrient needs, including:

- Pregnant and nursing women, infants and preschool children;

- People living with HIV/AIDS and other chronic illness;

- People suffering from diverse micronutrient deficiencies; and

- Victims of extreme events or catastrophes.[25]

Pregnant and Nursing Women, and Children

In most cases, women require more nutrient-rich foods than men, that is, more vitamins and minerals as a share of total calories. Pregnant women need even more calories and nutrients as nonpregnant women,

for example, four times the iron. Women who do not get enough food or the proper variety of food during pregnancy are at greater risk of complications both while pregnant and during delivery.[26] Malnourished mothers often give birth to underweight babies, putting these children at a nutritional disadvantage from the start. Half the children in South Asia and nearly a third of children in Africa are underweight, and the physical and mental damage done by inadequate nutrition between birth and age 2 is irreversible.

HIV/AIDS and Other Chronic Illness

The HIV/AIDS pandemic is closely related with hunger. Hunger weakens the body. A weaker body is more likely to contract HIV. Once HIV-infected, hungry people are less able to absorb nutrients, and they become more susceptible to developing AIDS. Hungry people with AIDS die more quickly than those with proper nutrition.

The causality goes the other way too. People with AIDS often cannot work and care for themselves, so family members must help. These additional tasks can detract people from farming or earning a living in other ways, increasing the entire family's risk of hunger. Many families will sell their household assets to pay for food and medical care for the sick, further increasing the

About 42 percent of women – 51 percent of pregnant women – suffer from iron-related anemia. Iron deficiencies can diminish work productivity by 10 percent or more. For pregnant women, it also substantially increases their risk of death in childbirth, accounting for up to 20 percent of maternal deaths in Africa and Asia, according to the Food and Agriculture Organization of the United Nations.

likelihood that they will go hungry. As noted by the Southern African Regional Poverty Network, when one adult is ill with HIV/AIDS, families "suffer from marked reductions in agricultural production and income generation, leading to earlier engagement in distress coping strategies and, ultimately, a decline in food security."[27]

Poverty and hunger also can drive young people to behave in ways that increase their risk of HIV infection. As such, HIV/AIDS is contributing to the breakdown of social bonds, labor shortages and reliance on crops that are easier to produce but less nutritious and economically valuable, adversely affecting food and nutrition security for entire communities and countries.

Other chronic illness, such as malaria and tuberculosis, similarly impact families' well-being and increase food insecurity.

Micronutrient Deficiencies

More than 2 billion people worldwide suffer from micronutrient deficiencies, often called "hidden hunger." Over half of these people consume adequate amounts of calories and protein, but their diets include inadequate amounts of micronutrients such as folate, iodine, iron, selenium, vitamin A, vitamin C and zinc. Most often, these deficiencies occur when diets lack diversity, espe-

cially of fruits, vegetables, dairy products, meat and fish. Similar to other forms of malnutrition, micronutrient deficiencies can reduce productivity and impair health, and eventually lead to premature death.

Extreme Events

Earthquakes, floods, landslides, droughts, storms, war and hyperinflation or other economic shocks also can disrupt food production and people's ability to earn livings, quickly plunging thousands or even millions of people into food insecurity and hunger. Victims of such extreme events make up between 6 percent and 8 percent of hungry people each year.[28]

People who are chronically hungry and food insecure are more vulnerable to personal or large-scale disasters. Illness, accidents, economic and political shocks, or other uncontrollable problems easily can push vulnerable people into poverty and hunger. Unfortunately, such vulnerable people also are more likely to live in regions prone to drought, disease and natural disasters. Moreover, as they try to cope with one extreme event, they often are forced to make decisions that put them at greater risk of hunger if another crisis hits.

Take Nabiseko, an orphan brought up by her aunt and uncle in rural Malawi. She married young to a prosperous farmer, and for a while she and her husband were doing better than the average villager. But one day, a thief stole their 30 head of cattle. Without their most valuable asset to borrow against, they could not afford fertilizer and their crop yields waned. A year later, Nabiseko's husband died, leaving her with five children to care for. She now struggles like most of the families in her village. "I sometimes go without food and I lack good clothes," she says.[29]

How People Cope

People like Nabiseko try to shield their families from hunger in a variety of ways, with actions becoming more drastic as the experience of hunger grows more intense. When faced with early food and income shortages, one of the first steps women take is to cut back slightly on the variety and quality of food being prepared and eaten. This response alone is enough to begin eroding a family's overall nutrition. If shortages worsen, adults may begin reducing the amount they eat at each meal, eventually skipping some meals altogether. Ultimately, parents may be forced to reduce the amount of food that children eat. At this point, family labor often is diverted from other livelihood endeavors to scrape for food in the fields and/or beg for food and money in the streets.

Many poor families try to hedge against hunger by combining income from multiple sources. For example, a farmer may plant multiple crops and varieties, while also supplementing his or her income with a less labor-intensive trade or other work from a neighbor. If hunger hits, many families are forced to sell their economic assets, often starting with items that are easiest to liquidate, such as small livestock and farm implements. But before taking such drastic action, many people willingly endure a considerable degree of hunger in order to preserve seeds for next year's planting or to avoid selling their animals.[30] In Mali, one of the "shadow" indicators of drought, a major

Extended families and communities play an important role in helping people weather tough times. But as hunger evolves from a temporary condition to one that is chronic, these communal bonds can be strained.

cause of hunger in the country, is escalating small-livestock sales. Governments and emergency donors monitor these volumes to decide when preventive action may be needed to stave off widespread hunger and famine.

Extended families and communities play an important role in helping people weather tough times. But as hunger evolves from a temporary condition to one that is chronic, these communal bonds can be strained. Widespread food insecurity, which occurs regionally in many developing countries, impacts entire family and community networks, leaving no one to care for those affected, except for the occasional relative who lives elsewhere and can send money or other assistance. Increasing numbers of hungry people have only governments and donors to turn to for help.

Better Using What We Know

While much has been learned about hunger in the past three decades, better information is needed about who is hungry and why.

Information gathering must begin to focus on household and community indicators of hunger in addition to national hunger measures. Such analysis will lead to better-targeted policy interventions.

Hunger-fighting efforts also need to sharpen their focus on the most vulnerable groups, especially women and children. Research and case studies consistently show that women play a unique and vital role in sustaining the food security of families and communities. More gender-specific data and analysis are needed so that anti-hunger efforts adequately take into account the low status of women in many countries, the type of work they do and the many roles they assume in a household.

By empowering women through education and improved legal status, they are better able to care for their infants and children.

BFWI Photo/K. Burge

Daniel D. Karanja, Ph.D., research fellow with Partnership to Cut Hunger and Poverty in Africa, contributed to this chapter.

4

Getting Back on Track *in the* *United States*

USDA Photo/Ken Hammond

The federal nutrition programs substantially reduce hunger in the United States. On the whole, they are effective and efficient. The fastest, most direct way to reduce hunger in the United States is to improve and expand the national nutrition programs.

Fortunately, much has been learned in past years about hunger and food insecurity in the United States, and the programs designed to curb them. Further improvements are needed in areas of program integration, coordination, efficiency and integrity as well as nutrition. Among specific communities and states, people are building on these lessons to design new and redesign old programs in ways that better meet their needs. Many of these efforts should be looked at more closely and the information shared nationally and with other communities.

Fulfilling The Promise

The United States has less than seven years to achieve the official goal of reducing by nearly 20 million the number of people living in households at risk of hunger. And while some program changes can be made to improve efficiency and outreach in ways that help eligible people while limiting taxpayer costs, the goal of cutting hunger will require substantial expansion of the nutrition programs.

Congress is scheduled in 2004 to update the child nutrition programs, notably the school and summer feeding programs, which would present an important opportunity to begin reforming and expanding the nutrition assistance programs, key steps in helping the United States keep its promise to cut hunger in half by 2010. While the Bush administration seriously considered expanding the child nutrition programs, it instead decided to propose a long-term program of space travel to Mars. Bread for the World and other advocacy groups are trying to get Congress to proceed with needed improvements anyway. For example, some states have demonstrated ways to improve the bureaucracy that keeps many schools and community groups from running summer feeding programs. Such successful initiatives should be expanded.

Looking beyond 2004, all the national anti-hunger networks, including Bread for the World, together have outlined a vision of how to end hunger in the United States. They meet together as the National Anti-Hunger Organization (NAHO) Coalition, and their vision is explained in the Millennium Declaration to End Hunger in America (see related story, p. 55). It calls for reform and expansion of the nutrition programs, coupled

A young girl selects vegetables from the salad bar at St. Helens Middle School in St. Helens, Ore., where the school offers low-priced summer meals to the entire community.

with broader efforts to reduce poverty. It affirms the crucial roles of low-income families, charities and the public sector.

The NAHO organizations now are working on a more detailed blueprint of how to end hunger in the United States. This blueprint could become the basis for legislation designed to end hunger in the United States or, perhaps more modestly, to meet the officially accepted goal of cutting hunger and food insecurity in half by 2010. Additional analysis and discussion with stakeholders at federal, state and local levels are planned to develop and build consensus around the blueprint.

This chapter provides Bread for the World Institute's initial thinking about ways to strengthen the national nutrition programs.

Where Do We Stand?

The United States can take pride in the development of its nutrition programs over the last several decades. While the historical impact of the national nutrition programs on hunger and food insecurity is hard to measure because of data constraints, people at risk of hunger who participate in federal programs clearly have better access to food and eat healthier. Unfortunately, up to half the people who should be participating in these programs do not.

In 2003 more than 21 million people received food stamps, at an annual cost of nearly $24 billion.[1] The average monthly benefit per person was approximately $84, increasing his or her total food purchases by between $22 and $30.[2] Low-income families purchase more food with a dollar of food stamp benefits than with a dollar of cash.[3] Because food stamp benefits depend on need and because of program improvements approved by Congress in 2002, assistance has expanded during the recent period of high unemployment.

While improved nutrition does not always follow improved food security, the federal assistance programs designed specifically for that purpose, such as the Special Supplemental Program for Women, Infants and Children (WIC) and the child nutrition programs, appear to be doing their job. A wealth of research demonstrates that the National School Lunch Program, for example, is associated with greater daily consumption of protein and 10 vitamins and minerals in addition to overall calories.[4] Moreover, these nutritional gains are not due solely to more food being eaten, but also children eating foods of higher nutritional quality.

"The success of the nation's nutrition-assistance safety net, beginning with the National School Lunch Program in 1946 and later undergirded by the Food Stamp Program and special programs for unusually vulnerable groups, has meant that extreme forms of hunger, common in Third World countries, have been virtually eliminated in the United States," according to the U.S. Department of Agriculture (USDA).[5]

Despite these successes, the nation's nutrition-assistance safety net has two significant shortfalls: (1) a substantial number of people participating in the federal programs remain at risk of hunger; and (2) no program reaches all eligible people, and several programs reach less than half of the intended recipients.

In 2002 nearly 35 million people lived in U.S households at risk of hunger. Yet the federal nutrition programs designed to help them barely met half this need. Forty-five percent of food insecure households received no help from the three largest nutrition programs – food stamps, free or reduced-price school lunches, and WIC. Among those experiencing hunger, fully half (50 percent) received no help from these programs. Moreover, of the people who did participate in the federal nutrition programs, many remained at risk of hunger.[6]

Why Aren't People Who Need Help Receiving It?

The fact that many people who use the federal food assistance programs remain at risk of hunger may mean that the programs are attracting people with the greatest need. But it also reflects weaknesses within the programs, mostly that benefit levels are too low. Over the years, researchers at USDA, nonprofit think tanks, advocacy organizations and other groups have been analyzing the programs' effectiveness in fighting hunger among participants as well as the programs' low-participation rates. The question of why people who participate in food stamps, WIC or the other assistance programs may continue to be food insecure does not have a simple answer.

Some research suggests that benefits are not high enough, especially for specific populations, like single men and women. While the relationship between food expenses and food security are fairly consistent, actual food expenses can vary greatly across households. For example, a food insecure man who lives alone typically spends the most on food – 150 percent of the Thrifty Food Plan, the government's official estimate of an adequate household food budget. Meanwhile, a food insecure household headed by a single mother typically spends the least on food – 103 percent of the Thrifty Food Plan.[7]

USDA also has noted that among people living in food insecure households, those receiving food assistance spend substantially less on food than those who receive no help. In 2002 food insecure households typically spent on food about the full cost (98 percent) of the food plan. In contrast, families receiving food stamps

Families spend varying amounts of money on food. Typically, men living alone spend the most on food, and single mothers spend the least. On average, people who participate in the Food Stamp Program increase their monthly food expenditures by between $22 and $30.

THE MILLENNIUM DECLARATION TO END HUNGER IN AMERICA

The National Anti-Hunger Organizations (NAHO)

WE CALL UPON OUR NATION'S LEADERS AND ALL PEOPLE TO JOIN TOGETHER TO END HUNGER IN AMERICA

America carries the wound of more than 30 million people - more than 13 million of them children - whose households cannot afford an adequate and balanced diet. Hunger should have no place at our table. It is inconsistent with our commitment to human rights and objectionable to the American values of fairness, opportunity, family and community.

Our nation is committed to leaving no child behind. But children who are hungry cannot keep up. They cannot develop and thrive; they cannot learn or play with energy and enthusiasm. Hunger stunts the physical, mental and emotional growth of many of our children, and stains the soul of America.

Many different points of view unite us in this declaration. Some of us work to end hunger because of deeply held religious beliefs. Others are motivated by hunger's impact on health and cognitive development. Still others are driven by the long-term economic, human and ethical costs of hunger. But all of us are moved by the recognition that America's moral authority in the world is undermined by so much hunger in our midst. Regardless of our religious beliefs or political commitments, we share the conviction that we as a nation must act to end hunger—now.

Ending hunger is a two-step process. We can make rapid progress by expanding and improving effective initiatives like public nutrition programs. This, combined with strengthened community-based efforts, has the capacity to feed all in need. But we need to go even further, to attack the root causes of hunger.

Our nation's own past experience, and the successes of other countries, demonstrate that this two-pronged strategy can work.

ENDING HUNGER

America made great progress in reducing hunger during the 1960s and 1970s, as the economy grew and the nation built strong public nutrition programs - food stamps, school lunches and breakfasts, summer food, WIC, and elderly nutrition programs. These vital programs provide the fuel for children to develop and learn, and for adults to succeed at work and as parents.

As a country we did not sustain that momentum. One response has been the emergence of a strong private anti-hunger sector: food banks, pantries, soup kitchens, food rescue and other emergency feeding programs have become a key bulwark against hunger for many Americans. Volunteers, businesses, non-profits and religious organizations now help millions of needy Americans put food on their table.

But emergency feeding programs alone cannot end hunger. They cannot reach the scale essential to address the desperate need many people face, nor can they provide long-term security for the families they serve. Our country's experience over the past 20 years shows that charity can fill gaps and ameliorate urgent needs. But charity cannot match the capacity of government to protect against hunger, nor the capacity of the private sector to foster economic growth and provide living wages.

Ending hunger requires a sustained public commitment to improve federal nutrition programs, and to reduce red tape to reach every household and every individual in need:

- We can begin with the millions of at-risk children who start their school days without food, or who miss meals during the summer months, when they lose access to regular year school meal programs. Expanding programs for school lunch, breakfast, summer food, after-school meals for school age children, and child care food and WIC for pre-schoolers, is essential, cost-effective and a moral imperative.

- The food stamp program, the cornerstone of the nation's hunger programs, has the capacity to wipe out hunger for millions of families. We should reduce the red tape that often keeps working families and others from getting essential food stamp help. And the help families get should be enough so they do not run out of food toward the end of each month.

- We also must better protect elderly citizens whose frail bodies and meager incomes make them susceptible to hunger and nutrition-related diseases. Improving food stamps, home delivered meals, congregate feeding programs and commodity donations will ensure that increasing age does not also mean an empty cupboard.

These and related nutrition programs can become readily available through the support of innovative community efforts across our country. And all programs can be re-woven to deliver healthy, nutritious meals to ensure an end to hunger in America.

ENDING THE CAUSE OF HUNGER

The root cause of hunger is a lack of adequate purchasing power in millions of households. When individuals and families do not have the resources to buy enough food, hunger results. As a nation we must encourage work and also ensure all who work that the results of their labor will be sufficient to provide for the basic needs of their families. For those unemployed or disabled, or too old or young to support themselves, other means can ensure sufficient income to protect them from hunger.

Many steps can be taken to help families achieve independence and security: a strong economy; an adequate minimum wage that, like the one a generation ago, lifts a small family out of poverty; private and public sector provision of jobs and job training; strategies to create and increase assets among working families; social insurance protection for the unemployed and retired; and child care, refundable tax credits, food stamps and health insurance that reward work efforts of families trying to make ends meet.

A sustained and comprehensive investment in the efforts of all American families will ensure that inadequate income never again results in lack of needed nutrition for the children and adults of our country.

Taking these steps to reward work and effort, along with the ready availability of nutritious food programs, will ensure that residents of the United States are not hungry tomorrow or any time in the future. Ending hunger in America will reduce dramatically the deprivation that currently saps the lives of so many of our children and families. Ending hunger will make us a stronger nation.

This goal is achievable. The time is now. We call upon the President, Congress, and other elected leaders in states and cities provide decisive leadership to end hunger in America. Let us all work together, private and public leaders, community, religious and charitable groups, to achieve an America where hunger is but a distant memory and we live true to the values of a great nation.

WIC Brings a Bright Spot to A Struggling Family

By Melvin Durai

On a warm Saturday morning, Sophia Chiremba carries her 14-month-old son, William, around the bustling farmer's market in Lafayette, Ind., looking for vendors who accept WIC vouchers. About a third of them do and Chiremba spends $9 on peaches, potatoes and apples, hauling them to her second-floor apartment at Purdue University.

She and her husband, William Anong, both international students, seem unlikely participants in the WIC program (Special Supplemental Nutrition Program for Women, Infants and Children). Chiremba, 29, from Zimbabwe, is pursuing a Ph.D. in consumer sciences, while Anong, 36, a Cameroon citizen with a U.S. green card, is in the final stages of his Ph.D. in chemistry. Their assistantships pay them more than $2,000 a month, but with many expenses, including $400 a month for daycare and $600 for rent, they've found WIC essential.

> "I used to buy formula and (WIC) was a big help, because formula is expensive," Chiremba says.

"I used to buy formula and (WIC) was a big help, because formula is expensive," Chiremba says.

When a younger William was on formula, WIC saved them about $100 a month; nowadays it saves them about $50. "They're very generous with their quantities," she says. "They give us six gallons of milk."

Chiremba believes that without WIC she might not have met all her nutritional requirements during her pregnancy. "I probably wouldn't have bought other things that I needed, such as orange juice and fruits."

M. Durai

Sophia Chiremba and her 14-month-old son, William, shop for fresh fruit at a farmer's market in Lafayette, Ind.

She also benefited greatly from the nutritional advice WIC workers gave her. "It's a very helpful program," she says. "It's not all about giving us those checks, but it's also about educating us. You tell them what foods you eat and they do a nutritional assessment."

While her family isn't eligible for other government help, they try to save money by shopping at Aldi, a discount food store, and growing vegetables in a small plot of land they rent from the university.

They hope to harvest corn, pumpkins, green beans, shallots, cucumbers and tomatoes. "This will help a lot, especially the tomatoes," says Chiremba, scanning their weedy patch. "We usually buy canned tomatoes from Aldi, but it will be nice to have fresh tomatoes."

As she passes a neighboring garden, she stops to admire the rows of okra plants. "Their okra did well, our okra didn't," she says. "I'm jealous, because we eat a lot of okra."

Preferring their native cuisine, including sadza, a cornmeal dish from Zimbabwe, and yams from Cameroon, they rarely eat out. "It's expensive and we don't like the food," Chiremba says. "For us, eating out is going to someone else's house."

Melvin Durai is a freelance writer who lives in Lafayette, Ind.

M. Durai

Sophia Chiremba places her 14-month-old son, William, in his highchair as she prepares to feed him lunch.

typically spent 90 percent of the official food-plan costs on their food budgets.[8] While this difference could reveal greater income needs among households that seek help from the government, it also suggests that people seeking help likely need – and qualify for – more than one program's assistance.

Why are people not seeking additional help? Extensive research can be found on many participation barriers identified to date, ranging from a lack of awareness about the programs and eligibility criteria to people's distrust of the federal government and burdensome application processes (see related story, p. 59). While significant work already is underway to address some of the commonly cited problems, the government has yet to allocate additional money to help pay for necessary changes.

Moreover, additional research may be needed to better understand how the various nutrition and anti-poverty programs interrelate so reforms to one program do not lead to detrimental changes in another. Take the Food Stamp Program. Between 1994 and July 2000, the national food stamp rolls fell by nearly 40 percent, dropping from 27.2 million participants to 16.7 million.[9] Some of this decline could be attributed to the improved economy and better wages for lower-skilled workers in the mid- to late-1990s. However, the 1996 reform in federal welfare law (the Personal Responsibility and Work Opportunity Reconciliation Act) led to program changes that reduced eligibility for some groups, established work requirements for adults without children and limited future benefit increases for all participants. Welfare reform also led to administrative changes and new barriers for working people that decreased food stamp participation, with children bearing the brunt of about half that decline.

Congress asked the Government Accounting Office (GAO) – its investigative body – to examine this decline, and in July 1999 the GAO reported that some eligible people were having problems receiving food stamps because of various service- and program-related problems in state and local offices.[10] For example, the USDA's Food and Nutrition Service found that certain offices in the Portland, Ore., area required potential applicants to arrive at the office before 8:30 a.m. If not, these people were turned away and told to come back another day to fill out the application. Of those who did arrive before 8:30 a.m., the offices' "first-come, first-served" policy often meant that people would spend an entire day waiting to apply.

Several states since have modified their programs to improve customer service and accessibility and ease application and certification burdens. For example, some states have streamlined their food stamp applications and combined them with other program applications, such as Temporary Assistance for Needy Families (TANF) and Medicaid. In an effort to expand outreach, the USDA has translated its program applications and other information material into 32 languages. Many local food stamp offices also use "language lines," a service that provides an applicant a verbal translator by speaker-phone.

Legislative changes during this period also have helped raise participation rates. In 1996 Congress had decided that legal immigrants could not ever qualify for food stamps. In 2002 Congress reversed that decision. Congress also changed the law in ways that encourage states to reach more eligible people with assistance. Several states are using federal waivers to allow longer food stamp certification periods so that people who qualify for food stamps do not have to requalify every three months, a burden often cited among working recipients as a reason for not participating. Bread for the World and other advocacy groups played an important role in passing these 2002 food stamp reforms.

These efforts appear to be paying off. Since July 2000, food stamp rolls have increased fairly steadily to an estimated 23 million participants in December 2003.[11] Though some of this 35-percent increase is due to more people needing food stamps as jobs have become scarcer in the recent national recession, it far outpaces the 3-percent climb in poverty during this same period, suggesting that state efforts are working to help more eligible people receive food stamps.

Of course, more needs to be done to fill the hunger gap. Even with current changes, the Food Stamp Program – with the highest participation rates among food insecure households – still reaches barely half the people at risk of hunger.[12] In addition to programmatic and customer service changes, more money will be needed to get the job done.

Jobs, Hunger and the Nutrition Programs

A strong job market powerfully reduces hunger. Between 1995 and 2000 the country reduced hunger, largely due to low unemployment and rising incomes during the late 1990s. Declines in food insecurity and hunger were experienced regardless of where people lived or their demographics. In fact, declines were greatest for women with children, African Americans and Hispanics – traditionally some of the most economically disadvantaged groups. Job growth and higher incomes for lower-skilled employees accounted for most of the improvement in food insecurity during this period, and about half of the reduction in hunger.[13]

USDA food security data show that people living in households with incomes below the poverty line are at a higher risk of being hungry. But these same data also show that food insecurity is not necessarily tied only to

FIGURE 4.1
Where Are Food Insecure Households Located?

Prevalance of Food Insecurity by State, Average 2000-2002

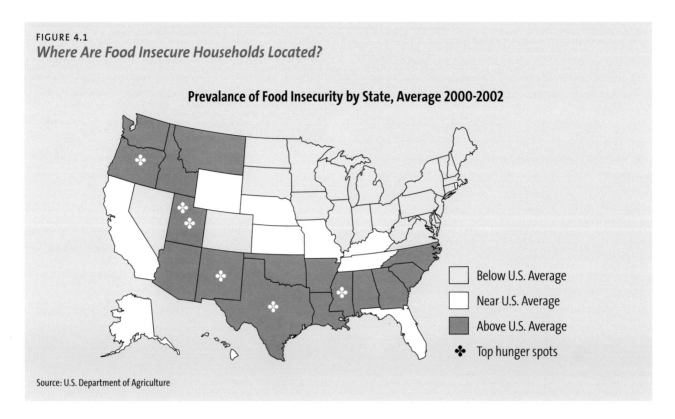

Below U.S. Average

Near U.S. Average

Above U.S. Average

✿ Top hunger spots

Source: U.S. Department of Agriculture

lower income. One in four people living in food insecure homes – 8.5 million people – report incomes at 185 percent of the poverty line or higher.[14] How do some poor households manage to remain food secure while some nonpoor households struggle to put food on the table?

Strikingly, growing numbers of employed people need and receive help from the nutrition programs. Among food stamp families with children, the percentage of those working increased from 27 percent in 1993 to 42 percent in 1999.[15] According to the Center on Budget and Policy Priorities, in 2002 nearly three-fourths (73 percent) of adults with children were working or engaged in some type of work-support activity.[16]

New thought and research need to be devoted to interactions between employment, hunger and the nutrition programs. The Food Stamp Program is one way the nation can make sure that people who work at least are able to feed their families.

Don't Forget the Children

When considering the programs' low participation rates and barriers, it is important to remember that the majority of people who benefit – or who should be benefiting – from these programs are children. In order to receive help, children need their parents or guardians to ask for them. Consequently, any barriers that serve to prevent adults from applying and possibly participating in the programs also hinder children's ability to receive help.

About one in six children lives in food insecure households, but the USDA has learned that children go hungry for a day or more in less than 1 percent of all U.S. households.[17] Even in households where adults report hunger, children rarely go hungry because parents often choose to skip meals rather than make their children go without eating. Typically, mothers take the brunt of hunger and moderate its impact on their children.

Still, the children suffer. In a nationally representative sample of food insecure families, researchers found that:

- 81 percent reported that at times they relied on only a few kinds of low-cost food to feed their children because they lacked enough money to buy the food they needed;

- approximately half (52 percent) reported that at times they could not afford to feed their children balanced meals; and

- one in four reported that at times their children were not eating enough because the family could not afford enough food.[18]

Poor nutrition and food insecurity have been found to have harmful effects on children's psychosocial development and learning. Malnutrition also weakens children's immune systems, increasing their likelihood for recurrent infections. Patterns of irregular eating and poor nutrition also are being cited in some early research linking hunger and poverty to obesity.

Many Program Barriers Keep People From the National Nutrition Programs

The United States supports an array of national nutrition programs designed to protect men, women and children from going hungry and suffering poor nutrition. Despite the programs' success, many eligible people continue not to use these programs.

For example, less the one-third of seniors eligible for food stamps receive them. While nearly 16 million children qualify for free or reduced-price breakfasts, only 6 million children receive them. Nearly three-fourths of people considered food insecure do not receive food stamps.

A wealth of research has identified barriers to program participation and how to improve the programs. The following is a short list of some of the more common reasons cited.

People are not aware of the programs, or think they are not eligible.

In one study, the overwhelming majority of food stamp nonparticipants estimated to be eligible said they were not aware they were eligible.[1]

People are not aware or do not understand program benefits.

Misperceptions exist about the level of program benefits available to people, which can discourage people from applying. For example, many seniors believe they are only eligible for $10 per month in food stamps, while the average benefit for elderly individuals living alone is $45.

Some of the most troubling misinformation exists among Hispanic and immigrant populations, where people report that they think they must pay back benefits later in life or that accepting food stamps will affect applications for citizenship.

People living in immigrant communities fear "outing."

Families with undocumented workers pose another area of concern. Although children living with undocumented workers are eligible for program benefits like food stamps, the fear that a family will be "outed" during the application process inhibits some parents from seeking help for their children. Once a person or family is outed during the application process, "The community shuts down," according to one community advocate.[2]

People are turned off by overly burdensome application processes.

While improvements are being made to application processes – they are getting shorter and some programs have combine forms – problems persist with applications that are extremely lengthy, complicated and difficult to complete without additional personal paperwork.[3]

Some programs have eligibility criteria that may be overly restrictive.

For example, an open site in the summer feeding program must be in a neighborhood where 50 percent of children have family incomes below 185 percent of the poverty line. But not all low-income children live in areas with high poverty rates.

Some programs' benefits do not cover the hidden costs people assume when they participate in a program.

Participating in the programs has costs associated with it (i.e., time away from work to apply for the program or to place children in child care so a parent can make an appointment). These costs may erode any perceived benefit to participating in a program. For example, the average benefit level of food stamps for a household of two-to-three people is $163 – or 84 cents per meal per person per day. A parent may decide participating in the program is not worth that amount of money. Program providers also report that federal reimbursements generally do not cover all program costs.

People associate a negative stigma with the programs.

According to a study by Mathematica Policy Research, almost half of people eligible for food stamps who were not participating indicated there was a stigma related to using this benefit. This had a statistically significant effect on participation in the Food Stamp Program.[4]

People lack transportation to get to a program office to apply or recertify for a program.

In nearly every program, transportation is cited as a barrier. Especially with the Summer Food Service Program, finding transportation can be a challenge to getting children to the site where food is provided.

[1] Michael Ponza, James Ohls, Lorenzo Moreno, et al., "Customer Service in the Food Stamp Program." (Washington, DC: Mathematica Policy Research Inc.) July 1999, xvi.

[2] Based on Bread for the World Institute field research.

[3] Ponza.

[4] Anne Gordon, Ronette Briefel, et al., *Feeding Low-Income Children When School Is Out – The Summer Food Service Program: Final Report.* Economic Research Service, U.S. Department of Agriculture, E-FAN No. (03001), March 2003, 79.

Understanding U.S. Nutrition Programs:
The Main Child Nutrition Programs

The National School Lunch Program (NSLP)

The National School Lunch Program (NSLP) provides reimbursements to schools for nutritious lunches served to students at more than 90 percent of schools around the country. Nearly 26 million students participate in the school lunch program, with almost 16 million low-income children receiving lunch for free or at a reduced price. For these children, the school lunch program provides a critical link to food security.

How it works

Children in households with incomes below 130 percent of the poverty level ($23,920 annually for a family of four) qualify for free lunches. In addition, children whose families receive food stamps or Temporary Assistance for Needy Families (TANF) automatically are eligible for free meals. Children with family incomes between 130 percent and 185 percent of the poverty line (185 percent is $34,040 annually for a family of four) qualify for reduced-price lunches. Schools may charge students no more than 40 cents for these lunches. Children whose family income is above 185 percent of the poverty level can purchase school lunch at full price.

Schools are reimbursed for each meal they serve. The reimbursement rates to schools are tiered – in 2003-2004 schools received $2.19 for each free lunch provided, $1.79 for each reduced-price lunch offered, and $0.21 for each full-price lunch. (Rates are higher for schools serving high numbers of free and reduced-price meals.) School meals are required to meet federal nutrition standards and have become healthier over the past several years as schools have increased the number of fruits and vegetables served and reduced the fat content of meals. The U.S. Department of Agriculture (USDA) also provides commodity assistance to select school lunch programs.

The School Breakfast Program

About 75 percent of schools that participate in the school lunch program also offer a breakfast program. However, only about 8 million children receive breakfast at school, with 6.7 million receiving free and reduced-price breakfasts. Research has shown that children who eat breakfast at school score better on tests, have lower rates of tardiness and absences, and are less likely to be anxious and depressed.

How it works

As in the school lunch program, schools receive reimbursements for each meal served ($1.12 for free breakfasts, $0.90 for reduced-price breakfasts and $0.22 for full-price breakfasts). The eligibility standards for free and reduced-price breakfasts are the same as for school lunches. Some schools provide breakfast in the cafeteria, and others have adopted breakfast-in-the-classroom to accommodate students who (due to bus schedules or other reasons) arrive too late to eat before school. Students receiving reduced-price breakfast pay no more than 30 cents.

The Summer Food Service Program

The Summer Food Service Program was created to help ensure that low-income children have food security in the summer. Unfortunately, this program is drastically underused, serving just over 2 million children. (And about 1 million are served during the summer through the school lunch program at year-round schools, for example.) Comparatively, nearly 16 million children receive free and reduced-price meals during the school year. Burdensome paperwork for sponsors, lack of transportation and high area-eligibility rates are impediments to fuller use of this program.

How it works

Organizations that run summer programs, such as schools, local government agencies, camps, colleges, and private nonprofit organizations (including churches, synagogues and mosques), can be reimbursed for meals served to children during the summer. In most cases, providers may qualify for reimbursements if (1) they are located in an area where 50 percent of the children have a family income below 185 percent of the poverty level or (2) over 50 percent of the children enrolled in the summer program have a family income below 185 percent of the poverty level. Summer meals are provided free to all participating children.

Generally, providers are reimbursed up to $2.41 for each lunch/supper, $1.38 for each breakfast and $0.56 for each snack, plus administrative costs. Most organizations can be reimbursed for two meals/snacks a day.

The Child and Adult Care Food Program

This program providers nutritious meals to more than 2.9 million children a day in child care. It provides an important support for child care, because providers must be licensed or approved to provide day care to participate. In addition, food often draws children whose parents must work to afterschool programs, which offer a safe and enriching environment.

How it works

This program provides reimbursements for meals served in child care centers, day care homes, homeless shelters, Head Start programs and afterschool programs. It also operates in adult day care centers serving those who are functionally impaired or aged 60 and over. The eligibility criteria and reimbursement rates differ depending on the sponsor and the type of care provided.

The Special Supplemental Nutrition Program for Women, Infants and Children (WIC)

The WIC program provides supplemental food high in nutritional value to low-income families. Serving about 7.5 million women, infants and children in 2002, WIC is one of the most effective government social programs. WIC has reduced low-birth weights, child anemia and infant mortality. WIC also reduces Medicaid costs and increases children's readiness to learn.

How it works

WIC is available to lower-income pregnant, postpartum and breast-feeding women, and to infants and children up to age 5. To qualify, a family must have an income at or below 185 percent of the poverty line and be at nutritional risk. Food such as milk, cheese, iron-fortified cereal, eggs, carrots, peanut butter, infant formula and tuna are provided through vouchers that can be redeemed at approved retail outlets. WIC also provides nutrition education, which enables families to learn about healthy eating and food shopping practices that will last a lifetime and can be passed on to children.

Elderly Nutrition Program

This program, established in the Older Americans Act (OAA), provides grants and meal subsidies to states to support congregate meals and meals delivered to homes, such as Meals on Wheels. It is administered by the Administration on Aging at the U.S. Department of Health and Human Services. The meals served in this program must meet nutritional guidelines.

How it works

The Administration on Aging provides funding to states based on Census Bureau data on the number of older adults in each state. States then distribute funding to area agencies on aging that either provide meal programs or contract with organizations that provide services. These are not means-tested programs, but there are extensive targeting goals and required criteria to ensure that the funding helps vulnerable older people. The OAA puts a very strong emphasis on helping those in economic need, low-income minority individuals and people in rural areas.

The Food Stamp Program

The Food Stamp Program is the nation's first-line of defense against hunger. With its origins in the Depression, the Food Stamp Program was made permanent in 1964 and served 19 million people by 2002. (The highest level of participation was in 1994, with nearly 28 million recipients.) The federal government pays for food costs plus one half of administrative costs, with states picking up the rest.

How it works

Households with income below 130 percent of the poverty level can be eligible for food stamps. In general, participants receive electronic benefit transfer (EBT) cards with which they may purchase food at most grocery stores. There are strict asset limits, such as a $2,000 limit on resources like savings accounts and other assets, and work requirements usually apply. Benefits are based on USDA's Thrifty Food Plan and differ depending on family size. Only food can be purchased with food stamps; items such as alcohol, household goods or pet food are not allowed.

More than 90 percent of schools in the United States participate in the National School Lunch Program, which provides children living in low-income households free or reduced-price lunches.

National Obesity Epidemic Raises Important Questions

Overweight and obesity quickly are becoming the primary public health concern in the United States. Nearly two-thirds of adults and more than one in 10 youth are considered overweight or obese. If this trend is not reversed, health experts predict that today's children will be the first generation in decades not to live as long as their parents.[19]

Obesity is a complex health problem that affects people at all income levels. But some low-income people's tendency to adopt irregular eating habits, so-called feast-and-famine patterns, has been associated with slightly higher rates of being overweight and obese. For example, recent work from Cornell University and the University of California at Davis suggests that obesity among poor women may be linked to their habit of periodically going without food so that their children can eat.[20]

Seeking Help Elsewhere

For too many people, the fight against hunger remains a constant struggle, sometimes undermining their productivity, earning ability, health and overall well-being. So it's no surprise that people who are faced with hunger and find little to no relief in the federal nutrition assistance programs look for help elsewhere.

Community and emergency food assistance efforts have burgeoned in the past few decades, to a limited extent making up for cutbacks in government programs dating back to the early 1980s. Some research also suggests that people seeking help from community food pantries and soup kitchens face fewer barriers, such as no application or screening process, and are more likely to use these services than apply for federal help.

The Need for a Flexible Federal Safety Net

Part of the debate about how best to improve the federal nutrition programs includes the issue of whether the federal government's role in administering the nation's nutrition programs should be diminished through block grants and "superwaivers" so that the role of community and faith-based efforts can be increased. While such community efforts deserve to be strengthened, certain aspects of the current system, including its flexibility to respond to economic changes while delivering standard benefits and services nationally, make it effective in fighting hunger and should be retained.

Most of the primary nutrition programs are designed in a way that allows them to respond to need as people enter and leave the labor force. During recessions, for example, caseloads for programs increase as unemployment increases. This is particularly true for the Food Stamp Program. As entitlements, food stamps and most child nutrition programs can expand and contract as the economy shifts. If funding for the programs is capped through block grants or superwaivers, they could lose this elasticity and the ability to help all eligible people in need.

A handful of policymakers also have suggested replacing the government's role in food assistance altogether with a private-sector effort run by charities and faith-based organizations. Expanding the role of churches and charities does make sense given the strong American value to give and the effective role that charities play in providing food assistance.

But private-sector programs, too, must contend with changes in the economy. Charitable organizations are heavily dependent on contributions of food and money from individuals and corporations, and donation levels often fluctuate with the economy. In economic down times, emergency food suppliers may have to limit the quantity of food distributed or the number of households aided, even if need increases.

Although strong, the private sector's capacity does not approach the level required for the kind of system needed to serve millions of Americans at current assistance levels. Ensuring that the nutrition programs retain entitlement status and enhancing public-private partnerships in ways that support rather than burden the role of churches and charities will keep the United States on track to meet the 2010 goal of cutting hunger in half.

Estimates of how many people use community and emergency food assistance vary. America's Second Harvest, a national network of food banks, reports that it serves 55,000 grassroots agencies that feed 23 million people in the United States every year.[21] The USDA reports that in 2002 more than 10 million people lived in homes that used emergency food services, such as community food banks and kitchens.[22]

Regardless of differences, all indicators point to these numbers rising. Many emergency food providers report that they cannot meet their community's needs and are forced to turn people away, reduce the amount of food being distributed and/or reduce the frequency in which people can receive help. The 2003 U.S. Conference of Mayors report on hunger and homelessness found that requests for emergency food increased by an average of 17 percent during 2002 in the 25 cities surveyed. In more than half of these cities, officials reported that they were unable to keep up with the need.[23]

Moreover, people's use of food pantries and emergency kitchens is strongly associated with them being food insecure and hungry. According to the most recent USDA data, food insecure households are 19 times more likely to obtain food from a food pantry than a food secure household, and 25 times more likely to have eaten at an emergency kitchen.[24]

Charity Alone Cannot Meet the Need

Local efforts to fill the hunger gap have been growing, and people who use these services often report that they prefer to receive this form of help versus using one of the federal assistance programs – strong reasons to strengthen charitable programs. But some politicians who praise charities also are inclined to curtail government programs, and there is no way that charitable programs can carry the full burden of overcoming hunger.

Most charitable, emergency services are provided locally through community food assistance agencies that rely heavily on volunteers.[25] Although most of the food distributed by food pantries and community kitchens comes from local resources, such as food drives and church donations, the USDA also supplements these efforts with commodities through The Emergency Food Assistance Program (TEFAP). Congress appropriated $190 million for TEFAP in fiscal year 2003 – $140 million to purchase food and $50 million in administrative support.[26]

While strong and constantly improving, the private food assistance network is vulnerable to the ebb and flow of the economy and changes in the food industry. For example, in recent years food producers and retailers have become more efficient in ways that have reduced overruns and slightly damaged goods. The food industry

TABLE 4.1

U.S. Federal Nutrition Program Participation By State

	Food Stamps	Meal Programs			
		Children in:		Average Daily Attendance	
State	Percent of Eligible Persons Receiving	School Lunch Program	School Breakfast Program	Children in Summer Food Program	Children and Adults in CACFP*
Alabama	62%	540,430	152,631	40,350	41,440
Alaska	74%	51,231	9,614	687	9,598
Arizona	48%	463,639	140,865	25,874	68,353
Arkansas	66%	307,521	121,728	10,010	22,642
California	49%	2,609,992	846,630	183,909	301,035
Colorado	49%	313,930	55,798	12,000	37,730
Connecticut	58%	270,989	49,316	28,058	18,106
Delaware	52%	71,634	17,335	7,492	9,797
District of Columbia	100%	50,931	20,259	20,442	6,202
Florida	53%	1,338,698	433,143	186,242	117,209
Georgia	55%	1,083,570	378,768	88,281	105,479
Hawaii	100%	140,731	39,071	4,954	8,701
Idaho	45%	141,600	28,450	6,672	6,074
Illinois	66%	1,072,234	206,701	84,472	105,201
Indiana	66%	627,004	114,366	19,277	45,978
Iowa	56%	380,810	65,766	5,111	28,137
Kansas	43%	310,902	72,436	7,721	48,587
Kentucky	75%	499,491	187,127	33,244	47,805
Louisiana	74%	635,740	237,026	43,675	50,290
Maine	80%	99,106	25,806	5,786	14,351
Maryland	55%	403,487	113,147	29,863	50,095
Massachusetts	43%	533,653	110,423	56,662	54,503
Michigan	65%	816,603	179,018	33,981	60,215
Minnesota	55%	561,822	103,110	32,469	112,912
Mississippi	61%	398,430	175,371	28,562	28,920
Missouri	69%	589,547	161,728	27,590	44,071
Montana	58%	77,943	15,929	8,067	14,495
Nebraska	60%	219,969	37,678	5,111	35,629
Nevada	35%	121,294	36,093	5,025	5,906
New Hampshire	46%	105,860	16,522	4,039	6,713
New Jersey	56%	590,164	89,932	58,876	58,382
New Mexico	64%	194,471	82,230	44,828	41,735
New York	62%	1,761,759	461,085	308,251	205,287
North Carolina	53%	832,732	286,278	40,085	118,029
North Dakota	55%	79,177	13,252	2,012	16,368
Ohio	55%	984,455	187,643	44,600	87,905
Oklahoma	64%	373,700	146,403	10,858	40,896
Oregon	66%	262,853	99,736	19,698	30,882
Pennsylvania	67%	1,026,267	194,940	141,450	75,066
Rhode Island	70%	64,654	15,169	9,201	9,673
South Carolina	62%	466,793	167,323	68,549	30,601
South Dakota	59%	103,772	17,772	5,003	10,324
Tennessee	72%	620,005	193,854	40,181	37,620
Texas	46%	2,489,841	1,007,355	82,913	180,772
Utah	55%	273,149	35,197	20,778	33,069
Vermont	76%	52,243	14,472	3,100	6,805
Virginia	55%	671,120	175,651	37,511	46,189
Washington	57%	474,659	119,581	29,754	63,410
West Virginia	92%	196,138	83,062	14,154	16,722
Wisconsin	48%	544,516	58,888	27,882	57,266
Wyoming	50%	49,806	8,758	481	7,572

Source: U.S. Department of Agriculture

*Child and Adult Care Food Program

Margaret W. Nea

Research shows that children who eat breakfast at school score better on tests, have lower rates of tardiness and absences, and are less likely to be anxious and depressed.

also is redirecting salvageable goods to secondary markets, such as discount food and thrift stores. These changes have reduced what food charities would otherwise have received.

As food donation levels have shrunk, food banks need to raise money for food purchases, says Dan Pruett of the Capital Area Food Bank in Austin, Texas. "That presents all kinds of problems," he adds. "If you don't know how to raise money, you're going to be in a heap of hurt."[27]

There are also limitations to a volunteer-based system: In some places of high need, volunteers are not available to maintain a food pantry. It is not unheard of for a program to shut down when volunteers go on vacation or for pantries to reduce the hours they are open due to declining volunteerism.

The entitlement nature of the federal nutrition programs ensures that a minimum level of help will always be there when people need it most. It also ensures an objective, no-strings-attached form of help that not all charitable and faith-based efforts may provide.

Bottom line: Charitable community efforts – while generous – lack the breadth of the government's resources and reach. The U.S. government spends about $44 billion each year on domestic food assistance programs.[28] In contrast, private sector contributions are much lower. A 2000 analysis by the Institute for Research on Poverty conservatively estimates that private sector assistance nationwide comes to approximately $2.3 billion, including the value of the food.[29] A more generous estimate puts national charitable food donations at $4 billion.[30]

Moreover, while millions of people receive help from local emergency providers, the USDA finds that the vast majority of people in households at risk of hunger (81 percent) did not use a food pantry even once during the year. One in four such households reports that they had no such resource in their community.[31]

As stated in The Millennium Declaration to End Hunger in America, which represents the voices of national anti-hunger groups, many of which provide these charitable services, "Emergency feeding programs alone cannot end hunger."

That said, these community efforts are of great value in the fight against hunger, and their many successes offer lessons that should be built on to improve government efforts. Working toward an end to hunger will require the United States to create a food assistance network that combines and manages federal, charitable and private efforts in a way that best complement each other.

Where Do We Go From Here?

How might the federal food assistance system be improved? A place to start would be serious commitment on the part of the president and Congress to the goal of cutting hunger in half by 2010. To get there, they should pursue reforms that:

- Increase participation in the food assistance programs;

- Build on what the programs do to encourage work;

- Further strengthen what they do to help children at risk;

- Improve participants' nutrition in addition to increasing their access to enough food (i.e., more calories);

- Better integrate programs with community-based efforts;

- Improve coordination among the nutrition and anti-poverty programs; and

- Take full advantage of recent successes in reducing program fraud and error.

Communities: Cornerstones of Change

The federal government should find ways to more fully support and collaborate with the huge network of food charities and anti-hunger coalitions that are working at the community and state levels across the nation. Federal legislation should provide funding to help grassroots organizations tackle the problem of hunger in their own states and communities, partly by promoting and expanding the federal programs.

Most anti-hunger charities are quite small. The people involved often are focused on meeting immediate needs. But food banks and food charities increasingly are helping families know that they may be eligible for food stamps or WIC, and sometimes helping them fill

Does the Thrifty Food Plan Reflect True Grocery Costs?

To determine how much the average family should receive in food stamp benefits, the U.S. Department of Agriculture (USDA) designs a food plan that specifies the amount and cost of food to provide adequate nutrition.

The Thrifty Food Plan (TFP) is one of four such plans. It is the cheapest food plan and is priced monthly using the price data collected for the Consumer Price Index. The monthly cost of the TFP represents a national average of prices (four-person household consisting of an adult couple and two school-age children) and is adjusted for other household sizes. For food stamp purposes, the TFP is priced each June and sets maximum benefit levels for the fiscal year beginning the following October.

A main criticism of the TFP is that it assumes that families cook all their meals from scratch (i.e., it includes no prepared meals, such as purchasing a rotisserie chicken from the grocery deli). It also does not accommodate cultural differences in diet.

To provide an example of the variation that can occur in grocer prices, quantity allotments and per unit pricing and so forth, the following chart compares the USDA's TFP of a week's worth of groceries for the average family of four and what could be purchased at the Mt. Pleasant Giant in Washington, D.C., on Sept. 3, 2003. While this plan estimates that a family will spend $174.49 on groceries, it actually would have cost $205.35 to purchase the groceries needed for this meal plan – $30 more than what food stamps would have covered.

TABLE 4.2

Grocery Store Selection of items priced on 9/3/03

Food Item	Price	USDA's Weekly Amount	Exact Price per Amount	Actual Amount per poundage	Total Price
Fresh Fruits and Vegetables					
Bananas	$0.59 per lb	2 lb 12 oz or 11 medium	$1.62	5 bananas	$1.60
Melon	$0.75 per lb	1 lb	$0.75	smallest melon = 4 lb	$2.99
Cabbage	$0.99 per lb	4 oz	$0.25	1 head = 20 oz	$1.25
Celery	$1.69 per bag	3 oz	$0.21	2 lb bag, eight sticks	$1.69
Green Peppers	$0.99 per lb	3 oz	$0.20	1 pepper = 8 oz	$0.50
Lettuce	$1.89 per lb	4 oz	$0.47	1 head = 12 oz.	$1.40
Canned Fruits and Vegetables					
Apple Sauce	$1.59 per jar	2 oz	$0.14	24 oz jar	$1.59
Spinach	$0.99 per can	10 oz	$0.73	13.5 oz can	$0.99
Tomato Paste	$0.55 per can	6 oz	$0.55	6 oz can	$0.55
Tomato Sauce	$0.59 per can	1 lb 1 oz	$0.67	15 oz can	$1.18
Frozen Fruits and Vegetables					
Green Beans	$0.89 per package	5 oz	$0.49	9 oz	$0.89
Peas	$0.99 per package	5 oz	$0.50	10 oz	$0.99
Breads, Cereals, and Other Grain Products					
Crackers, snack, low-salt	$1.99 per box	4 oz	$0.50	16 oz	$1.99
Oatmeal, quick, rolled oats	$1.89 per can	3 oz	$0.32	18 oz	$1.89
Ready-to-eat cereal flakes	$2.00 per box	6 oz	$0.89	13.5 oz	$2.00
Barley, pearl	$1.59 per bag	4 oz	$0.40	16 oz	$1.59
Milk and Cheese					
Evaporated Milk	$0.93 per can	16 fl oz	$1.24	12 oz can	$1.86
Milk, 1% lowfat	$3.09 per gal	2½ gal	$7.72	1 gallon jug + 2 quarts	$7.70
Meat and Meat Alternates					
Beef, ground, lean	$2.19 per lb	2.4 lb	$5.25	weights vary	$5.25
Chicken, fryer	$1.99 per lb	1.5 lb	$2.98	weights vary	$2.98
Beans, kidney, canned	$0.69 per can	1 lb 11 oz	$0.76	15.5 oz can	$1.38
Eggs, large	$0.75 per carton	16	$1.00	12 egg carton	$1.50
Total $ spent			**$174.49**		**$205.35**

Reducing Poverty Also Key to Curbing Hunger

While the United States can make rapid progress against hunger by improving and expanding the national nutritional programs, a durable end to hunger depends on a broader effort to reduce poverty.

The best solution to hunger is a decent job. Some people are elderly, disabled or, for other reasons, cannot work. They need safety-net programs. But when poor people are asked what they most need, they ask for a stable, well-paying job or an educational opportunity that will lead to a good job. Many people make tremendous efforts to gain employment, such as migrant farm workers who travel hundreds of miles in hopes of finding work. But people cannot always find jobs, and many jobs pay too little to support a family.

Helping people overcome poverty by finding jobs that pay a livable wage must be a part of any U.S. plan to end hunger.

Create Jobs

One of the most important steps to cutting hunger and poverty in the United States is for government leaders to reduce high unemployment. How best to achieve a strong economy and low unemployment is debated. Some believe in supply-side economics, including tax cuts for investors and corporations in order to stimulate job growth. Others argue that reducing taxes or providing assistance to families who live paycheck to paycheck (and who are likely to spend extra income immediately) is a more effective way to stimulate the economy. In fact, if low-income people receive more food stamps, research shows that they use them right away — both reducing hunger and boosting grocery sales. Every $1 in food stamps turns over five times in the economy.

Prepare People for Work

People also need to be prepared for the jobs that the business community needs. Improving U.S. public primary and secondary education systems is a tried and true way to help Americans fill jobs in the United States and remain competitive in a global marketplace. Access to higher education helps some Americans move up the economic ladder. For every demographic – Blacks, whites, Latinos, men and women – incomes rise as education rises.

Make Work Pay

The United States always will need people to take low-skilled jobs such as farm work or cleaning hotel rooms, which most often pay lower wages. But in order for many of these workers to get by – and to be food secure – they must receive more in compensation than the market is willing to pay for their skills and services. The Earned Income Tax Credit (EITC) systematically raises after-tax wages of low-income workers. It has become one of the most effective programs in lifting families out of poverty (see related story, p. 72).

Programs such as food stamps, affordable housing, and child care and transportation assistance also help low-income workers make ends meet.

Another way to make work pay is to increase the minimum wage. Today a minimum wage worker who earns $5.15 an hour cannot support a family. Increasing the minimum wage to $6.65 would mean an extra $42 (after taxes) for someone working 40 hours a week.

FIGURE 4.2
Poverty Again on the Rise in the United States

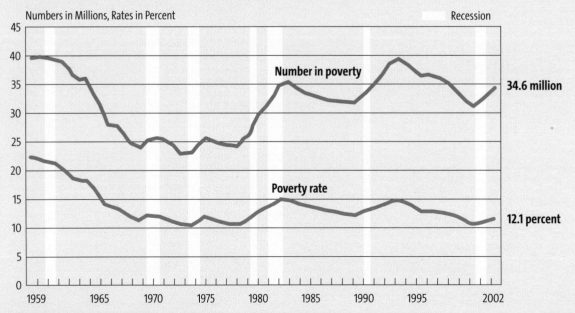

Note: The date points represent the midpoints of the respective years.

Source: U.S. Census Bureau, Current Population Survey, 1960-2003 Annual Social and Economic Supplements

out the necessary forms. Food banks also increasingly are involved in public-policy advocacy. The national food bank organization, America's Second Harvest, has developed an important advocacy program.

In many communities and some states, anti-hunger coalitions bring together charitable food assistance providers like churches, food banks and soup kitchens with leaders from business and government to develop strategies and tackle specific problems. They work to draw grocery stores and farmers' markets into low-income neighborhoods, promote broader participation in federal nutrition programs, and lobby state and federal legislatures to expand nutrition assistance.

For example, the Greater Philadelphia Coalition Against Hunger is partnering with two advertising firms on a year-long campaign to reach Philadelphians who qualify for food stamps but do not apply for them. At the prompting of USDA's Food and Nutrition Service, state-level coalitions in all the southeastern states (including federal, state and local officials) are working to develop and implement strategic plans to eliminate hunger. A key goal of these coalitions is to increase access to federal nutrition programs.

The Community Food Security Coalition now reports more than 250 members. Local food security coalitions work on various food-related issues, including hunger. As part of the 1996 Farm Bill, Congress established a competitive grants program to support community food security projects. In 2003 USDA awarded 28 grants totaling more than $4.6 million.

The Bush administration has promoted collaboration between USDA and community groups as part of the president's Faith-based and Community Initiative. But USDA began systematically expanding its connections to community groups during the Clinton administration.

Further expansion of such collaboration could become the centerpiece of a successful campaign to end hunger in the United States. Legislation could further expand federal assistance to the charities and coalitions that are working to solve the problem of hunger in their own communities. This would include more funding for them to help promote full use of the federal programs, monitor their effectiveness, and educate the public about hunger and its solutions.

Legislation also could encourage state and local officials of the nutrition programs to work with community groups. Closer collaboration between federal and community efforts would combine the financial power and reach of governmental programs with the local knowledge and flexibility of community efforts.

From what we know of U.S. public opinion, this is an approach that a large majority of U.S. voters would support.

In the United States, 6 percent of households with elderly are food insecure, and 1.5 percent of these households experience hunger at some point during the year. Income-boosting programs such as Social Security, Medicaid and Medicare likely explain higher food security rates among the elderly.

Improving Coordination

Pursuing a community-based approach to combating hunger also could lead to better coordination, integration, efficiency and accountability among the national nutrition programs.

The federal assistance programs typically are fragmented and difficult to navigate. Families often have to wade through a web of programs, each with its own application processes and requirements. The nutrition programs are no exception. Because of differing requirements, a family may receive free school meals but not qualify for food stamps. Among working adults, the programmatic barriers become even more difficult because many of the programs require certification or recertification during normal working hours and include a burdensome process that can consume an entire day.

As stakeholders consider modernizing and strengthening the federal food assistance programs, they need to question some basic program assumptions:

- Should the federal safety net include multiple nutrition-, food- and income-assistance programs, each with their own requirements, application processes and qualification periods?

- Could some programs streamline eligibility requirements so that one application could be used to verify eligibility for a package of help?

- Because monthly income often fluctuates among low-income families, should households found eligible be allowed to stay on a program for a full year?

- Given efforts to move adults into work, could the federal nutrition programs be coordinated with traditional work-support assistance, such as Unemployment Insurance and job training?

- Given today's technological advances and benefits garnered from computer database networks, can states better integrate programs both within their borders and nationally?

Such questions are not new. Many states and communities are taking the lead in better coordinating and integrating services as a way to increase program participation, cut expenses and improve accountability. Lessons from these examples point to new ways of thinking about the national nutrition programs and the federal safety net.

The Newmark Center: Career and Opportunity One Stop

In Coos Bay, Ore., state and local government offices have partnered with local nonprofit agencies since August 1994 to create The Newmark Center, one-stop shopping for adults seeking help. Whether a dislocated worker needing a new job, a single-mother seeking to apply for TANF and food stamps, or a disabled senior seeking health care, adults visit one building for all their needs.

The various social service agencies share personnel, office space and resources in order to more effectively serve Coos Bay county residents. More than just co-locating services, meaning that the different services are housed in one building, the Center tries to integrate services so that a single-mother seeking help to find a job also is screened for eligibility in TANF, food stamps, WIC, free or reduced-priced meals for her children, child care and medical care assistance, and any other help that she may qualify for at the state and federal level.

Integrating services involves a team of individuals from different service agencies conducting intake and managing cases together. In some instances, it also may mean consolidating or changing some caseworker job functions. In addition to major personnel and management changes, integrating services often requires consolidating governance structures, funding streams and information technology systems – all which take time, money and dedication.[32]

To date, The Newmark Center has had some notable success. In 2003 Coos Bay – an area with food insecurity rates higher than national averages – increased its food stamp participation to nearly 100 percent. But state

funding shortages threaten further program developments and possibly whether the program will continue in an integrated, one-stop fashion.

Coordinated Economic Relief Centers (CERCs): Voluntary Participation Low

In 2002 the Commonwealth of Virginia implemented a new one-stop program called Coordinated Economic Relief Centers (CERCs) to provide dislocated workers and other low-income people access to a broad range of services in one location. This effort grew out of the 1998 Workforce Investment Act, federal legislation that consolidated numerous federal employment and training programs and required states and localities to provide most federally funded employment centers through one-stop career centers.

Though most clients were expected to come to the centers to receive employment-related services, such as Unemployment Insurance, job service registration and job search assistance, the centers were designed to provide other services as well, notably accepting food stamp applications and directing people in need to charitable emergency food services.

A 2003 review of these centers found that while community programs' initial interest in coordinating services with the government was high, few could afford to provide on-site services and initial interest waned over time.[33] Moreover, most Center staff failed to inquire about clients' needs and did not offer food stamp applications or other service referrals unless directly asked. From the community's perspective, misinformation led some people to believe that the CERCs would promote economic development and create new jobs, and they were critical when this did not happen.

Such issues will need to be explored further if the coordination of nutrition programs and other work activities in a one-stop atmosphere are to be pursued.

Building on Success in Reducing Fraud

The nutrition programs have been successful in reducing fraud and the perception of fraud for years. For many people, just hearing the name "food stamps" conjures up images of people selling food stamps for cash to buy alcohol and drugs. But in fact, today's combined payment error rate for food stamps is the lowest in the program's history: 8.26 percent.[34] That includes overpayments as well as underpayments, in other words, honest mistakes as well as cheating. The extent of food stamp trafficking – selling benefits for cash – is quite low. The USDA reports, "Trafficking now amounts to two-and-a-half cents of every benefit dollar issued, a 29 percent decline in the rate of trafficking between 1996-1998 and 1999-2002."[35]

Does the U.S. Poverty Measure Reflect the Reality of Being Poor?

for some time now, researchers and experts have been debating whether the official poverty measure is a good indicator of need and whether it truly reflects what it means to be poor in the United States.

The debate is important because many of the federal food assistance programs use the poverty measure as a baseline for determining eligibility. But it also is highly political. Many of the proposed methods for improving the measure in effect would increase the number of people considered poor – and no politician wants to see poverty increase on his or her watch.

Current Definition

The federal government defines poverty based on a series of income thresholds that increase according to a family's size. Developed in 1965 by Mollie Orshansky for the Social Security Administration, the established poverty lines are based on the cost of "maintaining a nutritionally adequate diet," using the U.S. Department of Agriculture's Economy Food Plan. The figures then are tripled because in 1965, the average family of three spent about a third of its income on food. These thresholds are re-evaluated annually to reflect changes in the Consumer Price Index.

In 2003 the poverty line for a family of three was $15,260.

Gayle, who once worked for a national grocer, lives in Dignity Village, a mobile tent city for homeless people, located outside of Portland, Ore. After losing her job and medical insurance, Gayle was in a car accident that paralyzed her from the waist down. The mounting medical bills eventually left her homeless.

Many experts consider the thresholds to be inadequate measures today because families typically spend less than 20 percent of their incomes on food.[1] Families are spending more of their budgets on rapidly rising housing and medical costs. In 1999 a family had to earn $11.08 an hour to afford the national average monthly rent for a two-bedroom apartment or house. In 2003 that wage requirement was $15.21 – a 37 percent hike.[2] Meanwhile, between 2000 and 2003 the typical family's health insurance premium rose by $2,630 – a 41 percent increase.[3] It is little surprise that personal bankruptcies reached an all-time high in 2003, growing 7.8 percent over the year to more than 1.6 million filings.[4]

Wider Opportunities for Women calculates that in order to pay for housing, food, transportation, child care, health care and other basic expenses, a single mother with an infant and preschooler could need over three times the official poverty measure, or as much as $45,780 per year, depending on what kinds of work supports she receives and where she lives.[5]

What Is Income?

It has long been recognized that the official poverty threshold understates true need. It fails to consider a family's medical, transportation and child care costs. Critics also point out that it does not make adjustments for the effects of taxes, noncash benefits like food stamps and housing vouchers, or geographical differences. Assets, which can determine whether someone is able to move out of poverty, also are ignored. In fact, income limits for many food assistance programs – such as food stamps – already are set well above the poverty line. Many programs use the income threshold of 185 percent of poverty to determine eligibility.

The Census Bureau also has begun to incorporate alternative measures in its annual release of the U.S. poverty rate. Various alternatives incorporate the effects of taxes, medical expenses, social program benefits and other factors. But if and when such changes will be incorporated into social programs themselves remains to be seen.

1. Louis Uchitelle, "How to Define Poverty? Let Us Count the Ways." *The New York Times,* May 26, 2001.
2. National Low-Income Housing Coalition, Out of Reach 2003 Web site, http://www.nlihc.org/oor2003/introduction.htm.
3. Kaiser Family Foundation and the Health Research and Educational Trust, *Employer Health Benefits 2003 Annual Survey.* Accessed from Web site, http://www.kff.org/insurance/ehbs2003-abstract.cfm.
4. American Bankruptcy Institute, "Personal Bankruptcy Filings Continue to Break Records." American Bankruptcy Institute Press release, Nov. 14, 2003, accessed from Web site, http://www.abiworld.org/release/033Q.html.
5. Diana Pearce and Jennifer Brooks. *The Self Sufficiency Standard for the City of New York.* Wider Opportunities for Women, September 2002, accessed from Web site, http://www.sixstrategies.org/files/NYCstandard.pdf.

The innovation responsible for most of the progress that has been made on this front is the electronic benefits transfer (EBT) card. These debit cards have replaced actual food stamps in all states. EBT cards are harder to sell on the street because the card value is not visible. Recipients also have a more difficult time trading or swapping partial benefits, and each transaction is recorded and can be traced to individual stores and program participants, further deterring fraud.

What has been done to reduce waste, fraud and abuse saves money that can be used to expand services. It also shores up the public's trust in the programs. Moreover, such efforts improve the chances that people who qualify for help receive their full benefit.

The 8.26 percent error rate for the Food Stamp Program includes 6.16 percent overpayments and 2.1 percent underpayments. Dollarwise, this means that the program erroneously paid $1.2 billion in extra payments to people, while others received less – $382 million less nationally – than they were allowed.

When errors occur, it is hard to know whether the administrative office or the applicant simply made a mistake or whether income intentionally was misrepresented. The GAO has testified that applicants' honest mistakes caused about one-third (36 percent) of overpayment errors in 1996, with intentional errors accounting for about a fifth of errors (21 percent). Just under half of errors (43 percent) were due to caseworker error. The USDA, on the other hand, estimates that less than 1 percent of overpayments are due to intentional misrepresentation.

Nutrition: Building Blocks for the Future

The national nutrition programs already play an important role in overcoming disparities in access to healthy food. As discussed earlier, research shows that participation in food stamps, WIC and the school meals programs improve participants' overall nutrition as well as their access to food. But as scholars learn new things about nutrition and its impact on health, and as the U.S. population's overall nutrition needs change, these programs also must be reviewed to reflect better knowledge.

For example, comprehensive studies consistently associate the National School Lunch Program, which is available to 98 percent of public school children, with positive nutritional impacts. For many children, it is the most nutritious meal of the day. However, a recent GAO review of the program found that school lunches still are not meeting the 30-percent calories-from-fat limit. This finding is especially disconcerting given the rapid rise in overweight and obesity rates among children. As the GAO states, while "schools have reduced the average

The Food Stamp Program no longer uses paper coupons or stamps to convey benefits, but rather electronic benefit transfer (EBT) cards such as this. Switching to EBT cards has played a large role in reducing the program's payment errors.

proportion of calories from fat in lunches from 38 to 34 percent, nationwide," more still needs to be done.[36]

Indeed more can and should be done to make school lunches and other food-assistance programs as nutritious as possible. But there is a catch: Improving nutrition often comes at a higher cost.

Take the recent Farm-to-School pilot program that brings fresh fruits and vegetables into schools. According to the USDA's evaluation of the pilot, "School staff believed that the pilot lessened the risk of obesity, encouraged children to eat healthier food, increased children's awareness of a variety of fruits and vegetables, and helped children, who would otherwise be hungry, get more food."

In 2002 such programs provided free fresh fruits and vegetables to students in more than 100 schools across four states and one Indian Tribal Organization, to the accolades of parents and politicians alike. But to expand this fruit-and-vegetable initiative nationally, taxpayers would need to pay an estimated $4.5 billion more.[37]

Similarly, policymakers have been debating whether schools should remove vending machines and other "a la carte" items from campuses in an effort to improve students' eating habits during school hours. But because the federal school meal reimbursements do not cover all costs associated with the school lunch and breakfast programs, many schools rely on revenue from a la carte

Changing Tax Structure Could Signal Changes in Social Spending

The past several decades have seen significant changes in how Americans are taxed and how much they earn. Essentially, the richest 1 percent of taxpayers pays less tax and earns much more money, while everyone else pays slightly more in taxes and earns about the same.

While the factors driving these changes are complex, the U.S. tax structure clearly plays an important role. And tax cuts and the related federal deficit put nutrition and anti-poverty programs at risk.

Narrowing Tax, Widening Income Gap

Since 1960, the United States slowly has moved from a tax structure that placed a heavier burden on its wealthiest citizens to one that taxes everyone more the same, a "flatter" tax structure. The wealthiest people, who were paying more than half their federal income in taxes in the 1960s and 1970s, saw their rates reduced significantly in the 1980s, to 28 percent.[1] While these rates later jumped to almost 40 percent in the mid-1990s, they have fallen back again as a result of the 2001 tax cuts, which are scheduled to reduce the top rate to 35 percent by 2006.

The federal income tax rates for the bottom 99 percent of wage earners, meanwhile, rose from the mid-1960s to the early 1980s, from 22 percent to 30 percent. This rate then dropped to 23 percent during the Reagan years, and increased slightly to 26 percent during the 1990s.

But most striking is how as the difference in taxes between these groups narrowed, the gap in their incomes widened. While the average income of the bottom 99 percent of Americans barely budged during this period – a 13 percent increase – the average income of the top 1 percent more than doubled.

Economists who favor a flat-tax approach argue that by reducing the tax burden for people with higher incomes, these people are free to invest and spend more money, which keeps the economy growing. They also contend that it keeps government spending in check because everyone is equally vested. On the other hand, opponents maintain that a system that increases the tax burden incrementally as incomes rise – a progressive tax system – is fairer, because it allows the government to make up for the market's shortcomings.

Take low-income workers. As a matter of fairness, most Americans believe that a person who works full time should not be poor and hungry. However, the market dictates low wages for many low-skilled, but necessary jobs, keeping these people in poverty. Using taxes to pay for government services such as food stamps helps to ensure that low-income workers at least have enough food to eat. Low-income tax rebates, such as the Earned Income Tax Credit, help to reward people who work by relieving them of most taxes so they can spend their limited earnings on housing, food and other necessities, which are not always affordable. In that way, a progressive tax system helps ensure that people who have the greatest needs receive the help they might not otherwise get.

Less Money, More Spending

Reducing the taxes of the wealthiest people also reduces federal revenue, which potentially leads to less spending.

How much revenue has been lost? The Joint Committee on Taxation reports that as of 2003 the major tax changes beginning in 2001 cut revenue by $166 billion, with most of this loss from lower income taxes. According to the Center on Budget and Policy Priorities, total federal revenues (as a share of gross domestic product (GDP)) are at the lowest level since the end of the Eisenhower administration. Federal income taxes from individuals are at their lowest level since 1966 – 7.4 percent of GDP. Corporate income taxes are at their lowest level since 1937, just 1.2 percent of GDP.[2]

Meanwhile, government spending has increased to pay for the military actions in Afghanistan and Iraq and for the new Homeland Security Department. The combination of lower taxes and increased security spending has led to the United States' record-high budget deficit of nearly $500 billion.

How Low Will We Go?

If the president and Congress are to balance the budget again and reduce the federal deficit, tough decisions will need to be made. Will the tax cuts continue? If so, which programs and services will be reduced or eliminated? Or will taxes be raised? And if so, who will bear the brunt of the tax burden?

Many of the tax cuts recently enacted are scheduled to expire between 2004 and 2010. The Bush administration and key Republican congressional leaders are intent on extending the tax cuts.

Two economists at the Brookings Institute recently calculated the cost of extending these tax cuts another 10 years: $430 billion (or 2.4 percent of GDP).[3] To gain a sense of what this loss would mean for the federal budget, consider the angst gripping politicians as they grapple with how to pay for Social Security over the next 75 years. The 10-year tax-related revenue loss would be triple the size of the expected Social Security shortfall, as projected by the Social Security Trustees.[4]

Essentially, an extension of these tax cuts would put the country's budget on par with 1950 levels. Of course, back then many federal programs did not yet exist, including Medicare, Medicaid, most federal aid to education, and many environmental protection programs. That may be the point.

---

[1] By 1988, the marginal tax rate for the wealthiest 1 percent of Americans was 28 percent as a result of the 1986 Tax Reform Act.

[2] With the exception of 1983, which was a deep recession year.

[3] William G. Gale and Peter R. Orszag, "Sunsets in the Tax Code," *TaxNotes,* June 9, 2003, 1553-1561.

[4] The Social Security Trustees place the size of the Social Security shortfall at 0.73 percent of GDP over the 75-year period.

EITC Helps Low-Income People Benefit Most From Work

The Earned Income Tax Credit (EITC) has long been considered a success in helping low-income families battle poverty. However, like so many important social programs increasing participation is key. As many as 14 percent of the families with children that could benefit from the EITC fail to sign up for it.[1]

EITC is a refundable federal income tax credit for low-income working individuals and families. Congress originally approved the tax credit legislation in 1975 to help offset the burden of social security taxes while also providing an incentive to work. The credit reduces the amount of federal tax owed and can result in a refund check. When the EITC exceeds the amount of taxes owed, it results in a tax refund to those who claim and qualify for the credit.

Income and family size determine the amount of the EITC. To qualify for the credit, both the earned income and the adjusted gross income for 2003 must be less than $29,666 for a taxpayer with one qualifying child, $33,692 for a taxpayer with more than one qualifying child, and $11,230 for a taxpayer with no qualifying children.

Studies show that families use this money to help pay for child care, transportation and other costs associated with getting a job. Several studies have shown that the EITC helps move many people into work.[2]

---

[1] Len Burman and Deborah Kobes, *Urban-Brookings Tax Policy Center Policy Note*, 1/18/2002, accessed from Web site, http://www.taxpolicycenter.org/commentary/eitc_gao.cfm.

[2] Bruce Meyer and Dan Rosenbaum, "Welfare, the Earned Income Tax Credit, and the Labor Supply of Single Mothers." National Bureau of Economic Research Working Paper No. 7363, September 1999.

---

sales. It likely would cost additional taxpayer dollars to take the vending machines out of schools.

The U.S. obesity crisis – which affects people of all income groups – presents an opportunity for Congress and the public to re-examine low-income people's nutritional needs and how the current national assistance programs may be improved to better meet them. Much more is yet to be learned about this important public health issue, but certainly combating obesity will involve a broad cultural shift in people's eating habits, activity levels and social interactions with food. Bolstering nutrition education efforts is a likely place to start. Amid a society permeated with advertisements that satisfy "hunger" with double bacon cheeseburgers and king-size candy bars, objective nutrition education can help balance the mixed messages. Moreover, a few of the national nutrition programs already include nutritional educational components that can be strengthened and built on.

WIC, for example, was designed to meet pregnant women's, infants' and young children's specific nutrient needs. Most evidence points to the great success of this program, which includes a nutritional component. But the WIC food package was designed in the early 1970s and may need to be updated to conform to current nutritional advice. Also, WIC nutritionists may need additional time to talk with their clients about nutrition issues. As more women are encouraged to work, WIC approaches to family budget and menu planning may need to be updated to include more practical solutions for busy mothers.

Creating the Political Will

So how much money would it cost to reduce hunger, and would the public support strengthening anti-hunger efforts? Based on USDA data regarding food insecurity, Bread for the World Institute has estimated that an additional $5 billion to $6 billion in nutrition assistance annually would be enough to cut U.S. hunger and food insecurity in half.[38] But if anti-hunger advocates are to win an expansion of this scale, they also must push to make the programs more effective.

Over the years, anti-hunger advocates have been locked in a seesaw battle against critics of the national nutrition programs. Congress made huge cuts to the Food Stamp Program during the Reagan administration and again as part of welfare reform in 1996, which took away $60 billion from poor people over the subsequent six years. Considering 36 million people are under the poverty line, the average poor person lost almost $2,000 because of that one bill. Roughly half that loss was through cuts in the Food Stamp Program.

Welfare reform also marked a big shift in the perceived purpose of social programs and the need for greater accountability. The politicians and conservative think tanks who achieved the program cuts packaged them with a few attractive reform ideas – decentralization to states, moving people on welfare into jobs and the commonsense idea that children do better in stable marriages. While the deep cuts in welfare and food stamps have done a lot of harm to poor people, the reform ideas – especially the first two – have done some good. Some state governments have created more efficient, locally appropriate ways to manage welfare, and many people who were on welfare are now in the job market.

Voters care about ending hunger. Nearly three in four respondents say that the hunger issue is important to them in deciding whom they will vote for president in 2004. The same percentage say they are less likely to vote for a candidate who wants to make cuts in programs that affect children, such as school lunches.

Anti-hunger advocates have always worked to improve as well as expand the nutrition programs. In 2002, for example, anti-hunger organizations pushed successfully to change the federal incentives for states in ways that are reducing the red tape that keeps millions of hungry families off the Food Stamp Program. But opponents usually have been more outspoken on reducing waste and instituting tougher work requirements. Lately, some critics have begun to tap into widespread alarm about obesity, suggesting that the national nutrition programs contribute, in various ways, to obesity among low-income people, which has not been shown to be the case.

Recent polls commissioned by the Alliance to End Hunger provide new insights into how likely U.S. voters think about hunger.[39] Three polls in 2002 and 2003 demonstrate that most Americans support food assistance programs, and that a message combining expansion and reform would be attractive to nearly all likely voters and, thus, to politicians of both parties.

Voters care about ending hunger. Nearly three in four respondents say that the hunger issue is important to them in deciding whom they will vote for president in 2004. The same percentage say they are less likely to vote for a candidate who wants to make cuts in programs that affect children, such as school lunches; 64 percent say they would vote against a candidate who favored cutting the Food Stamp Program.

More than half of likely voters say the government is not spending enough to fight hunger. When asked whether they agree that "politicians should look for other places to save money in their state and local budgets and shouldn't be cutting food programs that help feed hungry people," 83 percent of likely voters agree.

But voters also are skeptical of big social programs. Many Americans like the idea of government working together with community groups. Americans believe deeply that people ought to work hard to get ahead and support their families. Welfare reform has had some harsh consequences among poor people, but is very popular among likely voters (87 percent), partly because it has pushed welfare recipients to get jobs. A very broad majority of survey respondents (82 percent) would support an expansion of the federal nutrition programs if combined with reforms to make them more effective and supportive of self-help efforts.[40]

The experience of anti-hunger groups over the decades and these recent survey findings suggest that advocates for the nutrition programs are more likely to win the sort of expansion that would dramatically reduce hunger if they put more emphasis on their commitment to reform as well as expand the nutrition programs. Attractive ideas about how to make the programs better also will help to justify added costs.

The Special Supplemental Nutrition Program for Women, Infants and Children (WIC) served 7.5 million women, infants and children in 2002 and is considered to be one of the most effective government programs.

Evelyn Knolle, a policy analyst at Bread for the World, contributed to this chapter.

5

Getting Back on Track Globally

IFAD/H. Wagner

The world has a fairly good idea of what to do to reduce hunger. A successful anti-hunger strategy must focus on both the immediate food and nutrition needs of hungry people and on long-term, sustained investment in reducing poverty. Both of these approaches cost money, significantly more than the world has been spending. And in a world racked with competing needs, interests and values, leadership and unwavering commitment are needed, even more than additional knowledge and development experience.

Of course, to secure that leadership and constancy, people want to see results, and the quicker the better. Fair enough, except that hunger is rooted in poverty. And even with adequate resources, breaking the poverty cycle for people, families and communities requires hard work, determination and time.

Developing country leaders need to commit to this endeavor and follow through with policies and other actions that support reducing poverty and hunger among their people. Each country bears the responsibility for its progress, but some countries suffer such widespread hunger and poverty that they also need help from the rest of the world.

Building on the Past

International development assistance can offer the help that is needed, but past impressions of foreign aid's ineffectiveness, white-elephant projects and diplomatic blunders have tainted foreign aid for many people. Fortunately, past failures – as well as successes – with foreign aid provide important lessons. When coupled with new analysis on how to grow economies, how to better distribute that growth, and how to focus aid more directly on poor and hungry people, these lessons can make international development assistance more effective than it has ever been.

Just a few years ago, 189 nations – including the United States – promised people living in the world's poorest countries that they would help improve their lives. Specific goals and measures were established – the Millennium Development Goals (MDGs) – which outline an interdependent, comprehensive strategy for reducing poverty and hunger. Enunciated as part of the U.N. Millennium Declaration in September 2000, the MDGs represent the distilled wisdom of 30 years of global development experience: that hunger, poverty, health, the environment, education, and even trade and aid all play a part in economic development, and that for results to happen, both rich and poor countries must do their share.

BFWI Photo/J. Stipe

Every $1 invested in nutrition intervention programs, such as vitamin and mineral supplements, results in $100 gained in healthier and more productive workers, according to the World Health Organization.

Each of the eight goals focuses on one factor in the poverty-reduction equation. The first seven goals address what developing countries must do and ways to move forward, such as increase child immunizations, protect forests, increase the number of births attended by a skilled professional and promote women's literacy (see related story, p. 88). The eighth goal sets out elements of a global partnership for development, underscoring the realization that developing countries cannot change global systems and injustices on their own. Development assistance, sustainable debt and market access are key pieces of this partnership.

Perhaps most significantly, the MDGs provide a unique opportunity to mobilize civil society and align national programs and actions to achieve the key targets.[1] They provide a framework in which to design, implement and analyze efforts to combat hunger worldwide. They also provide an opportunity for political pressure. The MDGs set up a public standard by which governments can be graded on their performance in areas such as combating hunger, poverty, HIV/AIDS and infant mortality. Citizens and civil society can use them as a scorecard to hold their governments accountable. As stated by the U.N. Development Program (UNDP), "Nothing short of a strong public advocacy is likely to ensure a genuine sense of national ownership,"[2] and history has shown repeatedly that ownership is essential to successful development.

Hope Is in the Trenches on a Malawian Farm

By Melissa Aberle-Grasse

Her head bound in a scarf against the late morning sun, Christian Chinkhuntha speaks with a quiet authority. She leads a group of nine farmer trainees around a field of deep green strawberry plants.

"We began with 100 square meters of land in 1982," Christian tells the group. "The local chief gave it up easily, as it was considered infertile. For seeds and fertilizer, we had 100 kwatcha (about $1)."

Today, the farm of Glyvins and Christian Chinkhuntha in central Malawi, known locally as Freedom Gardens, has grown to an abundant 20 hectares (about 50 acres). Thanks to hard work, an innovative irrigation system and other low-cost organic methods, a once marginal plot is now a thriving enterprise, selling a variety of fruits and vegetables at local markets. Today, too, the Chinkhunthas are planting new seeds: training others in what they've learned.

Their original parcel of land is common in Malawi lowlands: marshy in the rainy season, cracked and apparently infertile the other eight dry months. Now, however, water flows year-round through an ingenious, grid-like dirt trench system, framing each field. Built of nothing more than dirt and inexpensive pipes, the system is nonetheless effective at draining the fields in the rainy season and irrigating them throughout the dry. Indeed, its success is so locally celebrated, it earned Glyvins an honorary doctorate from Bunda College of Agriculture.

"Water was our first challenge," Glyvins explains. "But we learned to ask, what does the land have to give us, and how can we replenish with that?"

A nearby river, with banana trees thriving near its edge, provided a natural resource for controlling water flow to the property. Analyzing such details as slopes and water tables, and drawing upon their own hard-earned familiarity with the land, the Chinkhunthas calculated and reworked until they'd developed their irrigation system.

As the farming couple applied their ideas and learned other methods of sustainable farming, they expanded their small plot. They learned to maximize the use of composted materials in order to spend less on fertilizer. Other organic methods of cultivation, along with their irrigation, allowed them to harvest two-to-three times a year. Today, they sell tomatoes, green beans and cassava in local markets, and lemons and strawberries to hotels.

Christian Chinkhuntha helps train other local farmers in agricultural practices that boost productivity and profitability. She lives and works with her husband, Glyvins, on their farm, Freedom Gardens, in Malawi.

M. Aberle-Grasse

Viewing these productive fields, it is easy to forget how hard hunger has hit in Malawi recently. For the last several years, Malawi, like much of Southern Africa, faced a severe food shortage. Emergency food distribution was occurring in every district of the country. In June 2002 the U.N. World Food Program estimated that a third of Malawians were in immediate need of food aid.

Freedom Gardens felt the crisis, too; in 2001 and 2002, when rainfall was low, its production fell. However, with irrigation and a diversity of crops, Chinkhunthas still supported a reasonable harvest. Many people in nearby communities were not so fortunate, and the couple responded.

"Today, we have about twenty people working here," says Glyvins. "But when times were hard, we had nearly 200. If someone comes from our community and needs work, we never turn her away. I tell them, 'We have to cross this river together.'"

The acute food crisis in Malawi has passed, thanks to a solid 2002-2003 rainy season, and a drop in some commodity prices. But climbing out of the whirlpool cycle of drought and food shortage is a long-term process.

Hot and tired in the midday sun, the farmers meet in the shade to conclude the tour, passing around lemons from Freedom Garden's trees. The still greater communal harvest, however, is the training and insights received. Currently, a group of 15 farmers participate in long-term training, women and men who are leaders in their communities. At Freedom Gardens, they observe two widely supported keys to progress for small Malawian farms: crop diversity and low-cost irrigation. Though they celebrate their successes, the Chinkhunthas haven't forgotten their struggles and where they began.

"You always have to start with where you are," Glyvins emphasizes as his hand sweeps over the green vista. "We didn't start with this, we started small! By putting to proper use what we have – that's how we Malawians can be food secure."

Melissa Aberle-Grasse is a freelance writer who currently lives in Malawi with her husband and two children.

Snapshot: Botswana

Statistics:

Population – 1.5 million people

Life Expectancy – 37 (36 male, 38 female)[1]

Proportion undernourished – 24% (30% in 1979-1981, 18% in 1990-1992)

Number undernourished – approximately 400,000

Change in # undernourished, 1990-1992 to 1998-2000 – 200,000 person increase

Under-5 mortality rate – 101 (per 1,000 births)[2]

Botswana has experienced fairly consistent economic growth since the country gained independence in 1966, yet the number of people undernourished in the country continues to grow. Since the early 1990s, the number of people undernourished in Botswana has increased by 200,000, and most disturbingly, the proportion of people undernourished has increased from less than one in five in the early 1990s to nearly one in four today.

A few decades ago, Botswana was one of the poorest nations in the world, battling drought and famine. Today, the country's economy – largely dependent on diamond mining and beef exports – has continued to grow since the 1970s. Still, the country has not been able to forestall the nation's staggering HIV/AIDS infection percentages, hefty unemployment rates or high poverty levels, all factors directly feeding the rising hunger trend. The public sector dominance in the economy and lack of attention to rural areas has impeded private sector development, job creation and poverty alleviation.[3]

In Botswana, poverty is more prevalent and more severe in rural areas. Rural dwellers traditionally have raised cattle, while others living in remote areas rely on hunting and gathering for their subsistence.[4] However, the government has been reluctant to invest in rural development or agriculture, which is burdened with the country's difficult, arid climate and threat of drought. As a result, unemployment rates hover around 20 percent.[5]

The government of Botswana has functioned as a successful democracy since the country gained independence in 1966. Eight elections have been held, their legitimacy verified by the Botswana people. The Botswana Democratic Party has held control for over 30 years, winning the plurality in each winner-take-all contest. An Independent Electoral Commission was established in 1997 to officially oversee the elections. The people credit this success to their traditional system, Kgotla, in which policies are discussed openly among community members.[6] Despite the leadership's stability and popularity, the government has struggled to make wise economic decisions and synthesize its goals with those of the investment and donor communities that hold stakes in Botswana.[7]

The government of Botswana has made concerted efforts to link poor people with social services. Over the past two decades, officials have constructed a number of citizen economic empowerment programs, increased basic services, simplified the income transfer process and improved the general quality of life for many.[8] Yet the national poverty rate dropped from 59 percent to 47 percent from 1985 to 1994, and has hovered at 47 percent since that time.[9] Botswana lacks an overarching poverty reduction plan and the institutional structures with which to implement it. Major shortcomings of existing programs are that they are not consistent or coordinated, which results in fewer people using them.[10]

[1] Population Reference Bureau Web site, http://www.prb.org.
[2] Food and Agriculture Organization of the United Nations, *State of Food Insecurity in the World, 2002.* (Rome: FAO) 32, 36.
[3] Gervase S. Maipose, "Economic Development and the Role of the State in Botswana." *Development Policy Management Forum (DPMF) Bulletin,* April 2003, 1, 5.
[4] International Fund for Agricultural Development Web site, "Botswana: Female-Headed Households," http://www.ifad.org/gender/learning/challenges/women/bt_6_2.htm.
[5] Maipose, 4.
[6] Mogopodi Lekorwe, et al., "Public Attitudes toward Democracy, Governance and Economic Development in Botswana." AfroBarometer Paper No. 14, The Institute for Democracy in South Africa and the University of Botswana, 2002, 2-14.
[7] Maipose, 5.
[8] N. Baetsewe, "Botswana – Formulation of the National Poverty Reduction Strategy." Partnership in Statistics for Development in the 21st Century, 3.
[9] U.N. Development Program Web site, "Botswana Poverty Profile," www.unbotswana.org.bw/undp/poverty_country.html.
[10] Baetsewe.

Naysayers likely will argue against expanding development assistance, citing past failures. British musician and longtime Africa advocate, Bob Geldof, counters the argument this way: "Some argue Africa has had more than the Marshall Plan monies in aid over the years. True, but it has been incoherent, not conducive to anything but momentary support of dislocated development."[3]

However, throwing up our hands and walking away is not the answer either. The way forward must be to resist abandoning hopeful solutions because of past performance and instead learn from experience and do it better.

Hunger-Poverty Spiral

The most durable way to reduce hunger is to reduce poverty. Yet it can take decades for nations and people to escape poverty, creating a downward hunger-poverty spiral. In Afghanistan, for example, the Food and Agriculture Organization of the United Nations (FAO) estimates that rehabilitating the country's agriculture – which supports 21 million people – will take at least 10 years.[4] In the meantime, poor people continue to pay the price of being hungry. Too few calories leave people fatigued and more susceptible to illness. Micronutrient deficiencies can weaken eyesight, slow thinking and lead to life-and-death problems, especially during pregnancy,

Ethiopia Offers Lessons in Complexities of Fighting Hunger

Ethiopia's recurrent food crises provide an example of how complex the fight against hunger can be and how important integrated efforts are. After the 1984 famine, the government and international aid donors concentrated efforts on boosting food production and developing an early warning system to detect weather failures. Assistance was provided to help farmers buy seeds and fertilizers, and expand the ability of agricultural extension agents to work with farmers, all with the aim of increasing grain production.

These efforts worked. By the late 1990s, grain yields increased by more than 50 percent in a decade. Yet Ethiopia faced food shortages again in 2002. Why? The government miscalculated the importance of less obvious agriculture supports, such as roads, access to credit and systems to facilitate cross-border trade.

While the Ethiopian government strongly supported increasing agricultural production, it simultaneously withdrew from its activities related to broader agricultural needs, such as rural roads and crop storage units, assuming that this would open the door for private enterprise in these areas. Private businesses, though, did not yet extend to many rural areas and could not fill the gap. Consequently, as farmers harvested their bumper grain crops in the late 1990s and early 2000s, they watched as local market prices plunged: Corn was selling for less than half production costs. Prices were higher in more distant markets, but farmers and rural traders on donkeys could not reach them because of poor roads and national borders.

Having lost money, farmers reduced their costs the next year by planting less acreage; some only planted a fourth of what they had the year before. In 2002 these agricultural cutbacks met with severe drought, leading to massive crop failures that left millions of Ethiopians facing starvation.

The experience has been a wake-up call to government and donor officials, reinforcing the importance of a comprehensive approach to agriculture and rural development that includes market development, transportation and storage infrastructure, and rural credit.

early childhood and old age. Hunger undermines people's ability to earn a living and prepare for the future. By slowing economic development, hunger can undermine an entire nation's ability to move ahead.

In Kinshasa, the sprawling capital of the Democratic Republic of Congo (formerly Zaire), the average man consumes 1,500 calories per day, nearly 700 calories less than what the World Health Organization recommends. People who do not get enough to eat cannot live energetic or fully productive lives. In 2000 per capita gross national product (GNP) in sub-Saharan Africa averaged $470. FAO estimates that if undernourishment had been eliminated, GNP could have reached between $1,000 and $3,500.[5]

Because hunger in developing countries often is an all-consuming daily struggle – as described by one Ethiopian, "A life that cannot go beyond food" – food and nutrition assistance can help free people's time, directly improving productivity. Most hungry people also spend what income they have on food. Poor people in Tra Vinh, Vietnam, say, "Income is just enough to buy food, but rarely provides enough earnings for a household to build up assets and escape poverty."[6] In that way, food assistance programs directly free more of a family's money for other investments like livestock, tools and education that can be used to generate future wealth, reducing the likelihood that the family will need help again.

The Role of Nutrition Assistance

Though longer-term interventions that address poverty are critical in the fight against hunger, direct food and nutrition support can be a relatively inexpensive and highly effective way to help poor and hungry people now. With various programs ranging from food stamps to school feeding, nutrition assistance often is the best way to get food to the people who need it most. And because progress against hunger also contributes to progress against poverty, nutrition assistance is an important element of broader poverty-reduction development efforts (see related story, p. 85).

Micronutrient supplements for vitamin and mineral deficiencies work most quickly and directly, especially among specific populations like women and children. Vitamin and mineral supplement programs vary in how they are administered and financed, and are not without problems. Most supplements last only four-to-six months, so interventions must be repeated often and consistently, which can be difficult in some remote and volatile areas. The initial outlay of money needed to buy the drops or capsules also can be prohibitively expensive for some countries. But most experts agree that the programs' long-term benefits more than justify the initial costs. According to the World Bank, every $1 invested in vitamin and mineral supplements results in

FIGURE 5.1

Rates of Child Hunger Vary By Region

The world has agreed to cut hunger in half by 2015. Progress to date varies by region. Using underweight rates for children younger than 5 as a measure, the Caribbean, Latin America, and East and Southeast Asia are on track.[1] Rates have not changed in North Africa since 1990, and rates are rising in Southcentral and Western Asia, and sub-Saharan Africa.

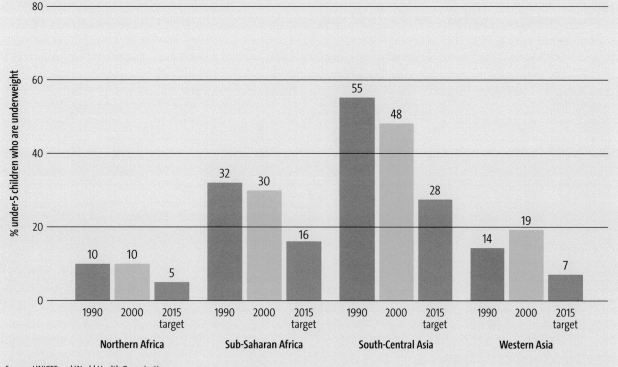

Prevalence Of Underweight Children In Selected Regions

Source: UNICEF and World Health Organization.

[1] In East Asia, 19 percent of children under 5 were underweight in 1990, dropping to 10 percent in 2000. The rates in Southeast Asia were 38 percent (1990) and 28 percent (2000); in Latin America and the Caribbean, 11 percent (1990) and 8 percent (2000).

$100 gained in healthier and more productive workers and public health savings.

During the past decade, the Canadian International Development Agency (CIDA), the Micronutrient Initiative, UNICEF and the World Health Organization have coordinated efforts through national immunization days, intensive health care sessions and regular health service to address micronutrient concerns, especially vitamin A deficiencies, which can cause preventable blindness in children and raise the risk of disease and death from severe infections. In pregnant women, a lack of vitamin A causes night blindness and may increase the risk of maternal mortality.

In June 1999 Niger held its first National Micronutrient Days, where health workers and volunteers distributed vitamin A capsules to 80 percent of children younger than 5, and iron/folate tablets to 75 percent of all pregnant women.[7] That same year, as part of the Indian state of Orissa's National Immunization Day,

children for the first time received a combined polio vaccination and vitamin A supplement. Because of such efforts, the Micronutrient Initiative estimates that 1.5 billion vitamin A capsules have been distributed in more than 70 developing countries, helping to reduce child mortality by approximately 20 percent.

Connecting Nutrition and Agricultural Development

The most effective anti-hunger programs combine improved food access and nutrition with long-term economic and community development. Historically, researchers have viewed food access issues – especially in rural communities – as agricultural productivity and income issues, relegating research and policy to agricultural science and state agricultural departments. Nutrition, on the other hand, most often has been regarded as a public health issue, with researchers pursuing biomedical solutions and policy makers being housed in health departments.

FIGURE 5.2

The World Has A Long Way To Go To Cut Poverty In Half By 2015

The fight against hunger goes hand-in-hand with the fight against poverty. The world has agreed to reduce the proportion of people living in extreme poverty – on less than $1 a day – by half by 2015. The target largely has been met in East Asia and the Pacific, but Latin America and the Caribbean, parts of Europe and Central Asia, and sub-Saharan Africa still fall drastically short of the mark.

Population Living in Extreme Poverty By Region

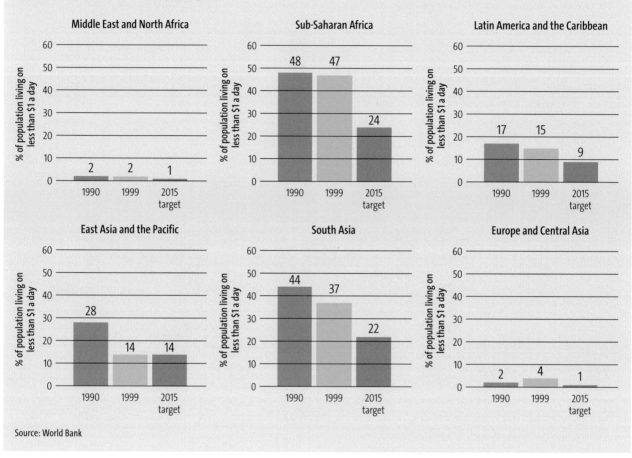

Source: World Bank

Moving forward, anti-hunger strategies increasingly will need to connect greater agriculture productivity and income with explicit nutrition goals. A project in Kenya to promote growth and consumption of orange-fleshed sweet potatoes provides such an example. Conceived and implemented by the Kenya Agricultural Research Institute, the International Potato Center and CARE-Kenya, the project sought to replace white-fleshed sweet potatoes native to Kenyan diets with orange-fleshed potatoes, high in beta-carotene (converted by the body into vitamin A). Since sweet potatoes are traditionally grown and sold by women, they also provide a way to target the people with the most direct control over household nutrition.

Special extension agents with nutrition backgrounds joined agricultural extension agents in working with communities to make the crop transition. The agriculture extension agents worked with women farmers in 10 communities to grow the new crop, which being drought resistant and having higher yields than the traditional potato quickly became popular among women. Meanwhile the nutrition agents shared the potatoes' nutritional benefits with the women as part of instruction on how to prepare the potato, use it in traditional dishes and market it to others. At the end of a 20-month intervention, researchers concluded, "It is likely that food-based strategies to promote the consumption of orange-fleshed sweet potatoes . . . will prove to be an effective way to improve the vitamin A status of young children and their families around the world,"[8] and that "deficiencies of vitamin A can be reduced within one year through an agricultural, food-based intervention."[9]

Snapshot: India

Statistics:

Population – 1 billion (second largest in the world)

Life Expectancy – 63 (62 male/64 female)[1]

Proportion undernourished – 21% (down from 25% in 1990-1992, 38% in 1979-1981)

Number undernourished – approximately 213.7 million people

Change in # undernourished, 1990-1992 to 1999-2001 – 800,000 person decrease

Growth in population, 1990-1992 to 1999-2001 – 147 million person increase

Under-5 mortality rate – 96 (per 1,000 births)[2]

India is home to the greatest number of hungry people in the world. And while its population has continued to grow – an increase of nearly 150 million people in the past decade alone – India still has managed to curb the tide of swelling hunger. Since the early 1990s, the number of hungry people has dropped by 800,000 and the rate of hunger has decreased from 25 percent to 21 percent.

India's centrally planned economy underwent extensive change in the 1990s, when the finance ministry kicked off market liberalization and privatization reforms. In the following years, India's economy grew significantly, with the gross domestic product climbing by 6 percent to 7 percent each year. Both inflation rates and fiscal deficits fell during this time, and the government greatly decreased tariffs and trade restrictions. Consequently, import and export levels shot up by over 20 percent. However, India's growth slowed considerably in 1998 with the Asian financial crisis and the imposition of sanctions, due to the build up of the country's nuclear arsenal.[3]

Seven out of 10 people in India live in rural areas and almost as many rely on agriculture for their livelihoods. Unfortunately, most of the growth that India experienced in the 1990s took place outside of the farming sector, within the industry and technology markets.

Nonetheless, economic liberalization reforms did have positive effects for agricultural trade by acting to increase India's trade volume, curtailing domestic surpluses and thus buoying prices. Public and private investments have spurred development for the agricultural sector, with groundwater projects extending irrigation and new research increasing productivity. Despite these advances, poverty and food access for rural populations is still a major difficulty. Many Indians lack sufficient income to provide nutritious food for their families.[4]

The Indian government runs a number of anti-poverty programs, such as subsidized food distribution, which consume a large portion of the national budget.[5] Although these projects reach some people living in poverty, they are neither financially sustainable nor keenly targeted to those most in need. More energy has been directed toward family planning and education than to basic needs such as health care and employment.[6] But more than anything, India lacks enough jobs for its labor force. Critical infrastructure also is lacking for disaster relief. Rural populations are left to struggle against natural disasters that wipe out crops and leave hundreds of thousands of people homeless.[7]

[1] Population Reference Bureau Web site, http://www.prb.org.

[2] Food and Agriculture Organization of the United Nations, *State of Food Insecurity in the World, 2002.* (Rome: FAO) 9, 35.

[3] Economic Research Service (ERS), U.S. Department of Agriculture (USDA), Briefing Room Web site, "India: Basic Information," www.ers.usda.gov/Briefing/India/basicinformation.htm.

[4] ERS, USDA, Briefing Room Web site, "India: Outlook," www.ers.usda.gov/Briefing/India/outlook.htm.

[5] ERS, USDA, Briefing Room Web site, "India: Policy,." www.ers.usda.gov/Briefing/India/policy.htm.

[6] World Bank PovertyNet Library Web site, "India – Achievements and Challenges in Reducing Poverty 1997," http://poverty.worldbank.org/library/view/8680/.

[7] PBS Web site, "Commanding Heights, India: Social. 2003," www.pbs.org/wgbh/commandingheights/lo/countries/in/in_social.html.

Food-for-Work and School Feeding

Community involvement and buy-in is critical to the success of food-assistance and broader development programs. Food-for-work and school feeding projects are prime examples of how to integrate people's immediate food needs with longer-term development goals in a way that empowers a community.

Food-for-work programs can provide a way to combine progress toward long-term development objectives with immediate food support. These programs essentially trade food for labor. The U.N. World Food Program (WFP); nongovernmental organizations (NGOs), such as the International Committee of the Red Cross; and bilateral donors, including USAID, use food-for-work schemes as part of agricultural recovery strategies.

The WFP's food-for-work projects often relate to irrigation, reforestation, terracing – all critical to agriculture. In the northern highlands of Ethiopia, for example, WFP for many years has been operating a food-for-work program that is focused on restoring the environment to make the land more productive.

Between July 2002 and September 2002, food-for-work projects in Afghanistan employed 1 million laborers per month. In August 2003, WFP food-for-work programs reached over a half million Afghanis with more than 7,000 million tons of food. The projects provided essential food assistance to the most vulnerable members of Afghanistan's population while enabling recipients to help rehabilitate local infrastructure and rebuild productive assets, such as roads and schools.[10]

School feeding projects are another example of combining food and nutrition needs and development objectives. Essentially, the programs entice students to attend school by providing them food. Improved

AIDS Deaths Continue To Rise Worldwide

The global HIV/AIDS epidemic killed more than 3 million people in 2003, and an estimated 5 million acquired the human immunodeficiency virus (HIV) – bringing to 40 million the number of people living with the virus around the world.
— AIDS Epidemic Update, December 2003

The number of people living with HIV/AIDS continues to increase in several regions, most markedly in sub-Saharan Africa, according to the most recent report by The Joint U.N. Program on HIV/AIDS, known as UNAIDS. In 2003 an estimated 26.6 million people in sub-Saharan Africa were living with HIV, including the 3.2 million who became infected during the past year. AIDS killed approximately 2.3 million people.

Sub-Saharan Africa remains by far the region worst affected by the HIV/AIDS epidemic. Southern Africa alone is home to about 30 percent of people living with HIV/AIDS worldwide, yet this region has less than 2 percent of the world's population.

For those people closely watching the numbers, they will notice that 2003 estimates appear lower than those released by UNAIDS in 2002. This decrease is not because of gains in the fight against HIV/AIDS, but because of improved measurement tools and methods that have resulted in better data. Based on these more accurate estimates, UNAIDS finds that both the number of people living with HIV/AIDS and the number of those dying from HIV steadily is increasing. Asia and the Pacific as well as Eastern Europe and Central Asia continue to experience expanding epidemics as well.

FIGURE 5.3
Number of Deaths Due to AIDS Globally, 1999-2003

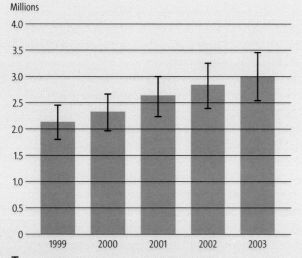

Millions

| bar indicates the range around the estimate.

Source: UNAIDS

To improve its effectiveness, development assistance must be targeted to programs that help the people who need it most, including small-scale farmers and people living in rural areas who comprise three out of every four poor and hungry people in the world.

nutrition has been linked with better school performance and attendance among students. On the flip side, improved education, especially for girls, is associated with a decreased chance of being poor and hungry. WFP's strategy of tying its distribution of staple foods to girls' school attendance has doubled the enrollment of girls attending school in Cameroon, Morocco, Niger and Pakistan.[11] If program administrators buy the food for schools locally, they also bolster area farmers' incomes.

Food stamps also can provide food assistance. Similar to the program in the United States, several developing countries provide vouchers to poor and hungry families so they can buy food. Because families receiving vouchers often spend some of the cash initially allocated for food on other necessities, these programs also boost families' overall income. Though most hungry people live in rural areas, food vouchers work best in more urban environments, where people live in more concentrated neighborhoods and have access to greater services and infrastructure like public transportation. Because the programs involve a fair level of bureaucracy and administration, they also tend to be most successful in middle- and upper-income countries.

Snapshot: *China*

Statistics:

Population – 1.275 billion (the world's largest)

Life Expectancy – 71 years, (69 male/73 female)[1]

Proportion undernourished – 11% (down from 17% in 1990-1992 and 30% in 1979-1981)

Number undernourished – approximately 135.3 million people

Change in # undernourished, 1990-1992 to 1999-2001 – 57.7 million person decrease

Under-5 mortality rate – 40 (per 1,000 births)[2]

China has seen the largest decrease in hunger since the early 1990s – a drop of 57.7 million people. Much of that success is attributed to China's recent economic reforms, which have encouraged rapid economic growth. Reforms include increased foreign trade, semi-privatization, encouragement of specialized production and free market practices, price increases and decollectivization.[3]

In recent years, China also has made strides to improve the quality of life for its rural population, which comprise two-thirds of the total population. Farmers have gained security in land rights and land tenure from a series of policy and legal reforms.[4] The central government also has committed funds for poverty reduction, focusing mainly on programs that develop agriculture, animal husbandry and agro-processing industries. Some programs have been implemented through local governments and some through microfinancing

techniques.[5] Per capita rural income has increased every year since 1978, and more than 140 million people have moved out of poverty.[6]

China's government also has instituted political reforms. New policies have decentralized power to an extent, granting more autonomy to local governments for their communities' development and revenue expenditure decisions.[7] As China's nonstate sector has expanded, the government has reformed social policy to create safety nets that are both cost efficient and flexible. The state-run systems that provide health care, pensions, housing and other fringe benefits in China still operate, but are sagging under the burden of too many workers.

---

[1]   Population Reference Bureau Web site, http://www.prb.org.

[2]   Food and Agriculture Organization of the United Nations, *State of Food Insecurity in the World, 2002.* (Rome: FAO) 9, 31.

[3]   L.X. Zhang, "Agricultural and Rural Development in China." Chinese Academy of Science, Center for Chinese Agricultural Policy, 2002, 4.

[4]   Rural Development Institute Web site, "China," www.rdiland.org/OURWORK/OurWork_China.html.

[5]   Zhang Lei, "Review and Outlook of Poverty Alleviation and Development in China." Manila Social Forum, PRC State Council, Leading Group Officeon Poverty, November 1999.

[6]   Lei, 5.

[7]   Justin Lin, Zhiqiang Liu and Funing Zhong, "Fiscal Decentralization and Rural Development in China." Hong Kong University, Sustainable Development Department, 1998.

Development Assistance

When it comes to lasting progress against hunger, there is no surer path than raising incomes. Poverty-focused development assistance can play an important role in helping poor nations and people become more productive, earn more money and achieve higher standards of living.

The World Bank estimates that it would cost an additional $50 billion a year in development assistance to achieve all the MDGs. While cost estimates to cut hunger in half by 2015 vary, all agree that more money is needed. But in making the case for more money, new ways of strengthening the effectiveness and accountability of assistance also must be pursued.

The Development Assistance Committee of the Organization for Economic Cooperation and Development (OECD) surveyed the best ways to deliver development assistance and found that countries receiving aid identified seven types of burdens that lessened aid's effectiveness. Topping the list were: donor-driven priorities and systems, difficulties with donor procedures, and uncoordinated donor practices.[12]

Most aid has been distorted by donor countries' self-interested motives. Much aid has been used to buy allies

in the Cold War or, now, the war on terrorism. Aid also is used to achieve foreign policy obligations (e.g., support for Israel or reduced drug trafficking) or the commercial interests of donor countries.

Too much aid has been designed in Washington, D.C., and European capitals. Projects have followed intellectual fashions in the donor countries instead of being grounded in the local realities of developing countries. Very poor countries especially are vulnerable to inappropriate interventions because they need aid to survive and have few local experts to help negotiate with external aid agencies.

Too much aid also has paid for temporary projects instead of longer-term, self-sustaining efforts. A World Bank assessment found that between 1994 and 1997, only one in five of its community development and integrated rural programs in Africa proved sustainable. Projects tended to be completely donor financed, temporary, focused on a single sector and implemented outside of local communities.

The World Bank concludes that its past rural development efforts in Africa most often failed because local priorities and local skills were not considered during the planning process.[13]

Young children who do not receive proper nutrition are more likely to suffer chronic illness later in life.

Margaret W. Nea

Improving Development Assistance

Improving a country's overall economic growth, while necessary, will not, in and of itself, reduce poverty and hunger. To succeed, poor and hungry people must participate in this economic growth as well. Toward that end, funding must be targeted toward:

- Small-scale farmers and people living in rural areas, who comprise three out of four poor and hungry people worldwide;

- Women and children, who are among the most socially, politically, economically and physically vulnerable to hunger; and

- People who are sick and infirm who often have greater nutrition needs.

Resources also should be directed toward very poor countries.

Yet because of the mixed motives of donor nations and political realities among and within both donor and recipient nations, aid often bypasses the groups (and countries) that most need it. In sub-Saharan Africa, for example, for every health and education $1 spent on people in the region's poorest quintile, $2.50 goes to the richest.[14] Similarly, though most poor people in sub-Saharan Africa live in rural areas dependent on agriculture, levels of development assistance for this region's agriculture declined precipitously during the 1990s.

Targeting Food-Insecure Communities: Rural and Urban

Rural Needs

Because most of the world's poor and hungry people live in rural areas, development efforts must focus on rural and agriculture development initiatives. Farmers need ways to better safeguard water, soil and soil fertility. Intensive working of the soil without enough nutrient replenishment has led to loss of soil fertility and decreasing production per acre. Indeed, food production per capita is declining in sub-Saharan Africa.

Greater crop yields would mean more food in poor rural communities and higher incomes. Not only do farmers rely on the money from their produce sales, but other people rely on farm income for their livelihoods as well. A woman who makes soap for a living likely sells her product to a farmer's family. A teacher who earns her wages in a rural school depends on the farmer, soap-maker and others to pay school fees so she can earn a living.

While important, increased productivity alone does not always translate into better food security or less hunger. The more remote and isolated a community, the more difficult it is for men and women to reach markets, get reliable pricing information and buy seeds and fertilizer. As such, farmers also need good roads,

FIGURE 5.4
Too Many Children Are Dying Before Their Fifth Birthday

By 2015, the world has agreed to reduce by two-thirds the number of children dying before age 5. In developing countries, for every 1,000 children born, more than 100 die before they reach their fifth birthday.

Under-5 Mortality Rates in 1990, 2000 and 2015 Goal

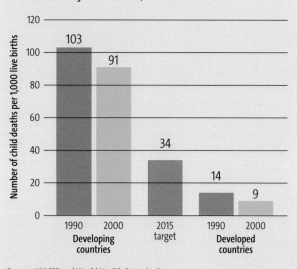

Source: UNICEF and World Health Organization

communication networks and opportunities to export to neighboring countries and far-off destinations. More efficient input and product markets and increased government support for small-farm research and agriculture extension also are needed.

Urban Needs

The development needs of urban people are not so different from their rural cousins: better-paying jobs, improved water and sanitation, expanded health and nutrition programs, more funding for schools, roads and public transportation. However, the approaches can be very different.[15] Open trade policies tend to help foster labor-intensive, job-enhancing manufacturing. Support for microenterprises and small businesses also can help to create jobs and raise incomes. Urban gardening projects encourage people living in cities to grow some of their own food. Up to 40 percent of the people in African cities are involved in urban or semi-urban agriculture.[16]

Fortunately, urban environments with their more concentrated populations and more complex bureaucracy often are at least marginally better equipped to meet these needs.

Targeting Food-Insecure People: Women and Children, Sick and Infirm

Women and Children

A wealth of research confirms that women are key to families escaping hunger. In most countries and cultures, women buy and prepare their families' food; they directly grow food to be eaten, especially fruits and vegetables. In many cases, they run a small business, such as a market garden, that helps pay for food, medicine, school fees, clothes and other necessities directly related to their children's well-being. By empowering women, communities directly strengthen families and help children.

The connection between a mother's health and her children's health is crucial, especially that of pregnant women and infants. Women who do not receive proper nutrition during pregnancy bear babies who are more likely to suffer disease later in life.[17] Similarly, young children who do not receive proper nutrition also are more likely to suffer chronic illness later in life.

Research in Egypt, Mozambique and elsewhere has shown primary education for women did more to reduce poverty than other factors.[18] Multiple studies also demonstrate that educating women is crucial to preventing infant undernutrition.[19] A vital step in reducing world hunger is to educate women and girls.

A Community in Ghana Creates Its Own Vision of Being Hunger-Free

By Isaac Akinyele

Some of the most successful development efforts are those that grow out of a community's assessment of its own needs. The Hunger Project in Ghana embraces such an approach.

In Taido-Anomabo, The Hunger Project worked with the community to improve its standard of living so that families would not have to fear the threat of hunger. Using a methodology it calls "Strategic Planning-in-Action," the project adopts catalytic efforts that not only help with poverty and hunger alleviation today, but also broader economic development issue so communities will be better protected from hunger tomorrow.

The community, which depends largely on agriculture for its livelihood, expressed the concern that people were suffering greatly from post-harvest losses. Many people also were not motivated to expand their farming efforts because the income from the sale of raw commodities was so low.

As a group, the community decided that it wanted to work toward creating a food processing plant so that farmers would be able to sell processed agricultural products at a higher price. The plant also would allow them to process the staple crops for easier storage, so that farmers could hold the crops longer and wait to sell them during the leaner seasons when prices are higher.

The Hunger Project helped establish this plant, and as a result, farmers in Taido-Anomabo are growing more crops, both for food and profit. The farmers now feel comfortable planting more acreage because they know that the produce will not go to waste.

To help keep the plant going, the farmers agreed to pay a small fee for every bowl of produce to be processed. This money is used to pay for the plant's upkeep and the attendant's salary.

Moreover, as other communities near Taido-Anamabo witness this success, they are being inspired to create a hunger-free community as well. In that sense, Taido-Anamabo's success is helping to build a network of community development that will strengthen the country.

This example is one among many successes which communities have recorded in the bid to improve their welfare. Stories from other communities in Africa especially in Nigeria and Zambia include improvements in access to health services, provision of safe potable water, provision of formal educational facilities, community-based transfer of knowledge and technology, access to micro-credit, enhanced productivity, diversification of income base, improved dietary practices and women empowerment in education, social and economic areas.

In achieving these successes some innovations and factors played significant roles. Prominent among these were strong and effective community organizational structure, use of indigenous technology, outstanding women initiatives, strong institutional linkages and integrated approaches, location of markets for produce, focus on priority needs, targeting on women and youths, and efficient use of available natural resources. These innovations and factors could be useful in addressing the problems of hunger and malnutrition in communities elsewhere.

Dr. Isaac Olaoluwa Akinyele is president of Food Basket Foundation International and a professor of the Department of Human Nutrition at the University of Ibadan, Nigeria.

Efforts to Meet Emergency Food Needs Are Strong, But Could Be Stronger

Early warning systems help predict natural disasters and have improved the international communities' ability to spot, prepare for and respond to impending food crises. But more can and should be done to prevent hunger during such emergencies. To get there, emergency food aid and its delivery network need continued support and strengthening.

The U.S. Agency for International Development (USAID) funds the Famine Early Warning System Network (FEWS NET), a group of organizations that work together to monitor weather, crop and rangeland conditions in Africa. The Global Information and Early Warning System on Food and Agriculture – run by the Food and Agriculture Organization of the United Nations (FAO) – also tries to stay on top of crop production and possible interruptions to predict and prepare for likely food shortages. As a result, famine deaths have declined steadily over the past two decades.

Still, risk-prone areas need vigilant monitoring, and the international community needs to remain alert and ready to help when the next hunger crisis emerges. In 2002 sub-Saharan Africa – a region in the midst of prolonged drought – received 1.9 million tons of emergency food. Eighty-three percent of this was delivered through the U.N. World Food Program (WFP). The rest either was donated directly from countries or channeled through nongovernment organizations. WFP alone undertook 130 relief operations in 72 countries, reaching 44 million people.

Yet more effort is needed. Many people still are at risk of famine. In Swaziland and Lesotho, families continue to face food shortages, and in Zimbabwe, escalating food prices, unemployment and political instability continue to leave many families without enough food to eat. In July 2003 WFP appealed for $311 million to feed 6.5 million people across the region, but received less than two-thirds of this appeal. Without ongoing food aid, many farmers will lack the energy to plant and harvest what they could.

More needs to be done. In 2003 the World Food Program appealed for $311 million to feed 6.5 million people in sub-Saharan Africa. Donors responded with less than two-thirds of this appeal.

FIGURE 5.5
More Aid Is Needed, But Levels Continue To Drop

The amount of money to help developing countries reach the Millennium Development Goals – including cutting hunger in half by 2015 – may be debated, but the fact that more money is needed is not. Net development assistance — as a percentage of donor countries' gross national income — has decreased over the last decade and is at an all-time low. Net aid to the least developed countries has decreased even more.

Net Aid As Percentage of Donors' Gross National Income (GNI)

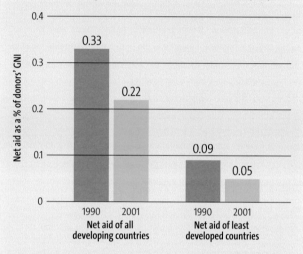

Source: Organization for Economic Cooperation and Development/Development Assistance Committee

The Sick and Infirm

Food security also is directly affected by a person's health and his or her body's ability to absorb calories and nutrients. Illness often prevents people from being able to fully absorb foods' nutrients. Compounding the problem, people who are sick and infirm most often need highly nutritious food.

Diseases such as HIV/AIDS, malaria and tuberculosis are endemic in many developing countries. These three diseases alone kill more than 6 million people each year. As such, countries need effective health care systems that reach and can be afforded by people most in need. In this way, a malaria vaccine, for example, would do a great deal to improve food security in sub-Saharan Africa, where 900,000 of every 1 million people die from malaria each year. Unfortunately, pharmaceutical companies generally do not invest in poor country diseases, like malaria. Demand is too uncertain for projected profits to justify large amounts of capital investment.

In cases where drugs and vaccines do exist to combat these diseases, poor countries often have a difficult time accessing them because the drugs are patented and expensive. In August 2003, an agreement was reached in the World Trade Organization that allows exportation of generic versions of essential medicines, which had previously been proscribed. This agreement has brought the costs of anti-retroviral drugs used to treat AIDS down from over $1,000 per year to roughly $300. Further efforts to work with generic producers, notably by the Clinton Foundation, show promise of halving costs again.

Cheaper drugs are a huge help, but do not obviate the need for stronger health infrastructures in poor countries. Drugs will not help if there is no way to distribute them.

Debt Relief and Trade

Development assistance is only one component of what an effective partnership with poor countries should include. Fairer trade rules and deeper debt relief also are essential to developing countries' being able to climb out of poverty and hunger. Oxfam America estimates that U.S. cotton subsidies cost Mali $43 million in 2001 cotton export earnings, while U.S. development assistance to that country totaled only $37 million

Many women in developing countries run small businesses, such as market gardens. Money from these ventures helps pay for food, medicine, school fees, clothes and other household necessities.

Agricultural Rehabilitation Moves Slowly in Afghanistan

Two years after the fall of the Taliban and despite many pledges of international commitment to Afghanistan's reconstruction, many Afghan people still suffer from hunger and food insecurity. The initial hope that these events would lead to a rebuilding of Afghanistan that eventually would help the Afghan people seems to be waning.

Eighty-five percent of Afghan people rely on agriculture for their livelihood, but decades of war, periodic drought and neglect have left this sector weak. The rehabilitation of agriculture is a top priority among both aid agencies and the Afghan government. All recognize that the money must come almost exclusively from international donors, but to date levels of aid have been inadequate and not used most effectively.

The U.S. General Accounting Office (GAO) undertook an assessment of efforts to rehabilitate agriculture in Afghanistan.[1] In July 2003 it reported serious problems in the ways both food aid and general development assistance, especially for agricultural redevelopment, have been disbursed. These problems have delayed improvement in the daily lives of Afghans, according to GAO.

The World Bank estimates that Afghanistan needs between $15 billion and $20 billion over the next five years, a projection in line with the Afghan government's estimates. Donors, including the United States, pledged $4.5 billion in 2003, but much of it has failed to materialize.

Agricultural assistance in 2003 was projected to total $230 million, less than half of what the Afghan government estimated it needed. Moreover, only 27 percent of the money received by the year's end had paid for long-term rehabilitation projects. Most of the money was needed to meet emergency humanitarian needs.

The lack of resources is undermined further by the failure of donors to coordinate their activities. Despite attempts to bring all agricultural redevelopment projects under the umbrella of a single strategy, including the establishment of two official committees, each donor agency still operates according to its own strategy.

Donors also have failed to coordinate activities with the National Development Framework developed by the Afghan government for that very purpose. This lack of coordination undermines the political development process in Afghanistan as well. GAO states: "Without an integrated operational strategy, jointly developed by the Afghan government and the international community, the Afghan government lacks a mechanism to manage the agricultural rehabilitation effort, focus limited resources, assert its leadership, and hold the international donor community accountable."[2]

The political development process is intimately tied to recovery and reconstruction in Afghanistan. The credibility of the nascent national government depends on the pace and progress of economic development and improvement in people's lives. As the Afghan people lose faith in the ability of the government to provide basic services, the government begins to lose its legitimacy and becomes more vulnerable to the resurgent power of local warlords. And if international donors do not respect the wishes of the national government, it is not likely that Afghan citizens will. Says Abdullah Abdullah, the Afghan foreign minister, "If in the year 2004 Kabul citizens are still in the dark because of [lack of] electricity . . . this government will lose credibility; its friends will lose credibility."[3]

[1] General Accounting Office (GAO), "Lack of Strategic Focus and Obstacles to Agricultural Recovery Threaten Afghanistan's Stability," June 2003.
[2] GAO, 37.
[3] James Morrison, "The Afghanistan Test," *The Washington Times*, July 15, 2003, A14.

Millennium Development Goals Reflect 'Human Dignity,' UN Campaign Director Says

The eight Millennium Development Goals (MDGs) constitute an agenda to significantly improve the health and well-being of people living in developing countries by 2015. The goals set clear targets for reducing hunger, poverty, disease, illiteracy, environmental degradation and discrimination against women.

These goals are not new ideas, but taken together they articulate the world's desire to ensure "human dignity" for all people, says Salil Shetty, director of the U.N. campaign to educate people about the MDGs and inspire them to take action. "A global movement to achieve the MDGs can exist," Salil says. "What will make the difference is if people, everyday citizens, start saying, 'We need this to happen.' This movement must start at the grassroots level and work from the bottom up."[1]

Goal 1: Eradicate Extreme Poverty and Hunger

Goal 2: Achieve Universal Primary Education

Goal 3: Promote Gender Equality and Empower Women

Goal 4: Reduce Child Mortality

Goal 5: Improve Maternal Health

Goal 6: Combat HIV/AIDS, Malaria and Other Diseases

Goal 7: Ensure Environmental Sustainability

Goal 8: Develop a Global Partnership for Development

---

[1] "'Human Dignity' at the Heart of the MDGs," NETAID, January 30, 2004, http://www.netaid.org/campaigns/mdg/story.pt?article_id=1226.

The Millennium Development Goals represent the distilled wisdom of 30 years of global development experience: That hunger, poverty, health, the environment, education, trade and aid all play a part in economic development.

FIGURE 5.6
Making Trade Work for the Poorest Countries

In recent years, the percentage of imports to developed countries (excluding arms and oil) admitted duty-free from developing countries has increased, based on dollar value. But the percentage of duty-free imports from the least developed countries has decreased.

Duty-Free Imports To Developed Countries, 1996-2000

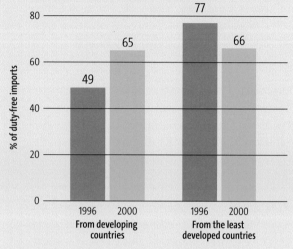

Source: Data based on estimates by UNCTAD in collaboration with the World Bank and World Trade Organization.

that same year. Hunger 2003, *Agriculture in the Global Economy,* outlines the inequities in the global agricultural trading system and their negative impact on developing country agriculture and agricultural trade. Also, many poor countries still carry heavy debt burdens despite the substantial debt relief achieved since 2000.

Sharing Responsibilities

The world essentially knows what to do to efficiently and successfully reduce hunger. Why, then, has so little progress actually been made?

The short answer is a lack of commitment from all sides. Developing countries themselves must take the lead in solving their problems. But the world's wealthy countries also could do a lot more to help. Experience shows that international assistance has the biggest impact when a poor country's government is seriously committed to development – when outside donors really are in partnership with local efforts.

At a 2002 U.N. conference in Monterrey, Mexico, the developing countries as a group committed themselves to improved governance and serious efforts to meet the MDGs. The industrialized countries committed themselves to increased development assistance and, in that context, President Bush proposed that the United States

Snapshot: Chile

Statistics:

Population – 15.2 million people

Life Expectancy – 76 years (73 male, 79 female)[1]

Proportion undernourished – 4% (down from 8% in 1990-1992 and 7% in 1979-1981)

Number undernourished – approximately 600,000 people

Change in # undernourished, 1990-1992 to 1999-2001 – 500,000 person decrease

Under-5 mortality rate – 12 (per 1,000 births)[2]

Chile's growing economy largely has contributed to its success in reducing by half the percent of people struggling with hunger since the early 1990s.

After a coup in 1974, the Chilean government adopted several "shock therapy" policies to restructure its economy, including rapid liberalization of trade, slashed government spending and the deregulation of business. The economy boomed in the late 1970s, followed by a bust in the early 1980s, at which time unemployment reached a high of 33 percent. Chile's economic fluctuations leveled off in 1990, helped in part by rising exports. More recently, Chile has sustained a more modest level of growth and benefited from enough stability to resist regional crisis.[3]

The change of rule from socialism to authoritarian-run free-market to a socially oriented democracy has formed a schizophrenic sort of political culture in Chile. In 1973 the socialist leader Salvador Allende Gossens was presiding over a massive state sector and fighting run-away inflation and eroded popular support. He was deposed by General Augusto Pinochet in a military coup that same year. Pinochet's subsequent 17-year reign saw the deconstruction of the state sector and the elimination of government programs.

During this period, the number of people living in poverty doubled.

When recession and unemployment destabilized Pinochet's government in 1989, elections ensued and the Christian Democrat Patricio Aylwin took over, establishing democracy in Chile. President Alywin reinstated social policies and directed programs at the poorest areas. With the increased spending, tax reform and an economic upswing, both unemployment and poverty rates fell significantly.[4]

Throughout the 1990s, a succession of democratic leaders have been successful in steering Chile's export driven economy, continuing decentralization while reestablishing social programs and rebuilding citizen trust in government.[5] Today Chile still faces unemployment, economic vulnerability and income inequality, yet services cover most basic needs and the quality of life for Chileans is high relative to other developing nations.[6]

---

1   Population Reference Bureau Web site, http://www.prb.org.
2   Food and Agriculture Organization of the United Nations (FAO), *State of Food Insecurity in the World, 2002.* (Rome: FAO) 9, 31.
3   PBS Web site, "Commanding Heights, Chile: Economic. 2003,"www.pbs.org/wgbh/commandingheights/lo/countries/cl/cl_economic.html.
4   PBS Web site, "Commanding Heights, Chile: Social. 2003," www.pbs.org/wgbh/commandingheights/lo/countries/cl/cl_social.html.
5   PBS Web site, "Commanding Heights, Chile: Political. 2003," www.pbs.org/wgbh/commandingheights/lo/countries/cl/cl_political.html.
6   FAO.

---

would provide more aid and channel it through a new Millennium Challenge Account (MCA). He said the MCA would direct additional development assistance to those poor countries that are democratic, have good economic policies, and invest in the health and education of their people.

Countries will be chosen for MCA money according to a set of objective, publicly available criteria. The way projects will be developed under the MCA also is a departure from traditional bilateral assistance. Under the MCA, governments of countries that meet the requirements to receive MCA funds will submit proposals for plans with which they want help. These proposals should be the result of consultations with the wide spectrum of stakeholders in the recipient country, from civil society organizations to businesses. The proposals can ask for anything from money to fund a specific project to general budget support for the central government. The proposal also can ask that the funding go directly to an implementing organization and not through the government of the recipient country.

Bread for the World and its allies have lobbied to keep the focus of the MCA on poor countries, to make it clear that the MCA will be evaluated according to how it helps to achieve the MDGs, and to mandate democratic participation in planning and implementing MCA activities. Bread for the World also has lobbied to make the MCA funding additional to ongoing development and humanitarian assistance, since many of the poorest countries will not meet the criteria for MCA participation.

Sept. 11, 2001, convinced President George W. Bush that the United States has a national security interest in reducing hunger, poverty and disease worldwide. He proposed the MCA and an expanded HIV/AIDS initiative, promising that they would be in addition to ongoing development and humanitarian assistance. In January 2004, Congress passed authorizing legislation for the MCA that included much of what Bread for the World had sought. Congress also increased funding for poverty-focused development assistance by 33 percent – from $6 billion in 2003 to $8 billion in 2004. The

New Malawi Program Bolsters Families Weakened by HIV/AIDS

By Jodie Fonseca

Most people in Malawi are subsistence farmers. For them, every missed day of working in the fields means a smaller harvest. Smaller harvests mean more hunger later in the year. Agnes Phiri[1] of Khongoni area in Lilongwe District knows first-hand how such cycles of food insecurity become even more daunting in the face of HIV/AIDS.

In past years, Agnes' family has been able to survive because two pairs of hands – hers and her husband's – were able to cultivate their fields. During the 2002 planting season, however, Agnes' husband – affected by AIDS – began to fall sick more frequently. Agnes attempted to work the fields alone, but often was called home to attend to her sick husband. The result was a below-average harvest that left her family's food supply stretched far thinner than it should have been.

As the 2003 planting season fast approached, Agnes' husband was completely bedridden and needed even more care. She wondered whether she would be able to cultivate the fields at all. Her 10-year-old daughter would not be able to help her as needed. Besides, Agnes wanted to keep her daughter in school. The only other family was Agnes' younger sister, who is blind.

Many agriculture-dependent families in sub-Saharan Africa are being devastated by hunger and HIV/AIDS. Fortunately, Agnes found help through the Consortium for the Southern Africa Food Security Emergency, or C-SAFE, a group of nine nongovernmental organizations implementing developmental relief programs in nearly all districts of Malawi.[2] The program, initiated in April 2003, includes food-for-work activities, supplementary feeding for malnourished children younger than 5 and malnourished pregnant and lactating women, and food distributions to households that are affected by "chronic illness," a proxy for HIV/AIDS.

C-SAFE recognizes that food is one of the most important needs for HIV-affected, agriculture-dependent families, both in managing the illness and in guarding against hunger. C-SAFE is groundbreaking among food distribution programs because it focuses on chronic illness as a marker of vulnerability. Depending in how poverty and food insecurity are defined by different organizations, Agnes' family may not have been eligible to receive assistance. However, C-SAFE specifically seeks out households made vulnerable by the types of prolonged, debilitating illnesses that are part of AIDS, such as chronic diarrhea, skin cancer and tuberculosis.

Rather than attempting to identify beneficiaries themselves, the consortium partners collaborate with community members to prioritize the households that have been made most vulnerable by chronic illness. Though each community approaches its targeting similarly, the C-SAFE program is designed to build in local variability. Most communities use the village AIDS committees or home-based care groups, made up of local citizens who have a personal understanding of their neighbors' circumstances, to prioritize affected households. As needed, C-SAFE staff provides guidance to the groups, and periodically follows up with communities to determine how well the food-distribution process is working.

Once chosen as beneficiaries, families receive monthly "household" rations of maize, corn-soya blend, vegetable oil and legumes. This food ration has been crucial in helping Agnes feed her family, stabilize her husband's body weight, and continue to send her daughter to school.

Women in Malawi line up to receive food from the Consortium for the Southern Africa Food Security Emergency (C-SAFE) as part of its food-for-work program.

Nationally, C-SAFE has a working group that meets frequently to share community experiences and harmonize approaches toward targeting the chronically ill. These lessons help shape future efforts to improve the program's design and better understand the interrelated issues of acute hunger, chronic food insecurity and HIV/AIDS.

Jodie Fonseca is a Mickey Leland International Hunger Fellow who works as an HIV/AIDS advisor with CARE International in Malawi.

---

1 Names have been changed to protect privacy.
2 The consortium includes Africare, The American Red Cross, CARE, Catholic Relief Services, Emmanuel International, The Salvation Army, Save the Children UK, Save the Children US, and World Vision International. Funding is provided by U.S. Agency for International Development's Food for Peace.

Snapshot: *Mali*

Statistics:

Population – 11.4 million people

Life Expectancy – 45 years (44 male/47 female)[1]

Proportion undernourished – 21% (down from 25% in 1990-1992, 60% in 1979-1981)

Number undernourished – 2.4 million people

Change in # undernourished, 1990-1992 to 1999-2001 – 200,000 person increase

Under-5 mortality rate – 233 (per 1,000 births)[2]

Sub-Saharan Africa has the highest rates of undernourishment in the world. But Mali, which has undergone significant economic and fiscal changes in the past decade, shows that progress against hunger can be made. Though the total number of undernourished Malians increased by 200,000 since the early 1990s, the rate of undernourishment dropped from one in four people to nearly one in five today.

Mali is a sparsely developed and heavily indebted nation in West Africa whose economy is susceptible to erratic swings. Its gross national product has fluctuated from 7 percent growth in both 1995 and 2002 to a 1.2 percent contraction in 2001. Agriculture is Mali's largest sector, employing 80 percent of the population and producing almost half the nation's gross domestic product, and these fluctuations primarily are due to annual variability in rainfall and commodity prices. Overall, trade liberalization reforms and currency devaluation have positively impacted the Malian economy during the past decade.[3]

The government has developed poverty-reduction strategies, working in tandem with aid agencies, to decrease the 71.3 percent of the rural population living below the poverty line. Relief efforts include expanding areas of cultivated land and diversifying the sector with cash crops for export. However, export markets are largely inaccessible to Malian crops because of poor infrastructure.[4]

Since independence from France in 1960, Mali has transitioned from a socialist government to a military dictatorship to a democracy. The first democratic elections were successfully held in 1992. Recent presidential elections were held in April 2002 with impressive results. A nascent civil society and media publicized the 24 broadly diverse candidates and their views. Malians widely accepted the outcome of the election and welcomed Amadou Toure as their new president.[5] While the democratic governments have cited decentralization as the main priority, mismanagement, corruption and lackadaisical privatization efforts have hindered Mali's potential for economic development.[6]

Since 1991, the centralized social service systems have given way to more local resource allocation through lower-level government. In the process, the national government has decreased much of the funding for these services in outlying rural areas. Aid agencies have scrambled to pick up the slack. The U.S. Agency for International Development and the Carter Center are among the major forces in rural Mali, working to enroll children in schools, raise the literacy rates, provide health care and vaccinations, and empower local communities. Aid agencies sometimes couple with government programs, but many prefer to work with private and civil society groups to avoid bureaucratic slowdowns and corruption.[7]

---

[1] Population Reference Bureau Web site, http://www.prb.org.

[2] Food and Agriculture Organization of the United Nations (FAO), *State of Food Insecurity in the World, 2002.* (Rome: FAO) 33, 36.

[3] U.S. Agency for International Development (USAID), "USAID's Approach to Poverty Reduction: The Case of Mali." Bureau for Policy and Program Coordination, January 2003, 5.

[4] Ibid., 6

[5] The Carter Center, "Observing the 2002 Mali Presidential Elections: Final Report." October, 2002, 6; and The Carter Center Web site, "Mali," www.cartercenter.org/activities/printdoc.asp?countryID=47.

[6] USAID, 6.

[7] Ibid., 11.

MCA received $1 billion; the new AIDS initiative received an additional $900 million, and the World Bank's fund for poor countries also received an increase.

These increases were less than President Bush had promised, but still substantial. Bread for the World is engaged in a major campaign called *Keep the Promise on Hunger and Health* to win the further increases in poverty-focused development assistance that President Bush has pledged for 2005. His budget proposal for 2005 includes further increases for the MCA and AIDS initiatives, but again less than he promised when they were announced. It also remains to be seen how hard President Bush will push on this issue during an election year, and how Congress will deal with development assistance as pressures to cut spending increase. Much depends on how much the president and Congress hear from constituents about keeping the promise on hunger and health.

Much also depends on whether poverty-focused development assistance for other humanitarian and development needs also is increased. Net development assistance – as a percentage of donor countries' gross national income – continues to fall and is at an all-time low. Moreover, aid levels have dropped most severely for the poorest countries. While commitment is needed from all sides, wealthier countries like the United States must take the lead and commit the money necessary to address world hunger and poverty once and for all.

In the summary of its 2003 Development Effectiveness Report, UNDP states, "In the end, partnerships matter. While the onus is on poor countries to put in place the pieces necessary to enable development, rich country support needs to add to this process. A business-as-usual approach cannot deliver on the MDGs."

Business-as-usual certainly will not achieve the goal of cutting hunger in half.

CHAPTER

6

Changing the Politics of Hunger

IFAD /A. Hossain

The prospect of making dramatic progress against hunger is tantalizingly close. World hunger increased in 2001, the latest year for which we have data. But over the last three decades, the world achieved heartening progress against hunger. In 1974, one in three persons was hungry; today it's one in six.

It's been 30 years since the World Food Summit of 1974, when leaders first committed themselves to end hunger in a decade. Even then, knowledgeable people agreed that the binding constraint was political. Indeed, in 1963 President Kennedy told delegates to the first World Food Congress, "We have the means, we have the capacity to eliminate hunger from the face of the earth in our lifetime. We need only the will."[1]

But now, as then, the question remains, How to build political will to end hunger in both developing and industrialized countries? The answers are as varied as the countries and cultures involved. Bottom line: Every country's solution must include grassroots activists and national leaders working together to ensure and sustain an end to hunger.

The United States exerts more influence in the world than any other nation, yet it is the least forthcoming of the industrialized countries in reforming its politics and policies in ways that directly benefit poor and hungry people. If the politics of hunger are to be played for the world's benefit, the United States must take the lead.

A Question of U.S. Priority

That said, reducing world hunger is certainly not at the top of the U.S. government's to-do list. Reducing domestic hunger fairs little better. In 1996 the United States only agreed to participate in the World Food Conference on the condition that the discussions would not call for any new funding. Since then, international and U.S. findings confirm that more money is needed to pay for programs that target reduced poverty and improved nutrition. In 2002 Bread for the World Institute estimated, based on U.S. Census data and a study by the U.S. Agency for International Development, that the United States could cut U.S. food insecurity in half by 2010 and do its share to cut world hunger in half by 2015 for an extra $7 billion a year.[2] Other organizations, from the World Bank to the Food and Agriculture Organization of the United Nations (FAO), have come up with their own approximations of what it would cost to end hunger and meet the Millennium Development Goals (MDGs). Obviously, such estimates are not etched in stone — changing circumstances and unforeseen events require flexibility (see related story p. 102). But though the estimates vary, all agree that more money is needed, and none of the predicted costs are prohibitively high.

The problem is not a lack of money or that lawmakers want children to go hungry, but that decision makers usually want something else more. In the end, the problem is a matter of priorities.

Public Values versus Political Realities

U.S. voters have indicated that they support spending more to combat hunger. Polls suggest that people want their government to support effective initiatives against hunger both at home and abroad.

But instead, domestic anti-poverty programs seem to remain at or near the top of the list for funding cuts when budgets get tight. On the international front, the United States gives less in development assistance — as a share of gross national product — than any other rich country.

Pursuing and safeguarding funding for social programs can be as difficult, if not more so, than fighting to put laws on the books. Many times, appropriations fall short of authorizations. It takes vigilance at every stage of the policymaking process to hold Congress and the president accountable. Last year, for example, President Bush toured several countries in Africa, heavily touting a recently enacted bill to fight global AIDS — introduced by the White House — which authorized $15 billion more in spending ($3 billion annually

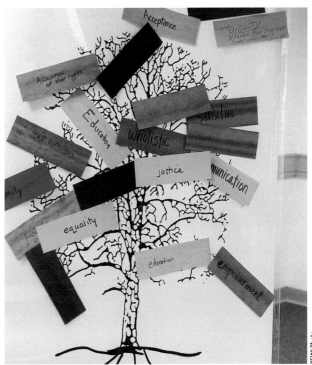

U.S. voters care deeply about hunger and want their leaders to seek justice for poor and hungry people both in the United States and worldwide.

Small Farmers at the Heart of Sustainable Cocoa Growing

By World Cocoa Foundation

Today more than 85 percent of the world's cocoa is grown by between 5 million and 6 million farm families in Asia, Latin America and West Africa. Many of these families depend on income from cocoa to survive. Without them, there would be no chocolate.

That's why the World Cocoa Foundation (WCF) believes that small farmers are the heart of sustainable cocoa growing. Yet these farm families face significant crop losses due to pests, diseases and a general lack of knowledge regarding the best way to care for their crops.

Since its founding in 2000, the WCF has been a leader in promoting sustainable, responsible cocoa farming to improve the well-being of millions of family farmers worldwide who grow cocoa. The WCF's comprehensive program takes science into the field, improving production efficiency, increasing farmer yields and using cocoa to promote reforestation of degraded tropical lands – all in a sustainable, responsible manner.

A global, industry-supported nonprofit organization, the WCF focuses on sustainable cocoa programs in all cocoa growing regions of the world. WCF members include exporters, processors, manufacturers, branded companies and allied industries.

The millions of small family-owned cocoa farms (5-12 acres) that produce the vast majority of the world's cocoa crop face critical needs. These farmers lack:

- adequate access to market information;
- improved tree stock;
- appropriate technologies to reduce disease and pest pressures that destroy a third of the crop each year; and
- farmer organizational support services.

Through targeted educational and scientific programs, WCF and its partners are working to address these constraints in Asia, Latin America and West Africa.

West Africa Regional Farmer Training Program

Cocoa is as vital to the economies of several West African countries as West African cocoa is to the global chocolate and cocoa industry. The region produces nearly 70 percent of the world supply and generates billions of dollars in export earnings to the region.

In West Africa the World Cocoa Foundation is part of a broad coalition of partners supporting the Sustainable Tree Crops Program (STCP) in Cameroon, Cote d' Ivoire, Ghana, Guinea and Nigeria. Program areas include: (1) grower and business support services; (2) research and technology transfer; (3) market system and information system development; labor practices and education; and (4) policy change.

The key partners include the global chocolate industry, host-governments in Africa, Institute of Tropical Agriculture (IITA), U.S. Agency for International Development (USAID), U.S. Department of Labor, International Labor Organization, The German Development Agency (GTZ), U.S. Department of Agriculture (USDA), The French Research Organization (CIRAD), and many nongovernment and private volunteer organizations.

Public-private partnerships, such as the World Cocoa Foundation, can play a crucial role in helping small-scale farmers in developing countries thrive, in turn helping to improve food security in these communities.

Currently, the program is providing support services to thousands of tree crops farmers, many of whom have seen their profits increase due to improved market information and support.

Southeast Asia Regional Farmer Training Program

In Indonesia, the Philippines and Vietnam, WCF is working with the USAID, USDA and a nongovernment organization called ACDI/VOCA on farmer training to control the spread of the cocoa pod borer. Results from Indonesia have been impressive: farmer adoption rates over 90 percent; crop losses have been halved; and farmers have decreased pesticide applications by over a third. The program has trained more than 35,000 farmers and training videos have been developed to accelerate the dissemination of information throughout the region.

Latin America Regional Farmer Training Program

The WCF has been working to develop a regional program for Latin America, but tailored to the individual needs of each country. Countries interested in participating include Bolivia, Brazil, Colombia, Ecuador and Peru. WCF recently launched a new farmer training and research initiative in Ecuador, along with its partners from the U.S. State Department and USDA. The Foundation is also part of an agroecology program in Brazil, being implemented by Conservation International.

Coordinated Cocoa Research

The WCF supports integrated crop management and breeding for genetic improvement. In the short-to-medium term, integrated crop management has shown promising results. A long-term strategy with potential impact is breeding new and improved trees that are more tolerant or resistant to diseases and pests. WCF is co-funding research with the USDA and other international research organizations to screen trees for resistance to witches' broom, frosty pod rot and black pod disease.

Through its targeted educational and scientific programs, the WCF is helping cocoa farming families in Africa, Asian and Latin America improve their quality of life.

For more information on the WCF and future cocoa farmer outreach efforts, please visit www.worldcocoafoundation.org.

over five years) for related programs. While in Nigeria, Bush told an audience, "I'm here to say you will not be alone in your fight" against AIDS.[3]

Although President Bush stated at that same event that Congress "must fully fund this initiative for the good of the people on this continent of Africa," later that mid-July week back in Washington, D.C., White House officials sought only $2 billion in funding – $1 billion less than promised. An amendment offered by Sen. Mike DeWine (R-OH) added more money to the AIDS fund, bringing the total to $2.4 billion, but the total still fell short of the expected $3 billion. A year later, President Bush's budget request to Congress proposed only $2.8 billion for the program's second year.

Who Is Responsible for Ending Hunger?

Given today's political realities, just who is responsible for the lack of progress in the fight against hunger? Does hunger continue because of public apathy or disenfranchisement, or are our leaders to blame for not listening to the people's mandate?

Ultimately, any decision to place food on the table rests with individual families, and that burden primarily falls on women running these households. But the broader community can make it more or less difficult to escape hunger. Poor and hungry people have little to no influence over the rules and institutions that shape and govern their communities and lives, and seldom do poor people use the potential power they do have. They tend to have little time, energy or resources to devote to defending their interests politically. In the United States, less than half of low-income voters turn out for presidential elections.[4] Thus, while the primary responsibility for a family's food security rests with the family, our humanity dictates that those who are materially better off must demand that today's economic and government systems change – the rules change – so that struggling families will be able to feed and care for themselves.

More than Words, Action Is Needed

Over the past several decades, multiple reports and conferences on world hunger have concluded with a call for more political will. That's not good enough any more. No report or conference should ever conclude that way again. The analysis instead should continue, explaining what practical steps will be taken – or can be taken – to build the necessary political will. As a hunger-fighting community, we have examples of success. Take the global Jubilee campaign of 1998-2000. It helped convince the nations of the world to write off $60 billion in unpayable poor-country debt, redirecting some debt service payments into basic health and education for poor people. The current energy around increasing development assistance to fight poverty and HIV/AIDS

again shows that sustained and consistent effort can create political movement on an issue that is important to hungry people.

Political will doesn't just happen, and political leaders seldom act from their own convictions. In its 30-year history, Bread for the World has learned a lot about how to build the political will in the United States to reduce hunger.

Seven Lessons on Building Political Will

#1: Advocacy Makes a Difference

First, anti-hunger advocacy makes a difference.

Bread for the World's experience is that citizens can bring about dramatic changes at home and in the world around them. Arthur Simon founded Bread for the World in 1974. He was a pastor in a low-income neighborhood, and his church helped needy families and contributed to international relief efforts. But he realized that to win significant changes in the lives of poor and hungry people, much more needed to be done. Bread for the World was founded because Art understood that the U.S. government could do more to help hungry people than charities alone. He also saw how members of Congress responded to their voters back home.

Bread for the World is broadly interdenominational, and works closely with secular, Jewish and Muslim organizations. Its 50,000 members, including 2,500 churches, mobilize about 250,000 letters to Congress each year.

Bread for the World members of the Lutheran Presbyterian Church in Truckee, Calif., are writing members of Congress asking them to support the Millennium Challenge Account, which expands development assistance in select poor countries.

These letters help win significant victories for hungry people almost every year. One of Bread for the World's biggest victories was U.S. support for the Child Survival Revolution of the 1980s. That initiative still saves thousands of lives every day. In 1999 and 2000, Bread for the World chaired the legislative coalition for debt relief for the poorest countries. Because of debt relief, in 10 or 15 of the world's poorest countries, more children now attend school, and more rural clinics stock much-needed medicines. In some countries, the process of debt relief also has strengthened democracy and reduced corruption.

The combined budgets of Bread for the World and Bread for the World Institute come to about $7 million a year. Over the last three years, Bread for the World has helped to win increases in annual funding for effective anti-hunger programs of about $2.8 billion. Bread for the World can reasonably take credit for about $1 billion of that — about $150 for each $1 in its budget. The organization's work also has improved the quality of programs, but the money figures alone demonstrate the remarkable impact activists can have to change the politics of hunger.

Fortunately, citizen participation in advocacy organizations worldwide is on the rise. Across Africa and much of the developing world, civil society networks are evolving as democracy takes hold. As these networks mature, increasing numbers of citizens will come to understand their political power and be motivated to advocate for an end to hunger in their communities.

#2: Religious Constituencies Count

A second lesson from Bread for the World experience shows that people of faith can be a core constituency in building political will to overcome hunger.

More than 90 percent of Bread for the World's members are Christian people who work for global justice as part of their religious lives. Many national religious bodies have strong assistance programs for hungry people, and most of them also make some effort to teach their people about relevant public policies. MAZON, the main Jewish anti-hunger organization, includes an advocacy component in 40 percent of its grants. Locally, more than three out of every four religious congregations engage their communities in helping hungry people.

Though religious leaders could do more to emphasize justice for hungry people, religious bodies overall are a stronger, more consistent voice on hunger policy issues than any other set of institutions in the United States.

Two volunteers, one from Zambia and the other from Canada, assist in the election process in East Timor.

People come to the political arena to fight hunger for a variety of personal reasons. Some people are moved by compassion or morality. Some people get involved because they've survived a personal struggle against poverty and want to ensure that their family and others do not have to endure such an experience. Others see material deprivation as a fertile ground in which instability flourishes and therefore a real threat to our national security.

But being an activist is not easy. It is time consuming and requires in-depth knowledge on specific issues as well as the intricacies of the U.S. political process. The religious association of many Bread for the World members makes them, as a group, exceptionally persistent. Their advocacy for justice is rooted in their experiences of God's love.

#3: Charitable Organizations Have Clout

A third lesson is that charitable organizations can speak powerfully for the people they serve.

One of the most hopeful developments in the U.S. politics of hunger is that charities increasingly have been active in advocacy and public policy education. Over the past decade, many charitable networks also have engaged with governmental institutions in new ways.

InterAction, which includes nearly all U.S. charities that work on relief and development assistance internationally, now leads campaigns to increase U.S. funding for and improve the quality of international relief and development government programs. InterAction has become an important partner to Bread for the World.

International School Feeding Programs: A Success Story

By Rep. James P. McGovern (D-MA)

Over the past five years, I have had the privilege of working with a number of U.S. and international nongovernmental organizations, and a bipartisan group of representatives and senators on ways to address international hunger and food security issues. This year, along with my colleague Rep. Jo Ann Emerson (R-MO), I became the co-chair of the Congressional Hunger Center, an organization committed to nurturing the next generation of leaders dedicated to ending hunger here at home and abroad.

I have been directly involved in promoting international school feeding programs, which help alleviate hunger among children by providing at least one nutritious meal each day in a school setting, and at the same time provide support to a broader set of development goals, such as achieving universal education, increasing educational opportunities for girls, stimulating local community development initiatives, and in the case of Africa, in particular, ensuring that HIV/AIDS orphans receive food and an education so that they do not face a future on the fringes of society.

I believe it is within our reach to alleviate hunger among children worldwide, and an important tool for achieving that goal is school feeding programs. Of the 300 million hungry children in the world, more than 120 million, mainly girls, do not attend school. In 2000 President Clinton launched a $300 million pilot program, the Global Food for Education Initiative (GFEI), to expand U.S. support of school feeding programs with the twin goals of reducing hunger among children and bringing more children – especially girls – into school by providing them with meals and/or take-home rations.

We know that education is fundamental to the upward mobility that can help poor children improve their standard of living, and to helping poor nations develop more productive, self-reliant economies. The United States long has been committed to providing school meals for children of low-income American families in order to improve children's minds and bodies. Under the GFEI, this commitment was extended to 7 million children through 48 school feeding projects in 38 countries.

In February 2003 the U.S. Department of Agriculture issued an evaluation of the pilot GFEI. The results showed measurable improvement in school enrollment, including increased attendance by girls.

> *"I believe it is within our reach to alleviate hunger among children worldwide, and an important tool for achieving that goal is school feeding programs."*

In projects implemented by the U.N. World Food Program (WFP), overall enrollment increases exceeded 10 percent, with an 11.7 percent increase in enrollment by girls. In projects carried out by U.S. private voluntary organizations, they reported an overall enrollment increase of 5.75 percent in GFEI-participating schools. In certain individual projects, the results were astounding – an increased enrollment of girls by 32.3 percent in Pakistan, 27.4 percent in Cameroon, 26.2 percent in Tanzania, 17.7 percent in Ethiopia, 13.8 percent in Honduras and 12 percent in Eritrea.

Benefits also went beyond those directly related to student attendance, enrollment and academic performance. Local employment increased and economic activity related to the projects picked up in addition to greater activity and participation in local infrastructure and community-improvement projects. Parents also became more involved in the schools and their children's education.

I have seen some of these projects in action. In February 2003 I visited a community of internally displaced people living on the outskirts of Bogota, Colombia, where WFP was carrying out a GFEI program in coordination with an education program sponsored by World Vision. The meals these children received at school often were their only food for the day, and their parents told me that the school and the meals were the only stable factors in their uncertain lives.

Congress recently established the GFEI as a permanent program, the George McGovern-Robert Dole International Food for Education and Child Nutrition Program. The McGovern-Dole program is now engaged in the same struggle confronting all domestic and international food aid programs – receiving sufficient funds to maintain and expand its programs so that even more children may benefit. President Bush requested only $50 million for the McGovern-Dole school feeding program in his FY 2004 budget. A bipartisan group of U.S. representatives and senators are working to increase that amount in the appropriations process. I hope we will be successful, not just this year, but in the coming years to ensure that developing nations reap the rewards of providing universal education to all their children and that none of them will sit in school suffering from hunger.

To review a copy of the GFEI pilot program evaluation, go to www.fas.usda.gov/excredits/gfe/congress2003/index.html.

Two girls are eating biscuits received as part of a school feeding program in Bangladesh, which is supported by the U.N. World Food Program, the government of Bangladesh and the Bangladesh Rural Advancement Committee.

M. Zeigler

The Politics of Hunger in Brazil: How Did We Arrive at Fome Zero?

"If at the end of my term every Brazilian person has three meals per day, I will have fulfilled my life's mission."

— President Luiz Inácio Lula da Silva, in his inaugural address.

Government programs to fight hunger are not new in Brazil, but with the election of Luiz Inácio Lula da Silva to president in October 2002, hunger moved to the top of the political agenda. A combination of factors resulted in what appears to be a qualitative shift in the level of commitment to fighting hunger in Brazil. Chief among them are Lula's personal commitment to hungry people and the Brazilian people's strong social consciousness.

Each president since Fernando Collor de Mello, Brazil's first elected president after military rule, has declared himself committed to combating hunger and poverty. Itamar Franco, who followed Collor in 1993,[1] designated the fight against hunger and poverty as the government's top priority and called on society to rally. In 1993 he established a National Food Security Council (CONSEA), which included nine ministers and 21 civil society representatives. Two years later, his successor, Fernando Henrique Cardoso, replaced CONSEA with his own anti-poverty program, called Community Solidarity. Its aim was to coordinate the different branches of government working on hunger and poverty reduction. Neither program, however, was fully funded or implemented. Brazil's weak economy limited the resources available for fighting hunger. Indeed, the focal point of Cardoso's administration (1995-2003) was the Plano Real, which finally brought inflation under control.[2]

For many years, even before the transition to democracy, a network of civil society organizations were active in helping hungry and poor people. They worked with farmers, rural workers and other poor people to help them defend their interests and strengthen their communities. The Roman Catholic Church helped to foment some of these popular institutions, and international nongovernmental organizations (NGOs) channeled financial and technical assistance to them. The Church's "base communities" taught liberation theology, which encouraged poor people to work for justice.

During the 1990s, poverty began to gain importance as a political issue. Social movements such as the Citizenship Movement against Hunger, the Movement of the Landless, and many smaller NGO movements helped to educate and energize the grassroots.[3] The federal government, itself, also helped with its Program of Communal Solidarity campaign. Says Simon Schwartzman, director of the American Institutes for Research for Brazil, these movements helped "shatter the centuries-old tradition of accepting poverty as natural and unavoidable and placed the goal of poverty eradication at the forefront of Brazil's political and social agenda."[4]

The Citizens' Action Against Hunger and For Life[5] campaign encouraged all Brazilians to do something about hunger in their communities and push for national change. The media also participated by helping to spread the campaign's message and better educate the public about hunger and poverty in Brazil.[6] The campaign articulated themes, such as solidarity with the hungry and freedom from hunger as an expression of full citizenship, themes that later would emerge in Lula's speeches and programs. Anti-hunger activist Fernanda Lopes de Carvalho notes how important these events were to changing social perceptions: "It is undeniable that the political perception of the problem has changed in favor of the view that poverty is not a natural scourge of Brazilian society."[7]

During his 2002 presidential campaign, Lula's message balanced the importance of budgetary prudence with the need to find ways to pay for social programs. This message resonated with millions of Brazilians tired of endemic poverty but also leery of radical economic shifts. Soon after taking office, Lula cancelled an order for military planes so that the money could be used to pay for social programs, signaling his commitment to shifting priorities.

The cornerstone of Lula's program to fight hunger and poverty in Brazil is Fome Zero (Zero Hunger), a collection of public programs that also calls on Brazilian people to participate in reducing hunger and poverty.[8] Essentially, Fome Zero combines direct service (such as school meals and a Food Card Program) and structural policies (including land reform and basic health care) with "participatory" food and nutritional security policy making. Through the "Mutirão" (community-based collective campaign), Brazilians are urged to donate food and money to local charities or to Fome Zero itself. The government set up accounts at two commercial banks so citizens and companies can make direct donations to the federal Fund to Fight and Eradicate Poverty.[9]

Lula's commitment to Fome Zero makes it different from earlier hunger and poverty programs. In Brazil, the president needs the cooperation of Congress to enact his policies, which often requires bargaining and deal making. Though this reality caused some political snags his first year – compounded by a lack of institutional support and ministerial

One of every three children under the age of 5 is malnourished, contributing to approximately 5 million deaths each year. Immediate anti-hunger programs, such as Fome Zero (Zero Hunger) in Brazil, can make a difference in reversing these statistics.

infighting – Lula's strong personal interest has kept hunger on the national agenda. Consequently, Fome Zero met its first-year target of reaching 1 million families.

The anti-hunger campaign itself also is a useful political tool. "It gives poverty a new sense of urgency and helps to forge a much needed social consensus," says José Graziano da Silva, special minister of Food Security and Hunger Combat – MESA.[10] Two out of three parts of Fome Zero focus on mobilizing society to fight hunger. It is both the result of political will to end hunger and an instrument for building political will to end hunger. Moreover, the fact that people both support and participate in Fome Zero helps Lula navigate federal politics.

In October 2003 Lula relaunched Fome Zero, with changes to resolve its initial problems, and combined it with assistance programs for education, health care and fuel. The new Bolsa Familia (Family Fund) will provide a single grant to families with the greatest needs. The 2004 budget for Bolsa Familia doubles the previous budget for all four programs, demonstrating again the power of both the idea and Lula's leadership and political skill.

Lula also has repeatedly taken his message to the international stage. In a speech at the 2003 U.N. General Assembly, he declared the eradication of hunger in the world a moral and political imperative. He proposed a Global Fund to Fight Hunger and challenged governments, NGOs and private organizations to fund it. On Jan. 30, 2004 he announced the establishment of a technical group to explore ways to fill the financing gap between the resources needed to eradicate hunger and those currently available. His charismatic leadership, both domestically and internationally, helps engage the general public and other national leaders in fighting hunger.

While it is too early to tell how successful Fome Zero and Bolsa Familia will be, the commitment of Brazil's president appears steadfast. Theoretically, political will can be generated either from above or below, but Brazil's experience shows how difficult it can be to separate one from the other. In the end, movement from both sides is necessary.

1   Collor de Mello was impeached for corruption and resigned from office Dec. 29, 1992.

2   Between 1989 and 1994, inflation averaged nearly 1,300 percent.

3   Simon Schwartzman, "Brazil: The Social Agenda." *Daedalus* (Vol. 129, No. 2) Spring 2000, 29-56.

4   Ibid.

5   Fornerly the Movement for Ethics in Politics.

6   Fernanda Lopes de Carvalho, "Brazilian Citizens Taking Action Against Hunger and Deprivation." *Sharing Innovative Experiences,* Vol. 6, 22-31, accessed from U.N. Development Program, Special Unit for Technical Cooperation among Developing Countries Web Site, http://tcdc.undp.org/experiences/v016/content6.html.

7   Carvalho, 37.

8   Personal email communication from Andrew MacMillan, FAO.

9   *Brazil's Food Security Policy, Fome Zero,* Ministerio Extraordinario de Seguranca Alimentar e Combate a Fome – Mesa. http://200.155.6.3/site/assets/cartilhas_fomezero/Security%20Policy%200K.pdf

10   Ibid.

"The time for making promises is over," U.N. Secretary-General Kofi Annan said at the June 2002 World Food Summit: Five Years Later. "It is time to act. It is time to do what we have long promised to do – eliminate hunger from the face of the earth." Two years later, his words still ring true.

A parallel movement is coalescing among anti-hunger charities in the United States. Take America's Second Harvest – a national network of food banks that supports about 50,000 agencies feeding hungry people.[5] About a million workers – mostly volunteers – work in these agencies, and America's Second Harvest has begun engaging them as advocates.

Governments also are reaching out to work more with charitable groups. The U.S. Department of Agriculture now makes grants to food banks and community groups to help poor people learn about and apply for federal nutrition assistance programs. The Bush administration's Faith-based and Community Initiative is part of this same broad trend.

Internationally, Bread for the World continues to work with the World Bank to help foster nongovernmental organization (NGO) involvement in World Bank-supported governmental programs in developing countries. What's most promising is that some community groups are using this opening to push for improvements in public programs. For example, churches and charities worldwide have worked together to monitor debt relief's implementation. Grassroots groups in poor countries continue to push from below to make sure that debt relief really benefits poor and hungry people. International charities like Oxfam and World Vision help such efforts with advocacy funding and political support in Washington, D.C.

Denny Lott of Truckee, Calif., teaches students at Glenn Duncan Elementary School. As a Bread for the World anti-hunger advocate, he also is a leader in his community, helping to organize educational workshops on hunger and poverty issues as well as leading letter-writing campaigns to support hunger-fighting legislation.

#4: Reach Far and Wide

Fourth, Bread for the World has learned that the anti-hunger movement must broaden its reach.

Advocacy, religious and charitable organizations are not strong enough to win the progress against hunger that is possible.

With that in mind, U.S. leaders from a diverse array of institutions have been meeting since 2001 as the Alliance to End Hunger. The Alliance is a coalition of diverse U.S. institutions that are working to strengthen political will to end hunger in the United States and worldwide. It includes advocacy organizations, charities, religious bodies, foundations, think tanks, universities, business corporations, unions, civil rights organizations, farm organizations and individuals. The Alliance helps its partner institutions deepen their work on the politics of hunger, partly by suggesting collaborative possibilities.

The Alliance has encouraged a number of influential institutions to do more to build political commitment on hunger issues. It also has spawned creative collaborative projects, notably a series of public opinion polls that have helped participating groups communicate more effectively about hunger issues (see related story, p. 104).

Early in 2003, the U.N. food agencies (based in Rome) launched the International Alliance Against Hunger. This effort has identified or helped to start national alliances against hunger in many countries, often including governmental representatives. At the suggestion of Bread for the World Institute, the U.N. food agencies also have helped a group of NGOs to forge a campaign to meet the goal of cutting world hunger and poverty in half. Toward that end, those involved in the campaign are asking for more and better development funding for rural and agricultural development as well as food assistance. This is the More and Better Campaign (www.moreandbetter.org).

These new international networks will share information on how people in different countries are working to build political commitment to end hunger. They also will suggest new ways that like-minded efforts in different countries might collaborate.

#5: Embrace Reform

Fifth, the Alliance to End Hunger polls have demonstrated that the U.S. public is ready to support reform-minded programs to reduce hunger.

Developing Future Leaders in the Fight Against Hunger

By Edward Cooney and Margaret Zeigler

for the past century, humanitarian leadership in the U.S. government has made a profound difference for millions of people impacted by hunger within our borders and overseas.

Beginning with the work of President Herbert Hoover during the Soviet famine of the early 1920s, and continuing with the efforts of Senate and House of Representative leaders over the next three decades, major relief efforts have been mobilized to save the most vulnerable people in famines across such countries as Bangladesh, Ethiopia, North Korea and Sudan. On the domestic front, important legislation was crafted and implemented to improve the nutrition and food security of millions of Americans.

These U.S. leaders advocated a course of action to save the lives of those suffering from famine and hunger, despite political and logistic circumstances that might have prevented humanitarian response. President Hoover encountered numerous obstacles to his famine relief efforts for war-affected people in Europe during World War I and to Soviet Russia during 1921 to 1923. Opposing views of the political value of aiding the enemy might have prevented him from achieving his goals, but his persistent belief that lives could be saved through effective diplomacy and mobilizing the generosity of American citizens resulted in many millions of tons of food and humanitarian assistance reaching those who needed it most. In the aftermath of World War II, President Truman led the rebuilding of war-torn Europe by proposing the Marshall Plan, securing billions of dollars for reconstruction and relief.

Sen. George McGovern (D-SD) worked tirelessly during the Kennedy administration to help establish the U.S. Agency for International Development (USAID) and the U.N. World Food Program, which today are responsible for delivering humanitarian relief and food services to millions of people impacted by hunger. More recently, his partnership with Sen. Robert Dole (R-KS) has resulted in the launching of a global school feeding initiative to reach the poorest children around the world (see related story, p. 97).

During the 1970s, the Senate Select Committee on Nutrition and Human Needs conducted hearings and published reports on such federal nutrition programs as school lunches and breakfasts, food stamps, summer meals, and elderly nutrition. This Senate committee was directly responsible for conducting the research necessary to launch the Special Supplemental Nutrition Program for Women, Infants and Children (WIC). Today, this program remains the most widely supported nutrition and hunger safety net in the United States.

In 1983 Rep. Mickey Leland (D-TX) worked with Rep. Benjamin Gilman (R-NY) to establish the House Select Committee on Hunger, which provided a bipartisan focal point on Capitol Hill in the fight against hunger. During its 10-year history, the Select Committee on Hunger held hearings, commissioned studies and served as an information clearinghouse for domestic and international hunger. Leland traveled across the globe, visiting numerous hunger hotspots, bringing along congressional delegations to investigate what could be done to mobilize rapid response. Along with other humanitarians on an investigative famine mission, he lost his life in August 1989, when his plane crashed over Ethiopia.

After the death of Leland, Rep. Tony Hall (D-OH) picked up the leadership mantle of the House Select Committee on Hunger and worked in a bipartisan spirit with his friends, Rep. Bill Emerson (R-MO) and Rep. Frank Wolf (R-VA). They traveled to dozens of famine stricken countries, including Haiti, North Korea, Somalia and Sudan, calling attention to the need for U.S. leadership to send food aid and subsequent humanitarian development assistance. A special reserve for emergency food aid, The Bill Emerson Humanitarian Trust, bears his name. The reserve is used for food aid needs in international famines today.

The current generation of U.S. leadership remains strong, with leaders emerging in the U.S. government and in nongovernmental organizations (NGOs). The current USAID administrator, Andrew Natsios, has been a passionate advocate for U.S. humanitarian relief and famine aid. Rep. Jo Ann Emerson (R-MO) and Rep. James McGovern (D-MA) currently co-chair the Congressional Hunger Center, a bipartisan leadership organization in Washington, D.C., that works on ending domestic and international hunger.

Many other congressional leaders, including Sens. Elizabeth Dole (R-NC), Byron Dorgan (D-ND) and Tom Harkin (D-IA) are placing hunger at the centerpiece of their legislative agenda. Other stalwarts include Sens. Thad Cochran (R-MS), Tom Dashle (D-SD) and Richard Lugar (R-IN), and Reps. Douglas Bereuter (R-NE), Michael Castle (R-DE), Benjamin Gilman (R-NY), Henry Hyde (R-IL), George Miller (D-CA) and Lynn Woolsey (D-CA).

Looking to the Future

How can we ensure that future government and NGO leaders emerge as voices for poor and hungry people? One way is to provide opportunities for specialized skills training, knowledge and experience for a new generation of young men and women who will take up the mantle of anti-hunger leadership.

The Mickey Leland International Fellows program, along with its domestic counterpart, the Bill Emerson National Fellows program, provide such an opportunity to hundreds of future anti-hunger leaders. These programs are living memorials to deceased members of Congress, Leland and Emerson, the bipartisan voices for hungry people on Capitol Hill during the 1980s and 1990s. The fellowships are unique in that they provide a combined field experience working alongside direct service organizations in the United States and dozens of countries overseas, with a structured hunger policy component in Washington, D.C. This combination equips the Leland and the Emerson fellows to be the next generation of leaders who will rally both government and private sector resources in the fight against hunger.

Edward M. Cooney is executive director and **Margaret M. Zeigler** is deputy director of the Congressional Hunger Center in Washington, D.C.

Understanding the Additional Costs of Reaching the MDGs

Various estimates exist as to how much it would cost to cut hunger in half and to reach the Millennium Development Goals (MDGs). The estimates vary, but all illustrate that the goals will not be met at current investment levels.

USAID

In 1998 the U.S. government commissioned a study of what it would cost to halve world hunger, which it updated in 2000. The researchers envisioned the specific types of investments that would be needed in different parts of the world, and used past U.S. Agency for International Development (USAID) projects to estimate costs and results. Their original estimate was that the world could halve hunger for an additional $4 billion a year – of which the U.S. share would be $1 billion. Their later estimate was that it would cost $6 billion, of which the U.S. share might be $1.5 billion.

FAO – Anti-Hunger Program

In its Anti-Hunger Program, the Food and Agriculture Organization of the United Nations (FAO) asserts that an additional $23.8 billion annually will be needed to cut the number of hungry people in half by 2015. Of this amount – $12.8 billion – should come from commitments of cash development assistance. The rest would come from the recipient countries themselves, the private sector and food aid.

FAO breaks down the costs in this way:

- Improve agricultural productivity and enhance livelihoods and food security in poor rural communities. Cost estimate: $2.3 billion per year.

- Develop and conserve natural resources. Cost estimate: $7.4 billion per year.

- Expand rural infrastructure (including capacity for food safety, plant and animal health) and broaden market access. Cost estimate: $7.8 billion per year.

- Strengthen capacity for knowledge generation and dissemination (research, extension, education and communication). Cost estimate: $1.1 billion per year.

- Ensure access to food for the most needy through safety nets and other direct assistance. Cost estimate: $5.2 billion per year.

World Bank

The World Bank uses two methods to come up with its estimate that between $40 billion and $60 billion a year in additional foreign aid is needed to meet all the MDGs.

First, Bank researchers focused exclusively on estimating the costs to reduce income poverty by half by 2015. Its logic is that by reducing poverty, countries will be able to afford schooling for all children as well as costs to achieve other MDGs.

Second, the Bank directly estimated the cost of attaining each MDG goal. Both routes yielded approximately the same costs. Total development assistance now provides roughly $50 billion a year, so using the Bank's estimates, donor nations would need to roughly double their efforts.

Like FAO, the Bank notes that by itself, this additional aid will not be sufficient to attain the goals, as many countries will have to reform their policies and improve service delivery to make the additional spending effective.

The Zedillo Report

The Report of the High-Level Panel on Financing for Development, chaired by former Mexican President Ernesto Zedillo, was prepared in 2001 ahead of the International Conference on Financing for Development. The Report's Appendix compiles the existing studies on achieving one or more or the MDGs into a single chart. The total estimated need comes to roughly an additional $50 billion per year.

The report cautions: "It is clear that our present knowledge does not suffice to put a convincing price tag, even a rough one, on the cost of meeting the human development goals." Individual countries will need to estimate their own costs if credible worldwide calculations are to be made.

Margaret W. Nea

Small-scale farmers in Africa could double or quadruple their harvests of staple crops, in turn increasing food security, by adopting simple strategies, such as using organic and mineral fertilizers to restore soil fertility, and by installing small-scale water storage and irrigation facilities. But such interventions require more and better-targeted money and sustained development efforts.

Most likely U.S. voters want their government to do more to reduce hunger in the United States and around the world. But public support broadens when a "liberal" call to do more is combined with a "conservative" commitment to making anti-hunger programs more efficient and supportive of self-reliance. Across the political spectrum, Americans are skeptical about government social programs. So any expansion of poverty- and nutrition-focused programs also must seek to make them more effective. Reform needs to be part of the anti-hunger message.

#6: More Money Is Needed

A sixth lesson of experience is that political work costs money. When Bread for the World began, it announced that it needed constituents to write letters to Congress, not necessarily to donate money. But the organization now is clear that building political will requires both people and money. Reaching out to more people and helping people get more deeply involved politically requires staff, and that means money.

Bread for the World and its allies spend roughly $10 million annually on advocacy and related education on policies that are important to poor and hungry people. Recent experience suggests that with $1 for advocacy and related education, Bread for the World can win $150 in public funding for anti-hunger programs. If that degree of leverage can be maintained, the annual funding for advocacy still would need to be increased by about $7 million for each $1 billion increase in official development assistance. The FAO estimates that cutting world hunger in half by 2015 will require some $12 billion more in annual development assistance – of which the U.S. share would be $3 billion. Just to achieve that goal, advocacy organizations might need to roughly triple their current budgets. The World Bank estimates that it would cost an additional $50 billion a year in development assistance to achieve all the MDGs. If the United States were to contribute $12 billion of this extra $50 billion, an additional $80 million would be needed for advocacy and related education.

Mali's population has increased from 9 million in 1992 to 11.4 million in 2001. Despite this growth, the country managed to reduce its proportion of hungry people from one in four to one in five.

Margaret W. Nea

These numbers are all guesstimates. But they give a rough sense of how much more financial effort is needed to change the politics of hunger. Existing efforts are only a fraction of what's required. But tens of millions of dollars more for U.S. advocacy and related education also is not impossible. The U.S. charities that work on international relief and development manage about $4 billion a year in grant funding. Why can't more of the charitable effort that is focused on world hunger and poverty be channeled into public policy advocacy? As a point of comparison, the U.S. environmental movement is spending some $150 million a year on advocacy and policy-related education.

#7: Calling All Leaders

Last, but not least: Quality leaders are needed.

Leaders reflect many occupations and personalities, including grassroots activists, church pastors, city council members, state governors, business executives, trade unionists, teachers, NGO staff, congressmen and women, and national presidents. And for the anti-hunger movement to gain speed, it needs quality leaders at all levels.

Fortunately, many countries have become more democratic over the past two decades, and some national leaders in developing countries are committed to overcoming hunger. In Brazil, Luiz Inácio Lula da Silva, known to his people as Lula, has shown that the presidency can be won on a hunger platform. In his inaugural address, Lula promised to eradicate hunger before his term's end. In Kenya, after peaceful elections and an orderly political transition from decades of corrupt one-party government, President Mwai Kibaki is focusing on long-neglected social issues, sparking renewed hope among a people tired of economic deterioration, rampant corruption and untold human suffering.

It is too early to tell how much impact these leaders will have, but there are reasons for hope. After a rocky start, Lula's Fome Zero (Zero Hunger) program in Brazil is "now on the right track."[6] By October 2003, less than a year after its inception, 1 million families were signed

American Voters Want Politicians To Do More To End Hunger

U.S. voters care deeply about hunger and want to make sure that anti-hunger programs remain a high priority and are protected against budget cuts.

In both national and regional studies, research indicates that U.S. voters want to hear more from political candidates about their ideas for fighting hunger and poverty. In many cases, hunger and poverty rank as a primary concern when compared to other important issues, outpacing even foreign affairs and terrorism.

Listed below are selected findings from research released by The Hunger Message Project, commissioned by Bread for the World and sponsored by Sodexho USA, both leading members of the Alliance to End Hunger coalition.[1]

In national polls, reducing U.S. hunger and poverty was described as the most important issue by many voters, easily outdistancing other important domestic concerns like the environment and ranking about as high as health care. (July 2002 and June 2003)

In an October 2003 study, 58 percent of likely Iowa caucus-goers and 48 percent of New Hampshire primary voters said that they would be more interested in hearing a candidate's position on reducing hunger and poverty in the United States than fighting terrorism.

Voters want our nation's leaders to take action on hunger: 93 percent of likely voters said that a candidate's position on "fighting the hunger problem" is important to them in deciding their vote for Congress. (July 2002)

Voters will reward those candidates that make hunger a priority – 64 percent said they would be less likely to vote for a candidate who cuts substantially from food stamps, and 65 percent would be more likely to vote for a candidate who makes hunger a priority. (June 2003)

Despite budget cuts and tough times, 94 percent of likely voters said explicitly that it was important to keep funding programs like school lunch and the Special Supplemental Nutrition Program for Women, Infants and Children (WIC). (June 2003) Similarly, 96 percent of likely Iowa Democrat caucus-goers and 94 percent of New Hampshire Democrat primary voters said that it is important to them that during these times of budget cuts and a sluggish economy, the government should fund anti-hunger programs such as the school lunch program, WIC, food stamps and programs to feed American seniors.

Nearly one of four likely voters said they were personally worried that they or someone in their family could go hungry in the future. More than 43 percent of voters said people in their own community go hungry. (June 2003 and October 2003)

The Hunger Message Project was conducted by Tom Freedman, Bill Knapp and Jim McLaughlin. Jim McLaughlin is a leading Republican pollster who works extensively with congressional Republicans including the National Republican Congressional Committee. Bill Knapp and Tom Freedman work with leading Democrats and worked against McLaughlin in the 1996 presidential campaign.

---

[1] The Hunger Message Project: July 2002, June 2003 and October 2003.

up to receive food aid. To ensure that poor families receive everything they need – education, fuel assistance and health care – not just bits and pieces, the government has decided to combine food assistance with other social programs, creating one "Family Fund" (Bolsa Familia) grant. Lula now also is engaging leaders of other nations, notably President Chirac of France, in the fight against world hunger.

In Kenya, within its first 100 days, the Kibaki government instituted free universal primary education and declared "zero tolerance" on corruption – one of Kenya's greatest social and economic ills. The World Bank and International Monetary Fund have resumed funding to Kenya in recognition of this crackdown on corruption.

In the United States, national leadership has been key to winning large gains for hungry people. A Columbia University research project on foreign aid found that the decisive factor in the three boldest foreign aid proposals since World War II – the Marshall Plan, the Point Four Programs and the Foreign Assistance Act of 1961 – was presidential leadership.[7] While President Bush's policies regarding Temporary Assistance for Needy Families (TANF) and some other domestic anti-poverty programs have been unfavorable to progress against domestic hunger, his policies regarding international development assistance have been remarkably progressive. Bipartisan leadership in Congress improved the president's proposals and secured funding for them.

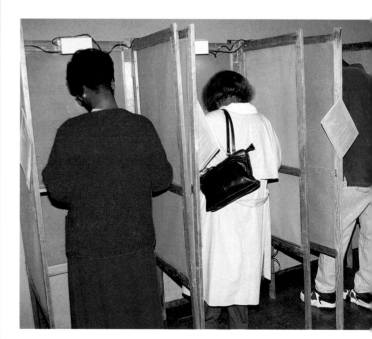

National and regional studies indicate that U.S. voters want to hear more from political candidates about their ideas for fighting hunger and poverty.

A wide chasm exists between current political promises to end hunger and the efforts to do so. To close this gap, political commitment and political action to end hunger must become objectives in their own right.

Local and community leaders also play important roles. The power of citizens who are organized and engaged in the political process cannot be denied. Such organization comes about through the efforts of people in communities who find ways to move their fellow citizens. Members of Congress listen to their constituents. Local leaders help amplify the voice of the community, forming a bridge between the individual and the collective community's needs. Bread for the World members are models of anti-hunger activism.

Taste the Victory

Something new is happening as democracy spreads and takes root in many parts of the world. Democracy gives decent people opportunities to insist on action against hunger. Nobel economist Amartya Sen has shown that famines simply are not tolerated in democratic countries. A critical press and active citizens compel authorities to keep people from starving to death.

But Sen did not find democracies without fault either. In his 1984 book, *Resources, Values and Democracy,* he noted that while there was no famine in India, a third of the population went to bed hungry every night. "The quiet presence of non-acute, endemic hunger leads to no newspaper turmoil, no political agitation, no riots in the Indian parliament. The system takes it in its stride."

Ironically, the shock of terrorism might make this an opportune time for progress against hunger. Economic problems may be increasing hunger, but the experience of Sept. 11, 2001, may have made people in the United States and other industrialized countries more supportive of efforts to reduce hunger. Political leaders in the world's most powerful nations also have become more inclined to take action to help poor countries reduce hunger and poverty.

Political will is not achieved overnight, and no one group can build it alone. But ending hunger within a decade or two remains a very real possibility. Taste the victory. It's tantalizingly close.

7 What You Can Do

BFWI Photo/K. Raisz

Progress against hunger is possible. Whereas in 1974, one in three persons was hungry, today it is one in six. In the past decade alone, 19 countries saw the number of hungry people decline by 80 million. These successes include more prosperous countries like Brazil and China, as well as smaller and poorer countries like Chad, Guinea, Namibia and Sri Lanka.

While progress against hunger now is experiencing disturbing setbacks in the United States and worldwide, the damage is not irreparable. The United States came close to ending domestic hunger in the early 1970s and logged reductions in hunger for several years in the late 1990s. Though past progress can be traced to many factors, the role of anti-hunger advocates and the wider advocacy community cannot be overemphasized. The key to fighting hunger has been and will continue to be building the political will necessary to bring about change.

Since the early 1970s, Bread for the World has been working to build such commitment. It began with a small group of Catholics and Protestants who realized that in addition to helping hungry people directly, churches could mobilize their members to call for more broad-reaching policy changes. In its 30 years, Bread for the World has made significant contributions to easing hunger among people living in the United States and around the world. What started in 1974 as a meeting in the apartment of Rev. Arthur Simon has become a national lobby that can get the attention of congressional leaders and the president.

What can you do to help in the fight against hunger? Read what a few people have to say about the power of one, joining the might of many.

'Stay the Course'

"Stay the course," says Patricia Ayres, who has been a Bread for the World activist since its beginning and repeatedly has served as a board member. She is active in the Baptist church, and her desire to fight for an end to hunger stems from her faith, as does her belief that the fight will be won. She is most proud of her part in the passage of the congressional Right to Food Resolution, which was Bread for the World's first legislative victory in 1975. This congressional promise to end hunger increased lawmakers' awareness of hunger and its serious social and economic consequences. It also led to the formation of the House of Representative's Select Committee on Hunger. How did she get started? She joined Bread for the World's movement in 1976 after attending a religious retreat in Dallas, Texas, where she first heard that part of leading a Christian life was seeking justice for all people.

'10 Times More Powerful'

It has been difficult for other advocacy and faith-based groups to get past the "soup kitchen syndrome," says Harold Stanton, who serves as Detroit conference chair of the United Methodist Committee on Relief's Hunger Program. Not everyone understands that helping hungry people is much more than simply giving them food, he says. By lobbying Congress for more foreign aid for developing countries and trying to change the system, "we are 10 times more powerful" than just sending food, he says. Harold is most proud of his role in the Jubilee 2000 USA campaign for debt relief in poor countries. Because of this win, countries are able to invest more money in social programs like expanding basic education to girls and boys. How does he make a difference? By writing one letter at a time.

For 30 years, Bread for the World members have been writing letters to members of Congress seeking policy changes to help people suffering from hunger and poverty worldwide. These millions of letters have helped to save countless lives.

'Giving Poor and Hungry People a Voice'

Glen Bengson joined the Bread for the World family soon after it was founded. He heard about the movement while attending a Lutheran seminary. While working as an intern at a church, he participated in the first Offering of Letters campaign on the right to food. Glen was drawn to Bread for the World's approach to advocacy because it combined Christian service based on the gospel call to feed the hungry with citizenship. Over the years, he has worked on many campaigns, though the Right to Food victory is most dear to him because it was the first. But even more significant has been "giving poor and hungry people a voice" in a national arena, he says. What inspires him? Responding to the gospel of Christ through citizenship.

Bread for the World:
Key Grassroots Victories on Domestic Hunger

By Barbara Howell

"Someone who sits down and writes a letter about hunger . . . almost literally has to be saving a life . . ."
– Paul Simon, who served as U.S. Senator (D- IL) from 1984 to 1997

For 30 years Bread for the World members have acted on the conviction that writing a letter on hunger to a member of Congress helps save lives. They have written millions of letters to their elected representatives, met them face-to-face, stimulated newspaper and television stories, and worked in a multitude of ways to help end the scandal of hunger in this "land of plenty."

The results have been remarkable. I experienced them first-hand as a Bread for the World Capitol Hill lobbyist on domestic hunger for 25 years. Representing a large, dedicated grassroots organization – working not for personal gain but for poor people – opened doors, changed minds, brought victories. Some times congressional staff asked us to visit them after an outpouring of letters. More than once a legislative aide would say, with a wry smile, If We support your bill, will you stop the letters (which have to be answered)?

Our lobbying efforts are done mostly in coalition with other anti-hunger groups. Many are think tanks that develop policy or have skilled lobbyists but no or few grassroots members. Bread for the World's main strength is its 50,000 members and the thousands of churchgoers who join us in the annual Offering of Letters to Congress. Our influence with congressional offices has always been much greater because of the letters and visits from their constituents that have preceded us.

The United States could eliminate hunger if the federal government fully funded social programs that are already in place and have demonstrated their effectiveness.

Our message has been that churches and charities can't do it all. The federal government should improve and expand the national nutrition programs so our nation's most vulnerable people won't go hungry. Our strategy is to find bipartisan congressional support. Hunger is not a partisan issue.

The timely interventions of Bread for the World's grassroots advocacy with members of Congress have been critical in helping the federal food programs remain a key component in the social safety net for poor people. This short article will address two of them. Bread for the World efforts have been especially important in assuring steady expansion through good economic times and bad of the Special Supplemental Nutrition Program for Women, Infants and Children (WIC) and the more politically vulnerable Food Stamp Program, as well as supporting the need for ongoing nutrition monitoring.

WIC

WIC is especially effective. It reaches low-income pregnant women and nursing mothers, infants and children younger than 5 who are not getting adequate nutrition. Numerous studies definitively show that WIC prevents fetal and infant deaths, improves children's health and saves money. An estimated $3.50 is saved in Medicaid costs for every $1 in WIC benefits to pregnant women.

One of the authors of the WIC program, the late Minnesota Sen. Hubert Humphrey, said, "[WIC] represents what is best in America – a dedication to our children and our future and an attempt to nip the poverty agenda in the bud."

Five Bread for the World Offerings of Letters throughout the 1980s and 1990s expanded WIC. Each one secured a commitment of millions of dollars to serve more eligible women, infants and children. A sixth Offering of Letters during the 1996 election year brought the issue of childhood hunger and effective programs like WIC to the attention of candidates for Congress, getting the commitment of 42 percent of the newly elected 105th Congress to support federal legislation to help overcome childhood hunger.

Unlike food stamps, WIC is not an entitlement program serving all eligible people seeking help. Bread for the World's goal has been to make WIC an entitlement program. So far Congress has not done so. WIC, therefore, must vie for annual funding with many other programs, including farm programs and international Food for Peace.

In the early 1980s, programs for low-income people were targeted for major cuts as economic recession, increased military spending and large tax cuts produced a looming budget deficit. Bread for the World's *Preventing Hunger at Home* Offering of Letters in 1982 effectively encouraged Congress to squelch proposed additional cuts to food programs of 25 percent to 30 percent. WIC was targeted for a $100 million cut, but instead received a $100 million increase, allowing 150,000 more women, infants and children to be served.

Every year as appropriations committees consider how much money to allocate to various programs, Bread for the World members from states and districts of committee members hound them to increase funding for WIC. In 1987, 1989, 1992 and 1994, the force of Bread for the World's Offering of Letters flooded Congress with up to a quarter of a million letters on WIC each year. In 1987 thousands of Mother's Day cards went to Congress urging that WIC be funded fully to serve all poor women and children who needed it.

Other actions helped spur advocacy. Churches were encouraged to visit WIC clinics to see how effective the program is. Congressional offices received birthday candles in letters from Bread for the World members in 1989 to emphasize the "Keep WIC Lit" theme, and WIC gained the biggest increase in five years.

Even during a time of severe budget cutting in 1992, Bread for the World's *Every Fifth Child* campaign secured an increase of $260 million for WIC, expanding the program an additional 350,000 women, infants and children. This campaign also increased funding for Head Start and Job Corps.

In 1987 WIC reached only 3.3 million out of an estimated 8.4 million eligible people. Now 7.5 million women, infants and children get WIC benefits, excluding only about 10 percent of those eligible. But when working on public policies, advocates can never rest.

BFWI Photo

Two members of Bread for the World discuss ways to fight hunger at the organization's 2003 National Gathering in Washington, D.C.

Food Stamps

For 20 million low-income people, food stamps provide the essential foundation to meet their food needs. It's not a feast. The average benefit is 90 cents per person for each meal.

Bread for the World's grassroots advocacy has stepped in frequently through the years to secure improvements and shore up support to prevent program cuts, especially in food stamps. One of the first domestic hunger actions by Bread for the World was to join the 1977 campaign to eliminate the purchase requirement in food stamps, opening the program to many people who were too poor to buy some stamps up front in order to get bonus stamps.

But the progress made in the 1970s was jeopardized in the early 1980s. From 1982 to 1985, $7 billion was cut from the program – reducing benefits and restricting eligibility. The major grassroots campaign, *Preventing Hunger at Home,* included sending letters on paper plates to emphasize that millions did not have enough to eat. The campaign supported a bipartisan congressional effort that prevented additional food stamp cuts and attempted to end federal oversight for food stamps and WIC by giving the states a set amount of money, called a "block grant," to run the programs. Attempts to block grant food stamps have been tried and defeated several times, including during the 1996 welfare reform legislation.

Bread for the World initiated local "Hunger Watch USA" surveys in 27 towns and cities in 1993 to emphasize the growing hunger problem exacerbated by the cuts in food programs amid a harsh recession. The recognition of a severe hunger problem in the latter half of the 1980s led to incremental improvements, but it took a decade of advocacy to finally win back 40 percent of the food stamp benefits cut in 1982.

The Republican "Contract with America" in 1995 supported increased military spending and tax cuts for middle- and upper-income people and tried to amend the Constitution to require a balanced budget. The subsequent pressure to slash spending set the stage for the major food stamp cuts that were part of the 1996 welfare reform bill signed by a Democratic president. The program lost $28 billion over six years. All recipients lost benefits, and 1.3 million people were dropped from the program.

The 1997 *Tell Congress: Hunger Has A Cure* Offering of Letters joined a campaign with other low-income advocates that won back a partial restoration of food stamps to legal immigrants who had lost benefits in welfare reform. By 2002, many of the 1996 cuts had been reversed and program changes reduced red tape that kept millions from getting help. Another growing budget deficit in 2003, however, brought food stamps and other food programs under attack and threatened to cut $13 billion from food stamps over the next 10 years. Bread for the World members once again moved into action and managed to block these cuts.

Nutrition Monitoring

Bread for the World in 1979 initiated an effort to make the federal government gather scientific data on hunger in America, providing an information base for national food and nutrition policies. A pilot program was approved that year. But it took 13 years for Congress to institute a comprehensive national nutrition monitoring system that includes a timely report on the dimensions of hunger. The most recent data report that nearly 35 million people live in households that experience hunger or live on the edge of hunger. Without the federal food programs and private efforts to provide food to hungry people, these dismal numbers would be much higher.

The government data add weight to the mounting evidence of steadily growing need for emergency food and shelter reported by food banks and churches, and the annual U.S. Conference of Mayors' report. But facts alone are not sufficient to change policies.

The political will to end hunger is still, as Bread for the World founder Rev. Art Simon said, a crying need. It is crucial, therefore, to keep writing letters, encourage more people to join the movement to end hunger, and force government leaders to address the needs of poor and hungry people.

Barbara Howell worked for 25 years at Bread for the World as both a domestic policy analyst and director of government relations.

No Guarantees

Emma Crossen became a Bread for the World activist about four years ago after attending a campus meeting at Bethany College in Lindsborg, Kan. She immediately became highly involved in anti-hunger legislative activities and in 2002 came to work for the organization's Washington, D.C., office as a summer intern. The 2002 campaign, *Working from Poverty to Promise,* which focused on the reauthorization of Temporary Assistance for Needy Families, proved frustrating. Congress continued – and, as of this report's printing, continues – to delay action on the important welfare legislation. "I learned how difficult it is for any group of concerned citizens to choose the best action, act on it and get the desired results," she says.

Especially in politics, she learned that there are no guarantees, making it all the more important for people to remain vigilant in fighting for poor and hungry people. "With our future in the hands of deep faith, hope and expertise, I trust that God's design will facilitate eventual success when we are right, and that humility will allow us to choose again when we are wrong."

Making A Difference

The 2004 Hunger Report, *Are We On Track To End Hunger?,* finds that no, the world is not on track to end hunger. But with steadfast leadership and continued commitment from people like you, we quickly can get back on track to cutting hunger in half and providing a better life for poor and hungry people around the world.

This year, 2004, marks a crucial election year in the United States. U.S. voters will be choosing leaders who will make important decisions. By voting for U.S. leaders who are committed to doing more to reduce hunger and poverty in the United States and worldwide, you can make a difference in the lives of poor and hungry people everywhere.

Volunteering and becoming an activist in your community and church is another way to help. Bread for the World and many other organizations – including many *Hunger 2004* sponsors – provide a way to help make a difference. The following list highlights just a few of these groups. (See the 2004 Sponsor List on p. 152, for additional information on service and advocacy organizations.)

Margaret W. Nea

Efforts to fight hunger and poverty over the past 30 years have reaped significant rewards. In 1980 UNICEF estimated that 40,000 children were dying from preventable diseases, about half related to hunger. Today that number has been cut to 27,400.

Bread for the World/Bread for the World Institute

Keep the Promise on Hunger and Health

Just a few years ago, nearly 200 countries – including the United States – made a promise to people living in the world's poorest countries: the Millennium Development Goals (MDGs). A key part of these goals is cutting hunger and poverty in half by 2015. It is urgent that this promise be kept.

In developing countries, nearly 800 million people are undernourished. The number of people with HIV/AIDS has nearly doubled in six years. In response to these challenges, President Bush proposed the Millennium Challenge Account (MCA), which would increase development aid for poor countries that can put it to good use. Time-tested, cost-effective measures have been quite successful in reducing hunger and disease. The president promised that the MCA – and the Emergency Plan for AIDS Relief – would add significant new funding to these efforts.

This year Bread for the World will be working with people like you to make sure that Congress and the president provide the funding that has been promised for these life-saving initiatives.

Bread for the World also will be campaigning to protect domestic nutrition and anti-poverty programs from the budget squeeze caused by war spending and tax cuts, mainly for wealthy people.

Bread for the World
50 F St. NW, Suite 500
Washington, DC 20001
Phone: (202) 639-9400
Fax: (202) 639-9401
Web site: www.bread.org

Some Other Voices for Hungry People

America's Second Harvest is the nation's largest domestic hunger relief organization. Through a network of more than 200 food banks and food-rescue programs, America's Second Harvest provides emergency food assistance to more than 23 million hungry Americans each year, 8 million of whom are children. Last year, America's Second Harvest distributed 1.7 billion pounds of food to needy Americans, serving all 50 states and Puerto Rico. Second Harvest has developed an important program of public policy advocacy. Its goal is to end hunger in America.

35 East Wacker Drive, Suite 2000
Chicago, IL 60601
Phone: (312) 263-2303
Fax: (312) 263-5626
Web site: www.secondharvest.org

Past and present, members of Congress and presidents have helped to pass legislation that benefits poor and hungry people everywhere. But if hunger is to be cut in half by 2015, even more must be done.

DATA (Debt, AIDS, Trade, Africa) is a new organization that is being spearheaded by rock star Bono of the Irish group U2. DATA seeks to help Africa through pressuring developed country governments to cancel unpayable debt, fight HIV/AIDS and reduce trade barriers. Bono is using his status as a public figure to bring attention to Africa and some of the major problems troubling the continent. In addition to talking to developed countries, DATA also is encouraging African governments to practice democracy and be accountable to poor people in their respective countries.

1317 F St. NW
Washington, DC 20004
(202) 639-8010
Web site: www.datadata.org

The Food Research and Action Center (FRAC) is a national organization working to improve public policies to eradicate hunger and undernutrition in the United States. Founded in 1970 as a public interest law firm, FRAC is a nonprofit and nonpartisan research and public policy center and hub of an anti-hunger network of thousands of individuals and agencies across the country.

1875 Connecticut Ave. NW, Suite 540
Washington, DC 20009
Phone: (202) 986-2200
Fax: (202) 986-2525
Web site: www.frac.org

Bread for the World's International Work: Persistent Themes and Impressive Victories

By James L. McDonald

Bread for the World tries to strike a balance between domestic and international hunger in its legislative work. But for its first seven years, its legislative agenda was heavily weighted toward the international dimensions of hunger. In 1974 U.S. poverty was at a historic low, just 10 percent, while television images of famine in Africa and reports from the World Food Conference in Rome heightened awareness and concern about world hunger. So it made sense then for the organization's work to be tipped toward international issues.

Bread for the World's first Offering of Letters in 1975 asked Congress to establish the right to food as a basic tenet of U.S. policy. Nearly a quarter of a million letters were generated, and in 1976 Congress passed a resolution declaring, "Every person in this country and throughout the world has the right to food – the right to a nutritionally adequate diet." The resolution became the foundation for Bread for the World's efforts over the next three decades. The campaign was "hugely successful," noted Bread for the World founder, Rev. Art Simon. "It brought in new members, galvanized activism across the country and motivated a large spread of church leaders to endorse our work."

There were other early victories as well. As a result of Bread for the World's next legislation campaign, *A World Food Reserve,* Congress created a U.S. farmer-held grain reserve that helped stabilize grain prices and assure sufficient food was available for humanitarian assistance even when harvests were meager. In 1980 Bread for World helped win an additional $43 million in emergency famine aid and 4 million tons of wheat for famine relief. These early efforts show that Bread for the World recognized how important food aid is in the effort to save lives in desperate circumstances.

But Bread for the World knew that food aid alone was not the answer. It also was important to encourage more local food production and rural development in poor countries. In 1979 Bread for the World convinced Congress to pass a series of food aid reforms designed to help countries become more self-reliant. The next year the U.S. Presidential Commission on World Hunger – appointed by President Carter as a result of Bread for the World's 1977-1978 Offering of Letters campaign – issued its report. Among its findings: "Food shortages may be more serious than shortages of energy within the next 20 years. Millions of human beings live on the edge of starvation. The most potentially explosive force in the world today is a frustrated desire of poor people to attain a decent standard of living. The anger, despair and often hatred that result represent a real and persistent threat to international order."

Africa Focus

Bread for the World's 1981 Offering, *Africa – Food for Life,* marks the first time that Africa was the specific campaign focus. That year Bread for the World members asked Congress to provide more development and humanitarian assistance targeted to Africa and to reform the way the assistance was delivered. They asked that more U.S. assistance be focused on the poorest countries and on the poorest people in those countries. They noted that women were the chief food producers in Africa and that more assistance needed to be directed to them. They also argued that assistance would be most effective if poor people themselves were involved in the decisions about how and where the money was spent. These policy reform themes continue to be sounded in Bread for the World's legislative work.

Bread for the World held its first Africa-focused legislative campaign in 1981, *Africa – Food for Life,* seeking more development and humanitarian aid for the poorest people in Africa, especially women who are the main food providers. This effort continues today.

Margaret W. Nea

Bread for the World now is widely recognized as an effective grassroots organization with a long-term commitment to ending hunger in Africa, where hunger is widespread and persistent. The 1991 Offering of Letters, *Horn of Africa,* resulted in legislation that mandated a shift in U.S. policy from Cold War purposes to peaceful development that has saved hundreds of thousands of lives. One provision, for example, made it illegal for the United States to give aid to dictators in Ethiopia, Somalia and Sudan.

The 1998 *Africa: Seeds of Hope* campaign succeeded in passing a bill that redirected U.S. resources toward small-scale farmers and struggling rural communities in Africa. The same bill set up the Bill Emerson Humanitarian Trust, which helps to make food available quickly in emergencies. In 2001 the *Africa: Hunger to Harvest* Offering of Letters successfully urged Congress to pass a resolution that called for significant new poverty-focused development assistance to sub-Saharan Africa and to increase the appropriations for sub-Saharan Africa by more than $400 million.

Child Survival Efforts

Bread for the World played a vital role in making child survival efforts an important emphasis of U.S. foreign assistance. When the visionary Jim Grant became head of the U.N. Children's Fund (UNICEF) in 1980, he began to promote a set of interventions that could dramatically reduce child mortality. At that time, 40,000 children were dying every day from preventable causes, half of them hunger-related. But Jim Grant was convinced that a focused global effort to support four low-cost techniques – growth monitoring, oral rehydration therapy, breastfeeding and immunization – could cut those numbers quickly and significantly improve child survival rates.

Recognizing that these four basic remedies were closely linked to improvements in child nutrition, Bread for the World undertook a campaign in 1985 that persuaded Congress to establish a Child Survival Fund within the U.S. Agency for International Development and approve an initial $25 million appropriation. The next year, Bread for the World and others asked Congress to double the appropriation to $50 million, and Congress agreed. Today the annual U.S. appropriation for child survival efforts is approaching $350 million.

International Debt Relief

Bread for the World long has recognized that one of the major impediments to developing country governments' efforts to fight hunger and poverty is the stranglehold of unpayable international debts. For most of its 30-year history, Bread for the World has been part of a broad coalition calling for measures to reduce the debt burden of poor countries and reform the policies of international financial institutions like the World Bank and the International Monetary Fund.

Bread for the World's 1999 *Proclaim Jubilee: Break the Chains of Debt* campaign worked with Oxfam America, the U.S. Conference of Catholic Bishops and other church groups on legislation that would significantly reduce poor country debt and direct the savings to poverty reduction efforts. Over the next two years, Congress freed more than $2.5 billion for debt relief, including $545 million toward the U.S. contribution to an international debt plan. The World Bank and other international financial institutions also announced a major shift in policy that tied debt relief efforts to poverty reduction. Because of the Jubilee debt campaign, many more children attend school, more rural clinics receive medications, and steps are being taken to improve accountability in many of the poorest countries.

The debt relief victory was one of a number of significant changes since the late 1990s that demonstrate a growing determination from leaders in the United States and other developed countries to tackle global poverty. Bread for the World's most recent campaigns have attempted to build on this mounting resolve. The 2003 *Rise to the Challenge: End World Hunger* campaign urged Congress to establish and fund a Millennium Challenge Account (MCA) focused on poverty reduction in the world's poorest countries. This year's Offering of Letters, *Keep the Promise on Hunger and Health,* asks Congress to fully fund the MCA and the HIV/AIDS initiatives without cuts to ongoing development and humanitarian assistance. If Congress complies, U.S. poverty-focused assistance will double to more than $12 billion.

As a result of Bread for the World's work and the collective efforts globally over the past three decades, the number of children dying every day had dropped in 2002 to 27,400. This is significant progress, but we have a long way yet to go.

James L. McDonald is vice president of policy and programs at Bread for the World.

InterAction is the largest alliance of U.S.-based international development and humanitarian nongovernmental organizations. With more than 160 members operating in every developing country, it works to overcome poverty, exclusion and suffering by advancing social justice and basic dignity for all.

1717 Massachusetts Ave. NW, Suite 701
Washington, DC 20036
Phone: (202) 667-8227
Fax: (202) 667-8236
Web site: www.interaction.org

MAZON: A Jewish Response to Hunger has granted more than $28 million since 1986 to nonprofit organizations confronting hunger in the United States and abroad. MAZON (the Hebrew word for "food") awards grants principally to programs working to prevent and alleviate hunger in the United States. Grantees include emergency and direct food assistance programs, food banks, multiservice organizations, anti-hunger advocacy/education and research projects, and international hunger relief and agricultural development programs in Israel and impoverished countries.

1990 South Bundy Drive, Suite 260
Los Angeles, CA 90025
Phone: (310) 442-0020
Fax: (310) 442-0030
Web site: www.mazon.org

The U.S. Conference of Catholic Bishops' Department of Social Development and World Peace is the national public policy agency of the U.S. Catholic Bishops. The department of Social Development and World Peace works on behalf of the Catholic bishops to advocate effectively for poor and vulnerable people, genuine justice and peace in the public policy arena, and to build the capacity of the Church to act effectively in defense of human life, human dignity, human rights and the pursuit of justice and peace.

Office of Social Development & World Peace
U.S. Conference of Catholic Bishops
3211 4th Street N.E.
Washington, DC 20017-1194
Phone: (202) 541-3000
Fax: (202) 541-3339
Web site: www.usccb.org/sdwp

Endnotes

Chapter 1

1. Barry Bearak, "Why People Still Starve." *The New York Times,* July 13, 2003.

2. David Brown, "Study Cites Opportunity to Lift Life Expectancy; WHO Says 20 Hazards Affect All Nations." *The Washington Post,* Oct. 31, 2002.

3. Food and Agriculture Organization of the United Nations (FAO), *State of Food Insecurity in the World, 2002.* (Rome: FAO) 6.

4. Ibid., 29.

5. Agriculture and Development Economics Division, Food and Agriculture Organization of the United Nations, "ESA and Food Security" Web site, www.fao.org/es/ESA/fsecurit.htm, accessed July 7, 2003.

6. Kay Sharp, "Voices of Hunger." Background Paper for Department for International Development Food Security Strategy Paper, April 2001, 6.

7. Ibid., 2.

8. Lisa C. Smith, "Can FAO's Measure of Chronic Undernourishment Be Strengthened?" International Food Policy Research Institute (IFPRI), Food Consumption and Nutrition Division Discussion Paper No. 44, May 1998, www.ifpri.org/divs/fcnd/dp/d044.htm.

9. U.N. Development Program, *Human Development Report 2003.* (New York: Oxford University Press) 2003, 5.

10. Sharp, 8.

11. Sara Scherr, "Halving Global Hunger." U.N. Millennium Project Task Force 2 on Hunger, Background Paper, April 18, 2003.

12. Smith.

13. U.N. World Food Program, "Southern Africa Crisis" Web site, http://www.wfp.org/index.asp?section=2, accessed Dec. 9, 2003.

14. Reports from Economist Intelligence Unit says estimates for North Korea range from 500,000 to 3 million dead of starvation since 1995; the *Korea Times* reports between 1 million and 2 million people died from starvation in the late 1990s.

15. FAO, 29.

16. FAO, 24.

17. Sharp, 3.

18. Centers for Disease Control and Prevention, "Overweight and Obesity Among Adults" Web site, http://www.cdc.gov/nccdphp/dnpa/obesity/defining.htm, accessed Sept. 17, 2003.

19. U.N. General Assembly Resolution 217 A(III), Article 25, Dec. 10, 1948, www.un.org/Overview/rights.html.

Chapter 2

1. Based on an interview with family during June 2003 research trip to Shelby, Miss., by Bread for the World Institute. The woman's name has been changed to protect her privacy.

2. Foreign Agriculture Service, U.S. Department of Agriculture (USDA), "Discussion Paper on Domestic Food Security," Feb. 13, 1998, www.fas.usda.gov/icd/summit/1998/discussi.html, accessed June 25, 2003.

3. Mark Nord and Margaret Andrews, "Reducing Food Insecurity in the United States: Assessing Progress Toward a National Objective." Economic Research Service (ERS), USDA, May 2002, www.ers.usda.gov/publications/fanrr26/fanrr26-2/fanrr26-2.pdf.

4. In 1995 the baseline used for the 2010 goal was 30.4 million people living in food insecure households. To reach the 2010 goal of cutting hunger in half, the number of people living in food insecure households would need to be reduced to 15.2 million – a difference of about 20 million people as of 2003. The USDA bases its performance on the rate of food insecurity. In 1995 the rate of household food insecurity was 12 percent, so the 2010 goal would be 6 percent. As of 2002, the food insecurity rate was 11.1 percent.

5. USDA, National Nutrition Monitoring and Related Research Act, Public Law 101-455, www.reeusda.gov/1700/legis/nutmontr.htm.

6. For full list of questions, see Mark Nord, et al., *Household Food Security in the United States, 2002.* ERS, USDA (Washington, DC: USDA) October 2003, Appendix A.

7. Foreign Agriculture Service.

8. America's Second Harvest, *Hunger in America 2001* Web site, http://www.secondharvest.org/site_content.asp?s=81, accessed July 12, 2003.

9. Nord, *Household Food Security in the United States, 2002,* 32.

10. Ronette Briefal, et al., "The Emergency Food Assistance System – Findings From the Client Survey." ERS, USDA, Food Assistance and Nutrition Research Report No. 32, July 2003, i.

11. Nord, *Household Food Security in the United States, 2002,* 16.

12. Ibid., 5.

13. Ibid., 9.

14. "Rural" here refers to "outside metropolitan area" as defined by the USDA and used in Current Population Survey data.

15. Nord, *Household Food Security in the United States, 2002,* 9.

16. Children's Defense Fund, *The State of Children in America's Union 2002;* Business Research Bureau, South Dakota KIDS Count 2003 Fact Book, http://www.usd.edu/brbinfo/kc/factbook.htm.

17. Food Research and Action Center, "WIC in Native American Communities: Building a Healthier America." April 26, 2001, 7-8, www.frac.org/html/news/wic01summary.html#anchor211289.

18. Ibid., 12.

19. Janet S. Kurzynske, Suzanne M. A. McGough, "Assessing Food Insecurity in Kentucky." Southern Rural Development Center, Dec. 15, 1999, http://srdc.msstate.edu/focusareas/health/fa/kurzyn_final.pdf.

20. U.S. Department of Labor, "Findings from the National Agricultural Workers Survey (NAWS) 1997-1998." Research Report No. 8, March 2000.

21. Alicia Bugarin and Elias S. Lopez, "Farmworkers in California," California Research Bureau, July 1998, 26.

22. Gary Huang, "Health Problems among Migrant Farmworkers' Children." U.S. Department of Education, ERIC Digest, ED357907. January 1993.

23. USDA, "Regional Estimate of Food Insecurity in Delta Counties of Arkansas, Louisiana and Mississippi Exceed National Rates." Technical Abstract, available from www.nps.ars.usda.gov/publications/publications.htm?SEQ_NO_115=125876.

Endnotes

24 Margaret Bogle and Tim Kramer, "Lower Mississippi Delta Nutrition Intervention Research Initiative, 2003 Annual Report." Agricultural Research Service of USDA, www.ars.usda.gov/research/projects/projects.htm?ACCN_ NO=402026&showpars=true&fy=2002.

25 Children's Defense Fund, *Children in the States 2003* Web site, http://www.childrensdefense.org/familyincome/childreninthestates2003/default.asp; U.S. Census Bureau, 2000 Census. Calculations by Bread for the World Institute.

26 Nord, *Household Food Security in the United States, 2002,* 9.

27 U.S. Census Bureau, "Income in the United States, 2002." September 2003, 3.

28 Nord, *Household Food Security in the United States, 2002,* 9.

29 Ibid., 7.

30 Mark Nord, "Food Security Rates are High for Elderly Households." USDA, *Food Review,* Summer-Fall 2002, 19-24.

31 USDA and U.S. Department of Health and Human Services' Nutrition Center for Health Statistics, "The Food Security Measurement Study." 1997; According to USDA's "Household Food Security in the United States, 1999," 16.7 percent of elderly people who lived alone and had incomes of less than 139 percent of the federal poverty line were food insecure; 6.4 percent of them experienced hunger.

32 Nord, "Food Security Rates are High for Elderly Households," 24.

33 Nord, *Household Food Security in the United States, 2002,* 7.

34 Food and Nutrition Service (FNS), USDA, Summer Food Service Program Web site, "Summer Food Service Program: Daily Average Attendance," http://www.fns.usda.gov/pd/sffypart.htm.

35 FNS, USDA, WIC Program Data Web Site, http://www.fns.usda.gov/pd/wichome.htm.

36 Nord, *Household Food Security in the United States, 2002,* 9 and 16.

37 Ibid., 10.

38 Ibid., 9.

39 Ibid.

40 Araminta Wordsworth, "U.S. Study: Medical Bills Main Culprit in Bankruptcies." *National Post (Canada),* April 27, 2000, accessed from Commondreams.org, www.commondreams.org/headlines/042700-03.htm.

41 U.S. Department of Housing and Urban Development, "Home Rent Limits," Homes & Communities Web Site, Feb. 4, 2004, www.hud.gov/offices/cpd/affordablehousing/programs/home/limits/rent/index.cfm.

42 Center on Budget and Policy Priorities, "The Food Stamp Shelter Deduction: Helping Households with High Housing Burdens Meet Their Food Needs." June 2002, 4-6, www.cbpp.org/7-1-02fs.pdf.

43 Tracy L. Kaufman, *Housing America's future: Children at risk.* (Washington, DC: National Low Income Housing Coalition) 1996.

44 ChildStats.gov Web site, "America's Children 2002," www.childstats.gov/ac2002/indicators.asp?IID=17&id=3.

45 Ibid.

46 America's Second Harvest, *Hunger in America 2001* Web site, http://www.secondharvest.org/site_content.asp?s=81, accessed July 12, 2003.

Chapter 3

1 Sara Scherr, "Halving Global Hunger." U.N. Millennium Project Task Force 2 on Hunger, Background Paper, April 18, 2003, 6.

2 Ibid., 1.

3 Food and Agriculture Organization of the United Nations (FAO), *State of Food Insecurity in the World, 2003* (Rome: FAO) 4.

4 The U.N. Conference on Trade and Development (UNCTAD) says there are no immediate prospects for a strong global recovery in 2004; "FDI Policies for Development: National and International Perspectives," UNCTAD World Investment Report, July 2003.

5 Other Millennium Development Goals cited in the U.N. Millennium Declaration include education, gender equality and women's empowerment, health and communicable diseases such as HIV/AIDS and Malaria, and environmental sustainability.

6 FAO, 6.

7 For a detailed discussion about the efforts to improve the FAO's hunger measurement, see Lisa C. Smith, "Can FAO's Measure of Chronic Undernourishment Be Strengthened?" Food Consumption and Nutrition Division Discussion Paper No. 44, International Food Policy Research Institute, May 1998.

8 FAO, "New Hunger Maps Released," FAO News Stories Web site, Dec. 22, 2003, http://www.fao.org/english/newsroom/news/2003/26659-en.html.

9 Pedro Sanchez and M. S. Swaminathan, coordinators, "Halving Hunger by 2015: A Framework for Action." Millennium Project Hunger Task Force, Interim Report, Feb. 1, 2004, 69 and 76.

10 Anthropometry measures dimensions of physical body size, such as height or weight, and can be used to compare distributions of measurements in two or more populations.

11 The repeated measurement process is referred to as "growth monitoring" and can be used to determine if small children are growing normally. Current widespread use of U.S. growth standards is questionable.

12 FAO, *State of Food Insecurity in the World, 2003,* 6.

13 Ibid., 31-32.

14 Ibid., 8.

15 Ibid., 32.

16 Ibid., 31.

17 The current annual reduction in the number of hungry people is 2.1 million, according to FAO.

18 This is one of 10 task forces set up by the United Nations to guide the implementation of the Millennium Development Goals. For more information, visit www.unmillenniumproject.org/html/task_force.shtm.

19 Scherr, 14.

20 Sanchez, 43.

21 Scherr, 23.

22 Ibid., 27.

23 Sanchez, 45.

24 Scherr, 25.

Endnotes

25 Ibid., ix.

26 FAO, *State of Food Insecurity in the World, 2003,* 11.

27 Ibid.

28 Scherr, 32.

29 Deepa Narayan and Patti Petesch, "Voices of the Poor From Many Lands." (Washington, DC: The World Bank) 2002, 72.

30 T.R. Frankenberger and M.K. McCaston, "The Household Livelihood Security Concept." *Food, Nutrition and Agriculture* (Rome: Food and Nutrition Division of FAO) 1998, 3.

Chapter 4

1 Food and Nutrition Service (FNS), U.S. Department of Agriculture (USDA), "Food Stamp Program Participation and Costs," Food Stamp Program Data Web site, www.fns.usda.gov/pd/fssummar.htm, accessed Dec. 12, 2003.

2 Elizabeth Frazao, *America's Eating Habits: Changes and Consequences.* Economic Research Service (ERS), USDA, (Washington, DC: USDA) May 1999, 312; Based on calculation of increases in food purchases of between 26 percent and 36 percent.

3 Kenneth Hanson and Elise Golan, "Effects of Changes in Food Stamp Expenditures Across the U.S. Economy." ERS, USDA, August 2002, 1.

4 J. William Levedahl and Victor Oliveira, "Dietary Impacts of Food Assistance Programs." *America's Eating Habits: Changes and Consequences,* 318; The 10 vitamins and minerals include calcium, iron, niacin, thiamine, riboflavin, magnesium, phosphorus, and vitamins A, B-6 and B-12.

5 FNS, USDA, "Guide to Measuring Household Food Security: Revised 2000." Food Security Studies Web site, www.fns.usda.gov/oane/MENU/Published/FoodSecurity/FSGuidesum.htm.

6 Mark Nord, et al., *Household Food Security in the United States, 2002.* ERS, USDA (Washington, DC: USDA) October 2003, 7 and 31.

7 Ibid., 23.

8 Ibid., 24-25 and 30; The maximum food stamp benefit equals the Thrifty Food Plan costs. Only about one-fifth of food stamp recipients receive the full benefit.

9 FNS, USDA, "Trends in FS Participation, 1994-2000." June 2002, Office of Analysis, Nutrition and Evaluation, Food Stamp Program Participation Studies Web site, www.fns.usda.gov/oane/MENU/Published/FSP/participationhtm#National.

10 General Accounting Office, "Food Stamp Program: Various Factors Have Led to Declining Participation." GAO/RECD-99-185, July 1999.

11 FNS, USDA, "Food Stamp Monthly Data, National Level." Food Stamp Program Data Web site, www.fns.usda.gov/pd/fsmonthly.htm, accessed Dec. 12, 2003.

12 These estimates are based on households with annual incomes below 185 percent of the poverty line. Not all of these households are eligible for certain programs. For example, households without pregnant women or children and with incomes above 130 percent of poverty would not be eligible for any programs.

13 Mark Nord and Margaret Andrews, "Reducing Food Insecurity in the United States: Assessing Progress Toward a National Objective." ERS, USDA, May 2002, 3-4.

14 Nord, *Household Food Security in the United States, 2002,* 16; More than 10 percent of people living in food insecure households report their income as unknown.

15 Center on Budget and Policy Priorities, "Food Stamp Program Background." July 10, 2001, 2.

16 Center on Budget and Policy Priorities, "Work and the Food Stamp Program." Sept. 30, 2003, 10. Work-support activities include participating in an employment and training program such as the Workforce Investment Act or receiving Unemployment Insurance, which requires a recipient to search for a job.

17 Nord, *Household Food Security in the United States, 2002,* 10; For 265,000 households in the United States, hunger was severe enough that one or more of their children went hungry on one or more days during the year.

18 Mark Nord, "Food Insecurity in Households with Children." Food Assistance and Nutrition Research Report Number 34-13, ERS, USDA, July 2003, 1.

19 Susan Combs, "Growing Pains: In American Children, Bigger is not Always Better." Texas Department of Agriculture, May 8, 2002.

20 M. Townsend, J. Peerson, B. Love, C. Achterberg and S. Murphy, "Food Insecurity Is Positively Related To Overweight In Women." *Journal of Nutrition,* Vol. 131, 2001, 1738-1745; C.M. Olson, "Nutrition and Health Outcomes Associated with Food Insecurity and Hunger." *Journal of Nutrition,* Vol. 129 (2 Suppl), 1999, 521S-524S.

21 America's Second Harvest, *Hunger in America 2001* Web site, http://www.secondharvest.org/site_content.asp?s=81.

22 Nord, *Household Food Security in the United States, 2002,* 32.

23 U.S. Conference of Mayors, *Sodexho Hunger and Homelessness Survey 2003.* Dec. 18, 2003, www.usmayors.org/uscm/news/press releases/documents/hunger_121803.asp

24 Nord, *Household Food Security in the United States, 2002,* 33.

25 James Ohls, Fazana Saleem-Ismail, Rhoda Cohen, Brenda Cox and Laura Tiehen, The Emergency Food Assistance System Study – Findings from the Provider Survey, Volume II: Final Report, prepared by Mathematica Policy Research Inc. for ERS, USDA, 2002.

26 USDA, "Frequently Asked Questions About TEFAP," Food Distribution Programs Web site, http://www.fns.usda.gov/fdd/programs/tefap/tefap-faqs.htm#Q8.

27 Based on interviews during July 2003 research trip to Austin, Texas, by Bread for the World Institute.

28 Testimony of USDA Under Secretary Eric Bost, Agriculture Subcommittee Hearing, May 22, 2003, http://appropriations.senate.gov/hearmarkups/record.cfm?id=204148.

29 Beth Osborne Daponte and Shannon Lee Bade, "The Evolution, Cost and Operation of the Private Food Assistance Network." Institute for Research and Poverty, Discussion Paper No. 1211-00, September 2000.

30 Bill Shore, *Revolution of the Heart* (New York, NY: Riverhead Books) 1995, 100.

31 Nord, *Household Food Security in the United States, 2002,* 33.

32 Mark Ragan, "Building Better Human Service Systems: Integrating Services in Income Support and Related Programs." Prepared for the Annie E. Casey Foundation, Casey Strategic Consulting Group, by the Rockefeller Institute of Government, April 2002.

Endnotes

33 ERS, USDA, "Using One-Stops To Promote Access to Work Supports – Lessons From Virginia's Coordinated Economic Relief Centers." Report No. E-FAN-03-010, November 2003.

34 Theodore F. Macaluso, "The Extent of Trafficking in the Food Stamp Program: 1999-2002." FNS, USDA, Office of Analysis, Nutrition and Evaluation, Report No. FSP-03-TRAF, July 2003.

35 Ibid.

36 General Accounting Office, "School Lunch Program: Efforts Needed to Improve Nutrition and Encourage Healthy Eating." GAO-03-506, May 2003, 1 and 3.

37 ERS, USDA, "The Food Assistance Landscape," Report No. 28-3, September 2003, 5-6.

38 Bread for the World Institute, *Hunger 2002: A Future With Hope* (Washington, DC: Bread for the World Institute) 2002, 4.

39 The Alliance to End Hunger includes organizations that focus mainly on ending hunger and a wider array of institutions (religious bodies, corporations, labor unions, foundations and others) that share an interest in overcoming hunger. The Alliance commissioned a bipartisan team of consultants to conduct focus groups and voter surveys as part of the Hunger Message Project.

40 Tom Freedman, Bill Knapp and Jim McLaughlin, "Alliance Hunger Message Project." Alliance to End Hunger/Bread for the World, July 2002-October 2003, www.bread.org/alliance_to_end_hunger/index.html.

Chapter 5

1 U.N. Development Program, *Development Effectiveness Report 2003* (New York, NY: UNDP Evaluation Office) November 2003, 32.

2 Ibid., 33.

3 Bob Geldof, "We Must Act Now To Prevent Apocalypse." *The Observer*, June 15, 2003, http://www.observer.co.uk/comment/story/0,6903,977791,00.html.

4 Of Afghanistan's total population of 25 million, 85 percent work in agriculture; *Future Harvest*, "Rebuilding Agriculture to Restore Afghanistan's Economy." Feb. 3, 2004, http://www.futureharvest.org/news/afghanistan3.shtml.

5 Food and Agriculture Organization of the United Nations (FAO), *State of Food Insecurity in the World, 2001.* (Rome: FAO) 2002, 19.

6 Kay Sharp, "Voices of Hunger." Background Paper for Department for International Development Food Security Strategy Paper, April 2001.

7 VM Aguayo et al., *Maintaining High Vitamin A Supplementation Coverage in Children. Lessons from Niger.* HKI-Africa Nutrition In Development Series, Issue 5, November 2003, 3.

8 Vital Hagenimana et al., "The Effect of Women Farmers' Adoption of Orange-Fleshed Sweet Potatoes: Raising Vitamin A Intake in Kenya." International Research for Women/Opportunities for Micronutrient Interventions Research Program, Research Report Series 3, June 1999, 22.

9 Ibid., 23.

10 GAO, "Lack of Strategic Focus and Obstacles to Agricultural Recovery Threaten Afghanistan's Stability." GAO-03-607 Foreign Assistance, June 2003, 16.

11 Sara Scherr, "Halving Global Hunger." U.N. Millennium Project Task Force 2 on Hunger, Background Paper, April 18, 2003, 61.

12 Organization for Economic Cooperation and Development, "Harmonizing Donor Practices for Effective Aid Delivery." Good Practice Papers-A Development Cooperation Directorate Reference, 13.

13 Africa Region, The World Bank, "The Community Driven Development Approach in the Africa Region: A Vision of Poverty Reduction Through Empowerment." December 2000, 5.

14 Ibid.

15 Daniel Maxwell, et al., "Urban Livelihoods and Food and Nutrition Security in Greater Accra, Ghana." International Food Policy Research Institute (IFPRI), Research Report 112, April 2000.

16 IFPRI, "Living in the City: Challenges and Options for the Urban Poor." Issue Brief, http://www.ifpri.org/pubs/ib/ib9.pdf.

17 Standing Committee on Nutrition, U.N. System, *Nutrition Throughout the Life Cycle, 4th Report on the World Nutrition Situation,* January 2000.

18 Agnes R. Quisumbing, et al., "Women: The Key to Food Security." *Food Policy Report,* IFPRI, August 1995.

19 Standing Committee on Nutrition.

Chapter 6

1 Bread for the World Institute, *Hunger 1994: Transforming the Politics of Hunger* (Washington, DC: Bread for the World Institute) 1994, 84.

2 Bread for the World Institute, *Hunger 2002: A Future With Hope* (Washington, DC: Bread for the World Institute) 2002.

3 White House press release, "President Bush Concludes Week Long Trip to Africa." Congress Hall, Abuja, Nigeria, July 12, 2003.

4 Timothy LeDoux, "Moving Toward Low-Income Voter Mobilization." *Hunger 2002: A Future With Hope* (Washington, D.C.: Bread for the World Institute) 2002, 68.

5 America's Second Harvest Web site, www.secondharvest.org/site_content.asp?s=316.

6 Raymond Colitt, "Brazilian President Signals Revamp of Poverty Program." *Financial Times,* Oct. 20, 2003.

7 New Perspectives on Foreign Aid, *Re-Engaging with the Developing World: The Aid Imperative* (USA: Columbia University Printing Services) 2002.

Table 1: Global Hunger – Life and Death Indicators

	Population						Life expectancy at birth		Infant mortality rate (per 1,000 live births) 2001	% of low birth weight infants 1995-2000y	% of 1-year-old children immunized (measles) 2001	Under-5 mortality rate per 1,000 live births		Maternal mortality rate per 100,000 live births 1985-2001y	Refugees 2002	
	Total (millions) mid-2003	Projected (millions) 2025	Projected population change (%) 2003-2050	Total fertility rate 2001	% below age 15 2003	% urbanized 2001	Male	Female				1960	2001		Country of origin	Country of asylum
Developing Countries	**5,112bb**	**6,647bb**	**55bb**	**3.0**	**..**	**41**	**63bb**	**66bb**	**62**	**14**	**70**	**216**	**89**	**440**	**..**	**..**
Africa (sub-Saharan)	**711.0**	**1,084.0**	**130**	**5.6**	**..**	**35**	**47**	**49**	**107**	**12e**	**58**	**261e**	**173e**	**1,100**	**..**	**..**
Angola	13.1	25.2	230	7.2	48	35	39	41	154	..	72	345	260	..	410,000	12,000
Benin	7.0	11.8	156	5.8	45	43	50	52	94	15	65	300	158	500	..	6,000
Botswana	1.6	1.0	−43	4.1	40	49	36	38	80	11	83	170	110	330	..	4,000
Burkina Faso	13.2	22.5	198	6.8	49	17	43	46	104	18	46	315	197	480	..	..
Burundi	6.1	10.1	152	6.8	46	9	42	44	114	16x	75	255	190	..	400,000	40,000
Cameroon	15.7	22.4	96	4.8	42	50	47	49	96	10	62	255	155	430	5,000	15,000
Cape Verde	0.5	0.7	76	3.3	39	63	66	73	29	13	72	164	38	35	..	..
Central African Republic	3.7	4.8	68	5.0	43	42	42	44	115	13x	29	327	180	1,100	15,000	50,000
Chad	9.3	16.7	215	6.7	47	24	47	51	117	24	36	325	200	830	7,000	15,000
Comoros	0.6	1.1	190	5.1	42	34	54	59	59	18	70	265	79	..	..	..
Congo, Dem. Rep. of	56.6	104.9	220	6.7	47	31	46	51	129	15	46	302	205	950	410,000	295,000
Congo, Republic of	3.7	6.8	186	6.3	47	66	49	51	81	..	35	220	108	..	25,000	120,000
Côte d'Ivoire	17.0	24.6	101	4.8	41	44	41	46	102	17	61	300	175	600	25,000	50,000
Djibouti	0.7	0.8	62	5.9	43	84	42	44	100	..	49	289	143	..	..	23,000
Equatorial Guinea	0.5	0.8	143	5.9	44	49	52	56	101	..	19	316	153	..	..	..
Eritrea	4.4	7.0	142	5.4	45	19	52	57	72	14	88	250	111	1,000	290,000	3,000
Ethiopia	70.7	117.6	145	6.8	46	16	41	44	116	12	52	280	172	870	20,000	115,000
Gabon	1.3	1.9	87	5.4	41	82	57	61	60	..	55	287	90	520	..	20,000
Gambia	1.5	2.7	177	4.9	41	31	51	55	91	14	90	364	126	..	..	10,000
Ghana	20.5	25.4	46	4.3	40	36	56	58	57	9	81	215	100	210x	10,000	40,000
Guinea	9.0	16.2	239	6.0	44	28	48	50	109	10	52	380	169	530	5,000	180,000
Guinea-Bissau	1.3	2.2	154	6.0	47	33	43	46	130	20	48	336	211	910	..	7,000
Kenya	31.6	35.3	27	4.3	41	34	46	46	78	9	76	205	122	590	2,000	220,000
Lesotho	1.8	2.1	24	4.5	40	29	37	38	91	..	77	203	132	..	..	..
Liberia	3.3	5.5	165	6.8	47	46	47	50	157	..	78	288	235	580	280,000	65,000
Madagascar	17.0	33.0	286	5.8	45	30	53	57	84	15	55	364	136	490	..	..
Malawi	11.7	17.7	149	6.5	46	15	39	40	114	13x	82	361	183	1,100	..	13,000
Mali	11.6	20.0	179	7.0	49	31	44	47	141	16	37	517	231	580	3,000	4,000
Mauritania	2.9	5.4	190	6.0	43	59	53	55	120	..	58	310	183	750	45,000	25,000
Mauritius	1.2	1.4	23	1.9	25	42	68	75	17	13	90	92	19	21	..	..
Mozambique	17.5	17.5	9	6.0	44	33	33	34	125	13	92	313	197	1,100	..	7,000
Namibia	1.9	2.1	37	5.0	43	31	50	49	55	15x	58	206	67	270	1,000	25,000
Niger	12.1	25.7	330	8.0	50	21	45	46	156	12	51	354	265	590	..	1,000
Nigeria	133.9	206.4	130	5.6	44	45	52	50	110	9	40	207	183	..	30,000	7,000
Rwanda	8.3	11.7	108	5.9	45	6	39	41	96	12x	78	210	183	1,100	50,000	35,000
Senegal	10.6	17.1	132	5.2	43	48	52	55	79	12	48	300	138	560	10,000	45,000
Sierra Leone	5.7	9.0	141	6.5	44	38	40	46	182	22	37	390	316	1,800	130,000	60,000
Somalia	8.0	14.9	218	7.3	48	28	45	48	133	..	38	294	225	..	300,000	..
South Africa	44.0	35.1	−26	2.9	33	57	53	54	56	..	72	130	71	..	..	65,000
Sudan	38.1	61.3	121	4.6	39	37	56	58	65	..	67	210	107	550	475,000	285,000
Swaziland	1.2	1.1	−2	4.5	43	27	47	44	106	..	72	233	149	230	..	..
Tanzania	35.4	52.0	109	5.2	..	33	44	46	104	11	83	240	165	530	..	520,000
Togo	5.4	7.6	78	5.5	44	34	53	56	79	13	58	267	141	480	5,000	11,000
Uganda	25.3	47.3	226	7.1	50	15	43	46	79	13	61	224	124	510	25,000	220,000
Zambia	10.9	13.6	60	5.8	47	40	41	40	112	11	85	213	202	650	..	250,000
Zimbabwe	12.6	12.8	16	4.7	43	36	43	40	76	10	68	159	123	700	8,000	10,000
South Asia	**..**	**..**	**..**	**3.4**	**..**	**28**	**..**	**..**	**70**	**26**	**59**	**239**	**98**	**430**	**..**	**..**
Afghanistan	28.7	45.9	134	6.8	43	23	47	45	165	..	46	360	257	..	3,500,000	..
Bangladesh	146.7	208.3	73	3.6	38	26	59	59	51	30	76	247	77	400	7,000	122,000
Bhutan	0.9	1.5	117	5.2	41	7	66	66	74	15	78	300	95	380	127,000	..
India	1,068.6	1,363.0	52	3.1	33	28	62	64	67	26	56	236	93	540	39,000	332,000
Maldives	0.3	0.4	77	5.5	42	28	71	72	58	12	99	300	77	350	..	..
Nepal	25.2	37.8	102	4.6	40	12	59	58	66	21	71	297	91	540	1,700	132,000
Pakistan	149.1	249.7	134	5.2	41	34	60	60	84	21x	54	226	109	..	10,400	1,518,000
Sri Lanka	19.3	21.7	11	2.1	25	23	70	74	17	17	99	133	19	90	155,000	..

Table 1: Global Hunger – Life and Death Indicators

	Total (millions) mid-2003	Projected (millions) 2025	Projected population change (%) 2003-2050	Total fertility rate 2001	% below age 15 2003	% urbanized 2001	Life expectancy at birth Male	Life expectancy at birth Female	Infant mortality rate (per 1,000 live births) 2001	% of low birth weight infants 1995-2000y	% of 1-year-old children immunized (measles) 2001	Under-5 mortality rate per 1,000 live births 1960	Under-5 mortality rate per 1,000 live births 2001	Maternal mortality rate per 100,000 live births 1985-2001y	Refugees 2002 Country of origin	Refugees 2002 Country of asylum
East Asia and the Pacific	..	..	..	2.0	..	39	..	..	33	8	77	201ᶠ	43	140	..	..
Brunei	0.4	0.5	90	2.6	30	73	74	79	6	..	99	87	6	0	..	..
Cambodia	12.6	18.5	94	4.9	41	18	54	58	97	9	59	217	138	440	16,000	280
China	1,288.7	1,454.7	8	1.8	23	37	69	73	31	6	79	209	39	55	..	396,000
Hong Kongᶜ	6.8	8.4	10	..	15	..	78	85	..	..	..	..	..	..	..	..
Fiji	0.9	1.0	15	3.0	32	50	65	69	18	12ˣ	90	97	21	38	..	..
Indonesia	220.5	281.9	43	2.4	30	42	66	70	33	9	59	216	45	380	11,500	29,000
Korea, DPR (North)	22.7	24.7	10	2.1	26	61	61	66	42	..	..	120	55	110	100,000	..
Korea, Rep. of (South)	47.9	50.6	−8	1.5	20	82	72	80	5	..	97	127	5	20	..	1,200
Laos, PDR	5.6	8.5	102	5.0	42	20	52	55	87	..	50	235	100	650	..	..
Malaysia	25.1	34.3	86	3.0	33	58	70	75	8	9	92	105	8	41	..	59,000
Mongolia	2.5	3.2	45	2.4	32	57	63	68	61	6	95	185	76	150	..	..
Myanmar (Burma)	49.5	59.7	30	3.0	32	28	54	60	77	16	73	252	109	230	510,000	..
Papua New Guinea	5.5	8.3	102	4.4	41	18	56	58	70	..	58	204	94	370ˣ	..	5,200
Philippines	81.6	111.5	63	3.4	36	59	67	72	29	18	75	110	38	170	59,000	160
Singapore	4.2	4.8	6	1.5	21	100	77	81	3	8	89	40	4	6	..	..
Solomon Islands	0.5	0.8	118	5.4	42	20	69	74	20	..	..	185	24	553ˣ	..	..
Thailand	63.1	72.1	15	2.0	25	20	68	75	24	7	94	148	28	44	..	336,000
Vietnam	80.8	104.1	45	2.3	31	25	70	73	30	9	97	219	38	95	302,000	16,000
Latin America and the Caribbean	540ᵈ	690ᵈ	46ᵈ	2.6	..	76	68ᵈ	74ᵈ	28	9ᵍ	91	154ᵍ	34ᵍ	190	..	..
Argentina	36.9	47.2	48	2.5	27	88	70	77	16	7	94	72	19	41	..	2,700
Belize	0.3	0.4	110	3.0	38	48	65	69	34	4	96	104	40	140	..	..
Bolivia	8.6	12.2	79	4.1	39	63	61	64	60	8	79	255	77	390	..	..
Brazil	176.5	211.2	25	2.2	28	82	65	73	31	9	99	177	36	160	..	3,700
Chile	15.8	19.5	41	2.4	27	86	73	79	10	5	97	138	12	23	..	..
Colombia	44.2	58.1	52	2.7	32	76	68	75	19	7	75	130	23	80	59,000	205
Costa Rica	4.2	5.6	51	2.7	30	60	76	81	9	6	82	112	11	29	..	12,750
Cuba	11.3	11.8	−2	1.6	20	75	74	78	7	6	99	54	9	33	34,200	1,000
Dominican Republic	8.7	11.1	54	2.8	32	66	68	70	41	13	98	149	47	230ˣ	..	250
Ecuador	12.6	17.5	73	2.9	33	63	68	74	24	16	99	180	30	160	..	9,100
El Salvador	6.6	9.3	86	3.0	35	61	67	73	33	13	97	210	39	120	..	..
Guatemala	12.4	19.8	120	4.6	43	40	63	69	43	12	90	202	58	190	..	730
Guyana	0.8	0.7	−34	2.4	30	37	60	67	54	14	92	126	72	110	..	..
Haiti	7.5	11.1	100	4.1	38	36	50	52	79	28ˣ	53	253	123	520	33,200	..
Honduras	6.9	10.7	114	3.9	40	54	67	74	31	6	95	204	38	110	..	..
Jamaica	2.6	3.3	38	2.4	30	57	73	77	17	11	85	76	20	95	..	..
Mexico	104.9	133.8	46	2.6	32	75	73	78	24	9	97	134	29	55	22,100	4,000
Nicaragua	5.5	8.3	98	4.0	42	57	66	71	36	13	99	193	43	150	..	..
Panama	3.0	4.2	68	2.5	31	57	72	77	19	10	97	104	25	70	..	1,700
Paraguay	6.2	10.1	142	3.9	38	57	69	73	26	9	77	90	30	190	..	..
Peru	27.1	35.7	58	2.7	33	73	66	71	30	10	97	234	39	190	..	900
Suriname	0.4	0.4	−18	2.1	31	75	67	72	26	11	90	98	32	110	..	..
Trinidad and Tobago	1.3	1.3	−7	1.6	22	75	68	73	17	..	91	73	20	70	..	..
Uruguay	3.4	3.8	24	2.3	24	92	71	79	14	..	94	56	16	26	..	60
Venezuela	25.7	35.2	62	2.8	33	87	71	77	19	6	49	75	22	60	..	1,100
Middle East and North Africa	..	..	..	3.7	..	57	..	..	47	11ʰ	89	241ʰ	61	360	..	..
Algeria	31.7	42.8	61	2.9	33	58	68	71	39	7	83	255	49	140	10,000	85,000
Bahrain	0.7	1.0	75	2.4	29	92	73	75	13	10	98	203	16	46	..	..
Cyprus	0.9	1.0	9	1.9	22	70	75	80	5	..	..	36	6	0	..	1,800
Egypt	72.1	103.2	77	3.0	35	43	66	70	35	10	97	282	41	80	2,000	80,000
Iran	66.6	84.7	45	2.9	32	65	68	70	35	7	96	233	42	37	38,000	2,210,000
Iraq	24.2	41.5	150	4.9	41	68	56	59	107	23	90	171	133	290	400,000	134,000
Jordan	5.5	8.7	115	4.4	38	79	69	71	27	10	99	139	33	41	..	151,100
Kuwait	2.4	4.6	192	2.7	26	96	77	79	9	7	99	128	10	5	..	65,000
Lebanon	4.2	5.2	35	2.2	29	90	72	75	28	6	94	85	32	100ˣ	..	409,000

Table 1: Global Hunger – Life and Death Indicators

	Population						Life expectancy at birth		Infant mortality rate (per 1,000 live births) 2001	% of low birth weight infants 1995-2000[y]	% of 1-year-old children immunized (measles) 2001	Under-5 mortality rate per 1,000 live births		Maternal mortality rate per 100,000 live births 1985-2001[y]	Refugees 2002	
	Total (millions) mid-2003	Projected (millions) 2025	Projected population change (%) 2003-2050	Total fertility rate 2001	% below age 15 2003	% urbanized 2001	Male	Female				1960	2001		Country of origin	Country of asylum
Libya	5.5	8.3	97	3.5	31	88	73	78	16	7[x]	93	270	19	75	1,000	12,000
Morocco	30.4	39.2	48	3.1	31	56	68	72	39	9[x]	96	220	44	230	..	..
Oman	2.6	4.4	139	5.6	37	77	72	75	12	8	99	280	13	14	..	..
Qatar	0.6	0.8	43	3.4	26	93	70	75	11	10	92	239	16	10	..	..
Saudi Arabia	24.1	46.1	208	5.7	39	87	71	73	23	3	94	292	28	..	..	246,000
Syria	17.5	27.6	99	3.8	37	52	69	71	23	6	93	201	28	110[x]	3,600	482,000
Tunisia	9.9	11.6	23	2.2	28	66	71	75	21	5	92	254	27	70	..	..
Turkey	71.2	88.9	37	2.4	30	66	66	71	36	15	90	219	43	130[x]	44,300	10,000
United Arab Emirates	3.9	4.7	27	3.0	25	87	73	77	8	..	94	223	9	3	..	..
West Bank and Gaza[a]	3.6	7.4	228	5.7	46	67	71	74	21	9	..	..	24	..	3,000,000	1,506,000
Yemen	19.4	39.6	268	7.6	49	25	58	62	79	26	79	340	107	350	..	81,700
Countries in Transition[b]	..	..	..	1.6	..	63	..	..	30	9[i]	95[i]	101[i]	37[i]	55	..	..
Albania	3.1	3.6	16	2.4	28	43	72	76	26	5	95	151	30	..	9,900	140
Armenia	3.2	3.4	4	1.2	20	67	70	74	31	9	93	48	35	35	11,900	256,000
Azerbaijan	8.2	9.7	41	1.6	29	52	69	75	74	10	99	74	105	80	4,900	11,400
Belarus	9.9	9.4	−14	1.2	16	70	63	75	17	5	99	47	20	20	..	3,600
Bosnia and Herzegovina	3.9	3.9	−15	1.3	17	43	69	74	15	4	92	160	18	10	160,000	34,200
Bulgaria	7.5	6.0	−40	1.1	14	68	69	75	14	9	90	70	16	15	4,800	1,200
Croatia	4.3	4.4	−1	1.7	17	58	71	78	7	6	94	98	8	6	251,000	8,100
Czech Republic	10.2	10.1	−10	1.2	15	75	72	78	4	6	..	25	5	9	3,000	6,300
Estonia	1.4	1.2	−35	1.2	16	69	65	76	11	5	95	52	12	52	..	..
Georgia	4.7	3.9	−43	1.4	19	56	75	80	24	6	73	70	29	50	8,700	4,200
Hungary	10.1	8.9	−25	1.3	16	65	68	76	8	9	99	57	9	15	..	1,200
Kazakhstan	14.8	14.7	−10	2.0	25	56	58	71	61	6	96	74	76	65	..	20,600
Kyrgyzstan	5.0	6.4	41	2.5	32	34	65	72	52	6	99	180	61	65	..	8,300
Latvia	2.3	2.2	−24	1.1	16	60	65	76	17	5	98	44	21	45	..	..
Lithuania	3.5	3.5	−10	1.3	19	69	66	77	8	4	97	70	9	18	..	200
Macedonia, TFYR	2.1	2.2	2	1.6	22	59	71	75	22	6	92	177	26	7	5,000	2,700
Moldova	4.3	4.6	8	1.5	20	42	65	72	27	7	81	88	32	28	..	..
Poland	38.6	38.6	−12	1.3	17	63	70	78	8	6	97	70	9	8	..	280
Romania	21.6	20.6	−21	1.3	17	55	67	74	19	9	98	82	21	42	9,200	75
Russian Federation	145.5	136.9	−18	1.2	16	73	59	72	18	7	98	64	21	44	25,300	17,400
Slovakia	5.4	5.2	−12	1.3	18	58	70	78	8	7	99	40	9	9	4,100	4,500
Slovenia	2.0	2.0	−15	1.2	15	49	72	80	4	6	98	45	5	11	..	380
Tajikistan	6.6	8.6	53	3.1	36	28	66	71	53	13	86	140	72	65	53,000	3,500
Turkmenistan	5.7	7.7	55	3.3	34	45	63	70	76	5	98	150	99	65	..	13,700
Ukraine	47.8	45.1	−20	1.1	16	68	62	74	17	6	99	53	20	25	13,400	3,600
Uzbekistan	25.7	33.2	45	2.5	34	37	68	73	52	6	99	120	68	21	2,700	38,000
Yugoslavia, FR[aa]	10.7	10.7	−4	1.6	19	52	70	75	17	5	90	120	19	9	32,000	353,000
Industrial Countries	..	..	..	1.6	..	79	..	..	5	7	90	37	7	12	..	..
Australia	19.9	25.0	48	1.8	20	91	77	82	6	7	93	24	6	..	..	25,000
Austria	8.2	8.4	1	1.3	16	67	76	82	5	7	79	43	5	..	..	30,900
Belgium	10.4	10.8	6	1.5	17	97	75	81	5	8	83	35	6	..	..	30,300
Canada	31.6	36.0	16	1.6	18	79	77	82	5	6	96	33	7	..	..	78,500
Denmark	5.4	5.9	8	1.7	19	85	75	79	4	6	94	25	4	10	..	5,200
Finland	5.2	5.3	−8	1.6	18	59	75	82	4	6	96	28	5	6	..	1,200
France	59.8	63.4	7	1.8	19	76	76	83	4	6	84	34	6	10	..	27,600
Germany	82.6	78.1	−18	1.3	15	88	75	81	4	7	89	40	5	8	..	104,000
Greece	11.0	10.4	−12	1.3	15	60	76	81	5	7	88	64	5	1	..	1,800
Ireland	4.0	4.5	18	2.0	21	59	75	80	6	4[x]	73	36	6	6	..	6,500
Israel	6.7	9.3	64	2.8	28	92	77	81	6	8	94	39	6	5	..	2,100
Italy	57.2	57.6	−9	1.2	14	67	77	83	4	6	70	50	6	7	..	5,200
Japan	127.5	121.1	−21	1.4	14	79	78	85	3	7[x]	96	40	5	8	..	6,500
Luxembourg	0.5	0.6	31	1.7	19	92	75	81	5	4	91	41	5	0	..	..

Table 1: Global Hunger – Life and Death Indicators

| | Population | | | | | | Life expectancy at birth | | Infant mortality rate (per 1,000 live births) 2001 | % of low birth weight infants 1995-2000y | % of 1-year-old children immunized (measles) 2001 | Under-5 mortality rate per 1,000 live births | | Maternal mortality rate per 100,000 live births 1985-2001y | Refugees 2002 | |
	Total (millions) mid-2003	Projected (millions) 2025	Projected population change (%) 2003-2050	Total fertility rate 2001	% below age 15 2003	% urbanized 2001	Male	Female				1960	2001		Country of origin	Country of asylum
Netherlands	16.2	17.7	11	1.5	18	90	76	81	5	..	96	22	6	7	..	17,200
New Zealand	4.0	4.7	27	2.0	22	86	76	81	6	6	85	26	6	15	..	1,700
Norway	4.6	5.1	22	1.7	20	75	76	82	4	5	93	23	4	6	..	5,940
Portugal	10.4	10.3	−10	1.5	17	66	74	80	5	7	87	112	6	8	..	..
Spain	41.3	43.5	0	1.1	14	78	76	83	4	6	94	57	6	6	..	160
Sweden	9.0	9.6	11	1.4	18	83	78	82	3	4	94	20	3	5	..	24,900
Switzerland	7.3	7.6	0	1.4	16	67	77	83	5	6	81	27	6	5	..	44,200
United Kingdom	59.2	62.9	8	1.6	18	90	75	80	6	8	85	27	7	7	..	79,200
United States	291.5	351.1	45	2.0	21	77	74	80	7	8	91	30	8	8	..	638,000
World	**6,314.0**	**7,907.0**	**46**	**2.7**	**..**	**48**	**65**	**69**	**57**	**14**	**72**	**193**	**82**	**400**	**..**	**13,000,000z**

.. Data not available.

a Palestinian Territory.

b Central and Eastern Europe/ Commonwealth of Independent States (the newly independent states of the former Soviet Union).

c Special administrative region, data exclude China.

d Data include Antigua and Barbuda, Bahamas, Dominica, Grenada, Guadeloupe, Martinique, Netherlands Antilles, Puerto Rico, St. Kitts-Nevis, Saint Lucia, and St. Vincent and the Grenadines.

e Data include São Tomé and Principe and Seychelles. Data exclude Djibouti and Sudan.

f Data include Cook Islands, Kiribati, Marshall Islands, Micronesia, Nauru, Nieu, Palau, Samoa, Tonga, Tuvalu and Vanautu. Data exclude Hong Kong.

g Data include Antigua and Barbuda, Bahamas, Barbados, Dominica, Grenada, St. Kitts and Nevis, St. Lucia, and St. Vincent and the Grenadines.

h Data include Djibouti and Sudan. Data exclude Turkey and the West Bank and Gaza.

i Data include Turkey. Data exclude Slovenia.

x Data refer to a period other than the one specified in the column heading, differ from standard deviation, or refer to only part of a country.

y Data refer to most recent year available.

z Table does not include all countries represented in this total.

aa Now Serbia and Montenegro.

bb Refers to "Less Developed" countries as defined by the World Population Data Sheet of the Population Reference Bureau.

Table 2: Global Food, Nutrition and Education

	Food supply							Educational enrollment (% of relevant age group)			
	Per capita dietary energy supply (DES) (calories/day) 2001	Food production per capita 2002	Vitamin A supplementation coverage rate (6 to 59 months) 2000	Adult literacy rate (% age 15 and above) 2001 Total	Female	Male	Total primary school (net)hh 2000-01	Primary school (net) 1995-99i Female	Male	Primary secondary, tertiary (gross %) 2000-01c Female	Male
Developing Countries	**2,675**	**125.7**	**56**	**74.5**	..	..	**82.0**	**76**	**82**	..	..
Africa (sub-Saharan)	**2,229**	**99.0**	**77k**	**62.4**	..	..	**59.0**	**49**	**54**	..	..
Angola	1,953	122.0	100	..	..	..	37.0	52	60	26kk	31kk
Benin	2,455	127.7	96	38.6	24.6	53.5	70kk	57	83	38mm	60mm
Botswana	2,292	73.5	..	78.1	80.6	75.3	84.0	85	82	81	79
Burkina Faso	2,485	125.5	93	24.8	14.9	34.9	36.0	28	41	18mm	27mm
Burundi	1,612	81.0	96	49.2	42.0	56.9	54.0	40	49	28	35
Cameroon	2,242	102.8	100	72.4	65.1	79.9	..	71x	81x	43mm,kk	52mm,kk
Cape Verde	3,308	110.7	..	74.9	67.0	84.9	99qq	99	98	79mm	80mm
Central African Republic	1,949	113.3	100	48.2	36.6	60.8	55.0	42	63	20pp	29pp
Chad	2,245	108.3	99	44.2	35.8	53.0	58.0	45	69	24kk	43kk
Comoros	1,735	95.4	6	56.0	48.8	63.3	56.0	50	60	36kk	44kk
Congo, Dem. Rep	1,535	57.7	93	62.7	51.8	74.2	33qq	32	33	24mm,qq	30mm,qq
Congo, Republic	2,221	92.5	100	81.8	75.9	88.2	..	93x	99x	53mm	61mm
Côte d'Ivoire	2,594	95.5	16	49.7	38.4	60.3	64.0	50	67	31qq	46qq
Djibouti	2,218	68.1	..	65.5	55.5	76.1	33.0	26	35	19kk	23kk
Equatorial Guinea	..	82.4	..	84.2	76.0	92.8	72.0	70	88	49kk	68kk
Eritrea	1,690	83.4	74	56.7	45.6	68.2	41.0	37	43	29	38
Ethiopia	2,037	109.7	65	40.3	32.4	48.1	47.0	28	34	27	41
Gabon	2,602	84.4	100	..	..	..	88.0	83	82	81mm	85mm
Gambia	2,300	61.2	87	37.8	30.9	45.0	69.0	65	75	43mm	51mm
Ghana	2,670	148.5	89	72.7	64.5	81.1	58.0	50	51	42	49
Guinea	2,362	124.8	99	..	..	..	47.0	41	56	26mm	41mm
Guinea-Bissau	2,481	106.3	91	39.6	24.7	55.2	54kk	45	63	34kk	52kk
Kenya	2,058	91.7	90	83.3	77.3	89.5	69.0	89x	92x	52	53
Lesotho	2,320	104.8	17	83.9	93.9	73.3	78.0	62	55	65	61
Liberia	1,946	75.9	83	..	..	..	..	64	100	..	..
Madagascar	2,072	82.7	58	67.3	60.6	74.2	68.0	67	66	43mm	45mm
Malawi	2,168	116.6	54	61.0	47.6	75.0	101.0	71	66	70mm	74mm
Mali	2,376	99.4	70	26.4	16.6	36.7	43qq	36	51	26mm	38mm
Mauritania	2,764	75.3	81	40.7	30.7	51.1	64.0	59	63	40	45
Mauritius	2,995	92.3	..	84.8	81.7	88.0	95.0	94	94	68	70
Mozambique	1,980	92.9	92	45.2	30.0	61.2	54.0	46	55	32	42
Namibia	2,745	69.8	81	82.7	81.9	83.4	82.0	82	77	75kk	72kk
Niger	2,118	94.1	92	16.5	8.9	24.4	30.0	22	21	14	21
Nigeria	2,747	113.9	79	65.4	57.7	73.3	..	33	38	41pp	49pp
Rwanda	2,086	107.0	59	68.0	61.9	74.5	97kk	97	97	51mm	52mm
Senegal	2,277	74.9	93	38.3	28.7	48.1	63.0	58	66	34mm	41mm
Sierra Leone	1,913	73.5	77	..	..	..	..	63	68	44	57
Somalia	..	82.4	100	..	..	..	..	7x	13x	..	..
South Africa	2,921	92.2	..	85.6	85.0	86.3	89.0	96	95	78	78
Sudan	2,288	126.5	99	58.8	47.7	70.0	46kk	41	49	32qq	36qq
Swaziland	2,593	79.3	..	80.3	79.4	81.3	93.0	94	92	75kk	78kk
Tanzania	1,997	79.5	45	76.0	67.9	84.5	47.0	48	46	31	31
Togo	2,287	95.6	100	58.4	44.0	73.4	92.0	82	100	53qq	80qq
Uganda	2,398	96.9	42	68.0	58.0	78.1	109.0	83	92	66	75
Zambia	1,885	80.8	86	79.0	72.7	85.8	66.0	66	67	43	47
Zimbabwe	2,133	74.9	..	89.3	85.5	93.3	80mm	80	80	58mm,kk	62mm,kk
South Asia	..	..	**42**	**56.3**	..	..	**79.0**	**66**	**79**	..	..
Afghanistan	..	..	70	..	..	..	..	15x	42x	..	..
Bangladesh	2,187	107.5	85	40.6	30.8	49.9	89.0	83	80	54	54
Bhutan	..	74.0	93	..	..	..	..	47	58	..	..
India	2,487	105.3	22	58.0	46.4	69.0	..	64	78	49mm,kk	63mm,kk
Maldives	2,587	103.9	93	97.0	96.9	97.1	99.0	100	100	79	78
Nepal	2,459	104.1	82	42.9	25.2	60.5	72.0	60	79	57	70
Pakistan	2,457	113.1	95	44.0	28.8	58.2	66.0	60	84	27mm	45mm
Sri Lanka	2,274	102.1	..	91.9	89.3	94.5	97mm,qq	97	97	64mm,qq	63mm,qq

Table 2: Global Food, Nutrition and Education

| | Food supply | | Vitamin A supplementation coverage rate (6 to 59 months) 2000 | Adult literacy rate (% age 15 and above) 2001 | | | Total primary school (net)[hh] 2000-01 | Educational enrollment (% of relevant age group) | | | |
| | Per capita dietary energy supply (DES) (calories/day) 2001 | Food production per capita 2002 | | | | | | Primary school (net) 1995-99[i] | | Primary secondary, tertiary (gross %) 2000-01[c] | |
				Total	Female	Male		Female	Male	Female	Male
East Asia and the Pacific	..	..	..	87.1[z]	..	..	93.0	93[h]	92[h]	..	..
Brunei	2,814	262.5	..	91.6	88.1	94.6	..	91[x]	90[x]	84	81
Cambodia	1,967	100.7	63	68.7	58.2	80.5	95.0	83	94	49	60
China	2,963	..	..	85.8	78.7	92.5	93[kk,mm]	95	92	62[mm,kk]	65[mm,kk]
Hong Kong[a]	..	..	..	93.5	89.6	96.9	..	..	..	66[pp]	61[pp]
Fiji	2,789	84.4	..	93.2	91.2	95.2	99[qq]	100	99	75[mm,qq]	77[mm,qq]
Indonesia	2,904	103.9	71	87.3	82.6	92.1	92[mm]	90	93	63[mm]	65[mm]
Korea, DPR (North)	2,201	80.4	96	..	..	..	..	..	..	..	..
Korea, Rep. (South)	3,055	119.0	..	97.9	96.6	99.2[i]	99[mm]	98	97	84[mm]	97[mm]
Lao, PDR	2,309	143.5	58	65.6	54.4	76.8	81.0	78	85	51	63
Malaysia	2,927	114.2	..	87.9	84.0	91.7	98[mm]	100	100	74[mm]	71[mm]
Mongolia	1,974	79.3	87	98.5	98.3	98.6	89.0	91	79	69	58
Myanmar (Burma)	2,822	150.2	67	85.0	81.0	89.1	83.0	83	84	48	47
Papua New Guinea	2,193	90.7	..	64.6	57.7	71.1	84[kk]	80	88	39[qq]	43[qq]
Philippines	2,372	111.9	90	95.1	95.0	95.3	93[mm]	93	98	81[mm]	79[mm]
Singapore	..	19.7	..	92.5	88.7	96.4	..	92[x]	93[x]	75[pp]	76[pp]
Solomon Islands	2,272	101.4	..	..	..	..	..	..	..	..	..
Thailand	2,486	105.2	..	95.7	94.1	97.3	85[mm]	80	83	69[mm]	75[mm]
Vietnam	2,533	148.7	61	92.7	90.9	94.5	95.0	94	95	61	67
Latin America and Caribbean	..	120.8	..	89.2	..	..	97.0	94	96	..	..
Argentina	3,171	123.6	..	96.9	96.9	96.9	107[mm]	100	100	94[mm,kk]	85[mm,kk]
Belize	2,886	140.2	..	93.4	93.3	93.6	100.0	100	100	76[mm]	75[mm]
Bolivia	2,267	118.1	73	86.0	79.9	92.3	97.0	97	97	80[mm]	88[mm]
Brazil	3,002	137.3	11	87.3	87.2	87.4	97[mm]	93	100	97[mm]	93[mm]
Chile	2,868	120.5	..	95.9	95.7	96.1	89[mm]	88	89	71[mm]	81[mm]
Colombia	2,580	99.1	..	91.9	91.9	91.9	89.0	88	88	72	69
Costa Rica	2,761	110.2	..	95.7	95.8	95.6	91.0	91	91	66	65
Cuba	2,643	66.2	..	96.8	96.7	96.9	97.0	99	100	77	75
Dominican Republic	2,333	91.5	9	84.0	84.0	84.0	93.0	91	90	77[mm]	71[mm]
Ecuador	2,515	121.5	25	91.8	90.3	93.4	99.0	98	97	71[mm]	73[mm]
El Salvador	2,512	86.2	..	79.2	76.6	81.9	81[kk]	87	74	63[qq]	63[qq]
Guatemala	2,203	101.8	..	69.2	61.8	76.6	84.0	79	83	54[mm]	61[mm]
Guyana	2,515	172.9	..	98.6	98.2	99.0	98[kk]	94	100	84[mm,kk]	85[mm,kk]
Haiti	2,045	83.4	32	50.8	48.9	52.9	..	83	78	51[pp]	53[pp]
Honduras	2,406	92.7	60	75.6	75.7	75.4	88.0	86	85	61[mm]	64[mm]
Jamaica	2,705	116.1	..	87.3	91.0	83.4	95[mm]	94	94	71[mm,kk]	67[mm,kk]
Mexico	3,160	111.9	..	91.4	89.5	93.5	103[mm]	100	100	74[mm]	74[mm]
Nicaragua	2,256	114.4	..	66.8	67.1	66.5	81.0	80	79	66[mm,kk]	63[mm,kk]
Panama	2,386	88.1	..	92.1	91.4	92.7	100.0	98	98	78[kk]	73[kk]
Paraguay	2,576	104.6	..	93.5	92.5	94.5	92[mm]	92	91	64[pp]	64[pp]
Peru	2,610	148.0	..	90.2	85.7	94.8	104[kk,mm]	100	100	78[mm,qq]	89[mm,qq]
Suriname	2,643	79.5	..	..	..	..	92.0	100[x]	100[x]	79[mm]	75[mm]
Trinidad and Tobago	2,756	121.8	..	98.4	97.8	99.0	92.0	93	93	68	65
Uruguay	2,848	118.1	..	97.6	98.1	97.2	90[mm]	94	93	89[mm]	79[mm]
Venezuela	2,376	106.9	..	92.8	92.4	93.3	88.0	92	84	70	65
Middle East and North Africa	..	..	..	60.8	..	..	77.0	73[n]	80[n]	..	..
Algeria	2,987	109.9	..	67.8	58.3	77.1	98.0	96	99	69[mm]	73[mm]
Bahrain	..	54.4	..	87.9	83.2	91.1	96.0	95	93	84[qq]	78[qq]
Cyprus	3,302	103.4	..	97.2	95.7	98.8	95.0	82	81	75[kk]	74[kk]
Egypt	3,385	126.7	..	56.1	44.8	67.2	93[mm]	90	95	72[pp]	80[pp]
Iran	2,931	130.0	..	77.1	70.2	83.8	74.0	74	75	63	66
Iraq	..	56.8	..	..	..	..	..	86	100	..	..
Jordan	2,769	104.9	..	90.3	85.1	95.2	94[kk,mm]	94	93	78[mm,kk]	76[mm,kk]
Kuwait	3,170	257.2	..	82.4	80.3	84.3	66[kk]	65	68	57[qq]	52[qq]
Lebanon	3,184	78.7	..	86.5	81.0	92.4	74.0	71	71	77	75
Libya	3,333	105.2	..	80.8	69.3	91.3	..	96[x]	97[x]	91[mm]	87[mm]

Table 2: Global Food, Nutrition and Education

	Food supply		Vitamin A supplementation coverage rate (6 to 59 months) 2000	Adult literacy rate (% age 15 and above) 2001			Total primary school (net)[hh] 2000-01	Educational enrollment (% of relevant age group)			
	Per capita dietary energy supply (DES) (calories/day) 2001	Food production per capita 2002		Total	Female	Male		Primary school (net) 1995-99[i]		Primary secondary, tertiary (gross %) 2000-01[c]	
								Female	Male	Female	Male
Morocco	3,046	87.9	..	49.8	37.2	62.6	78.0	70	79	46[kk]	56[kk]
Oman	..	108.6	..	73.0	63.5	80.9	65.0	65	66	56[qq]	59[qq]
Qatar	..	124.8	..	81.7	83.7	80.8	95[qq]	96	95	85	78
Saudi Arabia	2,841	75.3	..	77.1	68.2	83.5	58.0	56	60	57[kk]	60[kk]
Syria	3,038	128.8	7	75.3	61.6	88.8	96.0	89	96	61[pp]	65[pp]
Tunisia	3,293	82.2	..	72.1	61.9	82.3	99[mm]	97	99	76[mm]	76[mm]
Turkey	3,343	94.9	..	85.5	77.2	93.7	..	82	93	54[mm,kk]	65[mm,kk]
United Arab Emirates	3,340	395.0	..	76.7	79.8	75.2	87.0	79	78	74[mm]	64[mm]
Yemen	2,050	84.4	95	47.7	26.9	68.5	67.0	45	76	34[qq]	70[qq]
Countries in Transition[b]	..	73.6	..	99.3	..	..	91.0	88	92	..	..
Albania	2,900	145.5	..	85.3	77.8	92.5	98.0	100	100	70	67
Armenia	1,991	77.6	..	98.5	97.8	99.3[j]	69.0	..	..	63	57
Azerbaijan	2,474	79.6	..	..	..	..	91[kk]	90	89	69[kk]	69[kk]
Belarus	2,925	65.2	..	99.7	99.6[j]	99.8[j]	108.0	84[x]	87[x]	87	84
Bosnia and Herzegovina	2,845	65.6	..	..	..	..	..	100	100	..	..
Bulgaria	2,626	79.6	..	98.5	98.0	99[j]	94.0	94	96	79	76
Croatia	2,678	64.5	..	98.4	97.4	99.4[j]	..	72	72	69[pp]	68[pp]
Czech Republic	3,097	77.7	..	..	..[j]	..[j]	90[mm]	90	90	77[mm]	76[mm]
Estonia	3,048	47.7	..	99.8	99.8[j]	99.8[j]	98.0	97	98	93	85
Georgia	2,247	78.0	..	..	..	..	95.0	95	95	70	69
Hungary	3,520	79.2	..	99.3	99.2[j]	99.5[j]	90[mm]	90	90	83[mm,kk]	80[mm,kk]
Kazakhstan	2,477	83.0	..	99.4	99.2[j]	99.7[j]	89.0	100	100	78	77
Kyrgyzstan	2,882	118.6	..	..	..	..	82.0	82	82	80	79
Latvia	2,809	50.3	..	99.8	99.8[j]	99.8[j]	92.0	93	93	91	82
Lithuania	3,384	67.0	..	99.6	99.5[j]	99.7[j]	95.0	94	94	88	83
Macedonia, FYR	2,552	78.0	..	..	..	..	92.0	93	94	70	70
Moldova	2,712	56.2	..	99.0	98.4	99.6[j]	78.0	..	..	63	60
Poland	3,397	83.2	..	99.7	99.7[j]	99.8[j]	98[mm]	97	97	91[mm]	86[mm]
Romania	3,407	89.3	..	98.2	97.4	99.1[j]	93.0	93	93	70	67
Russian Federation	3,014	71.2	..	99.6	99.4[j]	99.7[j]	..	93[x]	93[x]	82[pp]	75[pp]
Slovakia	2,894	66.6	..	..	..[j]	..[j]	89[mm]	..	..	74[mm]	72[mm]
Slovenia	2,935	98.2	..	99.6	99.6[j]	99.7[j]	93.0	93	94	85[pp]	80[pp]
Tajikistan	1,662	54.2	..	99.3	98.9	99.6[j]	103.0	83	90	65	78
Turkmenistan	2,738	98.2	..	..	..	..	..	..	..	81[pp]	81[pp]
Ukraine	3,008	57.5	..	99.6	99.5[j]	99.8[j]	72[qq]	..	..	79[qq]	83[qq]
Uzbekistan	2,197	101.2	..	99.2	98.9	99.6[j]	..	89	87	74[pp]	79[pp]
Yugoslavia, FR	2,778	74.6	..	..	..	..	..	51	50	..	..
Industrial Countries	..	103.1[ff]	..	..	..	..	..	97[o]	97[o]	..	..
Australia	3,126	109.0	..	..	..[j]	..[j]	96[mm]	95	95	117[jj,mm]	112[jj,mm]
Austria	3,799	101.6	..	..	..[j]	..[j]	91[mm]	91	90	93[mm]	91[mm]
Belgium	3682[y]	110.6[y]	..	..	..[j]	..[j]	101[mm]	100	100	111[jj,mm,kk]	104[jj,mm,kk]
Canada	3,176	102.7	..	..	..[j]	..[j]	99[kk,mm]	99	98	96[mm,kk]	91[mm,kk]
Denmark	3,454	102.9	..	..	..[j]	..[j]	99[kk,mm]	99	99	102[jj,mm]	95[mm]
Finland	3,202	91.4	..	..	..[j]	..[j]	100[mm]	100	100	108[jj,pp]	99[pp]
France	3,629	100.2	..	..	..[j]	..[j]	100[mm]	100	100	93[mm]	90[mm]
Germany	3,567	91.7	..	..	..[j]	..[j]	87[kk,mm]	87	86	93[pp]	95[pp]
Greece	3,754	94.0	..	97.3	96.1[j]	98.5[j]	97[mm]	97	97	81[pp]	80[pp]
Ireland	3,666	95.0	..	..	..[j]	..[j]	90[kk,mm]	90	90	93[pp]	89[pp]
Israel	3,512	82.6	..	95.1	93.1	97.1	101.0	100	100	92	88
Italy	3,680	98.9	..	98.5	98.1[j]	98.9[j]	100[mm]	100	100	84[mm]	81[mm]
Japan	2,746	88.8	..	..	..[j]	..[j]	101[mm]	100	100	82[mm]	84[mm]
Luxembourg	..	..	..	..	..[j]	..[j]	97[mm]	97	95	74[mm,kk,gg]	72[mm,kk,gg]
Netherlands	3,282	91.1	..	..	..[j]	..[j]	100[mm]	99	100	99[mm]	100[jj,mm]

Table 2: Global Food, Nutrition and Education

| | Food supply | | Vitamin A supplementation coverage rate (6 to 59 months) 2000 | Adult literacy rate (% age 15 and above) 2001 | | | Total primary school (net)hh 2000-01 | Educational enrollment (% of relevant age group) | | | |
| | Per capita dietary energy supply (DES) (calories/day) 2001 | Food production per capita 2002 | | | | | | Primary school (net) 1995-99i | | Primary secondary, tertiary (gross %) 2000-01c | |
				Total	Female	Male		Female	Male	Female	Male
New Zealand	3,235	122.0	..	..	..j	..j	99mm	100	100	104jj,mm	94mm
Norway	3,382	85.6	..	..	..j	..j	101mm	100	100	102jj,mm	94mm
Portugal	3,751	100.4	..	92.5	90.3i	95.0i	..	100	100	97mm	90mm
Spain	3,422	118.0	..	97.7	96.9i	98.6i	102mm	100	100	95mm	90mm
Sweden	3,164	92.6	..	..	..j	..j	102mm	100	100	123jj,mm	103jj,mm
Switzerland	3,440	90.8	..	..	..j	..j	99mm	99	100	86mm	90mm
United Kingdom	3,368	90.1	..	..	..j	..j	99mm	99	99	119jj,mm	105jj,mm
United States	3,766	107.5	..	..	..j	..j	95mm	95	95	97mm	90mm
World	**2,807**	**109.3**	**56**	**..**	**..**	**..**	**84.0**	**78**	**83**	**..**	**..**

..   Data not available.

a   Special Administrative Region, data excludes China.

b   Central and Eastern European countries and newly independent states of the former Soviet Union.

c   Preliminary UNESCO estimate and subject to further revision.

h   Data excludes Hong Kong and Singapore.

i   Refers to most recent year available during the period specified in the column heading.

j   For purposes of calculating the GDI, a value of 99% was applied.

k   Data include São Tomé and Principe and Seychelles. Data excludes Djibouti and Sudan.

n   Data exclude Turkey.

o   Data include Andorra, Holy See, Ireland, Liechtenstein, Malta, Monaco, San Marino and Slovenia.

x   Data refer to a period other than specified in the column heading.

y   Data include Luxembourg.

z   Data exclude China, Hong Kong, Rep. of Korea and Mongolia.

aa   Data include Antigua and Barbuda, Bahamas, Barbados, British Virgin Islands, Cayman Islands, Dominica, Falkland Island, French Guina, Grenada, Guadeloupe, Martinique, Montserrat, Netherlands Antilles, Puerto Rico, St. Kitts and Nevis, St. Lucia, and St. Vincent and U.S. Virgin Islands.

cc   Data include São Tomé and Principe. Data excludes South Africa.

dd   Data exclude Afghanistan.

ee   Data exclude China, Fiji, Papua New Guinea and Solomon Islands.

ff   Data include Faeroe Islands, Iceland, Liechtenstein, Malta and South Africa.

gg   The ratio is an underestimate, because many students pursue studies in nearby countries.

hh   Enrollment ratios based on the new International Standard Classification of Education and may not be strictly comparable to years before 1997.

jj   For purposes of calculating the GDI, a value of 100% was applied.

kk   Data refer to the 1999/2000 school year.

qq   Data refer to the 1998/1999 school year.

mm   Preliminary UNESCO Institute for Statistics estimate, subject to further revision.

oo   Data refer to the 2000/2001 school year. Data for some countries may refer to national or UNESCO Institute for Statistics estimates. For details, see http://www.uis.unesco.org/. Because data are from different sources, comparisons across countries should be made with caution.

pp   Data refer to the 1999/2000 school year. They were provided by the UNESCO Institute for Statistics for Human Development Report 2001 (UNESCO Institute for Statistics 2001). The number '0' (zero) means zero or less than half the unit shown.

Table 3: Hunger, Malnutrition and Poverty

	Undernourished population		% under-5 (1995-2001[p]) suffering from:				% Population using improved drinking water sources 2000			Population in Poverty (%)			
	Proportion of the population undernourished (%) 1999-2001	Number of undernourished people (millions) 1999-2001	Underweight		Wasting	Stunting				Below national poverty line 1984-2002[p]			Below international poverty line $1 a day 1984-2002[pq]
			Moderate & severe	Severe	Moderate & severe	Moderate & severe	Total	Urban	Rural	National	Urban	Rural	
Developing Countries	**17**	**797.9**	**27**	**10**	**8**	**32**	**78**	**92**	**69**	..	..	..	..
Africa (sub-Saharan)	**33**	**198.4**	**29[h]**	**9[h]**	**10[h]**	**40[h]**	**57**	**83**	**44**	..	..	..	..
Angola	49	6.4	..	..	..	..	38	34	40	..	..	..	..
Benin	16	1.0	23	5	8	31	63	74	55	33.0	..	..	..
Botswana	24	0.4	13	2	5	23	95	100	90	..	..	..	23.5
Burkina Faso	17	1.9	34	12	13	37	42	66	37	45.3	16.5	51.0	61.2
Burundi	70	4.5	45	13	8	57	78	91	77	36.2	..	..	58.4
Cameroon	27	4.0	21	4	5	35	58	78	39	40.0	44.4	32.4	33.4
Cape Verde	..	..	14[x]	2[x]	6[x]	16[x]	74	64	89	..	..	..	..
Central African Republic	44	1.6	24	6	9	39	70	89	57	..	..	..	66.6
Chad	34	2.7	28	10	12	28	27	31	26	64.0	63.0	67.0	..
Comoros	..	..	25	9	12	42	96	98	95	..	..	..	..
Congo, Dem. Rep.	75	38.3	31	9	13	38	45	89	26	..	..	..	..
Congo, Rep.	44	0.9	14[x]	3[x]	4[x]	19[x]	51	71	17	..	..	..	..
Côte d'Ivoire	15	2.4	21	5	8	25	81	92	72	36.8	..	..	12.3
Djibouti	..	..	18	6	13	26	100	100	100	45.1	..	86.5	..
Equatorial Guinea	..	..	..	..	..	..	44	45	42	..	..	..	..
Eritrea	61	2.2	44	17	16	38	46	63	42	53.0	..	..	..
Ethiopia	42	26.4	47	16	11	52	24	81	12	44.2	37.0	45.0	81.9
Gabon	7	0.1	12	2	3	21	86	95	47	..	..	..	..
Gambia	27	0.4	17	4	9	19	62	80	53	64.0	48.0	61.0	59.3
Ghana	12	2.4	25	5	10	26	73	91	62	31.4	26.7	34.3	44.8
Guinea	28	2.3	23	5	9	26	48	72	36	40.0	..	..	..
Guinea-Bissau	..	..	23	5	10	28	56	79	49	48.7	..	..	..
Kenya	37	11.5	23	7	6	37	57	88	42	42.0	29.3	46.4	23.0
Lesotho	25	0.5	16	4	5	44	78	88	74	49.2	27.8	53.9	43.1
Liberia	42	1.2	20[x]	..	3[x]	37[x]	..	..	..	..	..	..	..
Madagascar	36	5.7	33	11	14	49	47	85	31	71.3	52.1	71.7	49.1
Malawi	33	3.7	25	6	6	49	57	95	44	65.3	54.9	66.5	41.7
Mali	21	2.4	43	..	..	..	65	74	61	..	..	..	72.8
Mauritania	10	0.3	32	10	13	35	37	34	40	46.3	25.4	61.2	28.6
Mauritius	5	0.1	16	2	15	10	100	100	100	10.6	..	..	..
Mozambique	53	9.7	26	9	8	36	57	81	41	69.4	62.0	71.3	37.9
Namibia	7	0.1	24	5	9	24	77	100	67	..	..	..	34.9
Niger	34	3.7	40	14	14	40	59	70	56	63.0	52.0	66.0	61.4
Nigeria	8	9.1	27	11	12	46	62	78	49	34.1	30.4	36.4	70.2
Rwanda	41	3.1	24	5	7	43	41	60	40	51.2	..	..	35.7
Senegal	24	2.3	18	4	8	19	78	92	65	33.4	..	40.4	26.3
Sierra Leone	50	2.2	27	9	10	34	57	75	46	68.0	53.0	76.0	57.0
Somalia	71[c]	6.2	26	7	17	23	..	..	..	..	..	..	..
South Africa	..	..	12	2	3	25	86	99	73	..	..	..	<2.0
Sudan	25	7.7	17	7	..	..	75	86	69	..	..	..	..
Swaziland	12	0.1	10	2	1	30	..	..	..	40.0	..	..	..
Tanzania	43	15.2	29	7	5	44	68	90	57	41.6	24.4	49.7	19.9
Togo	25	1.1	25	7	12	22	54	85	38	32.3	..	..	..
Uganda	19	4.5	23	5	4	39	52	80	47	55.0	..	..	82.2
Zambia	50	5.2	25	..	4	59	64	88	48	72.9	56.0	83.1	63.7
Zimbabwe	39	4.9	13	2	6	27	83	100	73	34.9	7.9	48.0	36.0
South Asia	**22[y]**	**293.1[y]**	**46**	**17**	**15**	**45**	**85**	**94**	**80**	..	..	..	..
Afghanistan	70[c]	15.3	48	..	25	52	13	19	11	..	..	..	..
Bangladesh	32	44.1	48	13	10	45	97	99	97	33.7	19.1	37.4	36.0
Bhutan	..	..	19	3	3	40	62	86	60	..	..	..	..
India	21	213.7	47	18	16	46	84	95	79	28.6	24.7	30.2	37.7
Maldives	..	..	30	7	13	25	100	100	100	..	..	..	..
Nepal	17	3.8	48	13	10	51	88	94	87	42.0	23.0	44.0	37.7
Pakistan	19	26.8	38	13	..	..	90	95	87	32.6	24.2	35.9	13.4
Sri Lanka	25	4.3	29	..	14	14	77	98	70	25.0	15.0	27.0	6.6

Table 3: Hunger, Malnutrition and Poverty

| | Undernourished population | | % under-5 (1995-2001p) suffering from: | | | | % Population using improved drinking water sources 2000 | | | Population in Poverty (%) | | | |
	Proportion of the population undernourished (%) 1999-2001	Number of undernourished people (millions) 1999-2001	Underweight Moderate & severe	Severe	Wasting Moderate & severe	Stunting Moderate & severe	Total	Urban	Rural	Below national poverty line 1984-2002p National	Urban	Rural	Below international poverty line $1 a day 1984-2002pq
East Asia and the Pacific	..	..	17^i	..	4^i	21^i	76^i	93^i	67^i	..	..	..	..
Brunei	..	..	..	..	..	..	..	..	..	..	..	..	..
Cambodia	38	5.0	45	13	15	45	30	54	26	36.1	21.1	40.1	..
China	11	135.3	10	..	3	17	75	94	66	4.6	<2.0	4.6	16.1
Hong Kong^a	..	0.1	..	..	..	..	..	..	..	..	..	..	..
Fiji	..	..	8^x	1^x	8^x	3^x	47	43	51	..	..	..	..
Indonesia	6	12.6	26	8	..	..	78	90	69	27.1	..	..	7.2
Korea, DPR (North)	34	7.5	60	..	19	60	100	100	100	..	..	..	..
Korea, Rep. (South)	..	0.7	..	..	..	..	92	97	71	..	..	..	<2.0
Lao, PDR	22	1.2	40	13	15	41	37	61	29	38.6	26.9	41.0	26.3
Malaysia	..	0.5	18	1	..	..	..	..	94	15.5	..	..	<2.0
Mongolia	38	1.0	13	3	6	25	60	77	30	36.3	38.5	33.1	13.9
Myanmar (Burma)	7	3.2	36	9	10	37	72	89	66	..	..	..	..
Papua New Guinea	27	1.3	35^x	..	..	..	42	88	32	37.5	16.1	41.3	..
Philippines	22	16.8	28	..	6	30	86	91	79	36.8	21.5	50.7	14.6
Singapore	..	..	14^x	..	4^x	11^x	100	100		..	..	..	..
Solomon Islands	..	..	21^x	4^x	7^x	27^x	71	94	65	..	..	..	..
Thailand	19	11.9	19^x	..	6^x	16^x	84	95	81	13.1	10.2	15.5	<2.0
Vietnam	19	15.1	33	6	6	36	77	95	72	50.9	25.9	57.2	17.7
Latin America and the Caribbean	10	53.4	8^j	1	2^j	16^j	86^k	94^k	66^k	..	..	..	..
Argentina	..	0.4	5	1	3	12	..	..	..	..	29.9	..	..
Belize	..	..	6^x	1^x	..	..	92	100	82	..	..	..	..
Bolivia	22	1.8	10	2	2	26	83	95	64	62.7	..	81.7	14.4
Brazil	9	15.6	6	1	2	11	87	95	53	17.4	13.1	32.6	9.9
Chile	4	0.6	1	..	0	2	93	99	58	17.0	..	..	<2.0
Colombia	13	5.7	7	1	1	14	91	99	70	17.7	8.0	31.2	14.4
Costa Rica	6	0.2	5	0	2	6	95	99	92	22.0	19.2	25.5	6.9
Cuba	11	1.3	4	0	2	5	91	95	77	..	..	..	..
Dominican Republic	25	2.1	5	1	2	6	86	90	78	20.6	10.9	29.8	<2.0
Ecuador	4	0.6	15	2	..	27	85	90	75	35.0	25.0	47.0	20.2
El Salvador	14	0.8	12	1	1	23	77	91	64	48.3	43.1	55.7	21.4
Guatemala	25	2.9	24	5	3	46	92	98	88	57.9	33.7	71.9	16.0
Guyana	14	0.1	12	..	12	10	94	98	91	43.2	..	..	<2.0
Haiti	49	4.0	17	4	5	23	46	49	45	65.0	..	66.0	..
Honduras	20	1.3	25	4	2	39	88	95	81	53.0	57.0	51.0	23.8
Jamaica	9	0.2	4	..	4	3	92	98	85	18.7	..	25.1	<2.0
Mexico	5	5.2	8	1	2	18	88	95	69	10.1	..	..	8.0
Nicaragua	29	1.5	12	2	2	25	77	91	59	47.9	30.5	68.5	82.3
Panama	26	0.7	7	..	1	14	90	99	79	37.3	15.3	64.9	7.6
Paraguay	13	0.7	5	..	1	11	78	93	59	21.8	19.7	28.5	19.5
Peru	11	2.9	7	1	1	25	80	87	62	49.0	40.4	64.7	15.5
Suriname	11	0.0	..	..	..	..	82	93	50	..	..	..	..
Trinidad and Tobago	12	0.2	7^x	..	4^x	4^x	90	..	..	21.0	24.0	20.0	12.4
Uruguay	3	0.1	5	1	1	8	98	98	93	..	..	..	<2.0
Venezuela	18	4.4	5	1	3	14	83	85	70	31.3	..	..	15.0
Middle East and North Africa	10^z	40.9^z	14^m	4^m	6^m	22^m	87^m	95^m	77^m	..	..	..	..
Algeria	6	1.7	6	1	3	18	89	94	82	22.6	14.7	30.3	<2.0
Bahrain	..	..	9	2	5	10	..	..	..	..	..	..	..
Cyprus	..	..	..	..	..	..	100	100	100	..	..	..	..
Egypt	3	2.3	4	1	3	19	97	99	96	16.7	22.5	23.3	3.1
Iran	5	3.8	11	2	5	15	92	98	83	..	..	..	<2.0
Iraq	27^c	6.2^c	16	..	..	22	85	96	48	..	..	..	..
Jordan	6	0.3	5	1	2	8	96	100	84	11.7	..	..	<2.0
Kuwait	4	0.1	10	3	11	24	..	..	..	..	..	..	..
Lebanon	3	0.1	3	0	3	12	100	100	100	..	..	..	..
Libya	..	0.0	5	1	3	15	72	72	68	..	..	..	..

HUNGER REPORT 2004 127

Table 3: Hunger, Malnutrition and Poverty

	Undernourished population		% under-5 (1995-2001[p]) suffering from:				% Population using improved drinking water sources 2000			Population in Poverty (%)			
	Proportion of the population undernourished (%) 1999-2001	Number of undernourished people (millions) 1999-2001	Underweight Moderate & severe	Severe	Wasting Moderate & severe	Stunting Moderate & severe	Total	Urban	Rural	Below national poverty line 1984-2002[p] National	Urban	Rural	Below international poverty line $1 a day 1984-2002[pq]
Morocco	7	2.1	9[x]	2[x]	2[x]	23[x]	80	98	56	19.0	12.0	27.2	<2.0
Oman	..	..	24	4	13	23	39	41	30	..	..	..	..
Qatar	..	..	6		2	8	..	..	..	..	..	..	..
Saudi Arabia	3	0.6	14	3	11	20	95	100	64	..	..	..	..
Syria	4	0.6	13	4	9	21	80	94	64	..	..	..	..
Tunisia	..	0.1	4	1	2	12	80	92	58	7.6	3.6	13.9	<2.0
Turkey	3	1.8	8	1	2	16	82	81	86	..	..	..	<2.0
United Arab Emirates	..	0.0	14	3	15	17	..	..	..	..	..	..	..
Yemen	33	6.1	46	15	13	52	69	74	68	41.8	30.8	45.0	15.7
Countries in Transition[b]	**8**	**33.6**	**7**[n]	**2**[n]	**4**[n]	**16**[n]	**91**	**95**	**82**	**..**	**..**	**..**	**..**
Albania	4	0.1	14	4	11	32	97	99	95	..	..	..	..
Armenia	51	1.9	3	0	2	13	..	..	..	55.0	..	..	12.8
Azerbaijan	21	1.7	17	4	8	20	78	93	58	68.1	..	..	3.7
Belarus	3	0.3	..	..	..	..	100	100	100	41.9	..	..	<2.0
Bosnia and Herzegovina	8	0.3	4	1	6	10	..	..	..	19.5	13.8	19.9	..
Bulgaria	16	1.3	..	..	..	..	100	100	100	..	..	..	4.7
Croatia	12	0.5	1	..	1	1	..	..	..	..	..	..	<2.0
Czech Republic	..	0.2	1[x]	0[x]	2[x]	2[x]	..	..	..	..	..	..	<2.0
Estonia	4	0.1	..	..	..	..	..	..	..	8.9	6.8	14.7	<2.0
Georgia	26	1.4	3	0	2	12	79	90	61	11.1	12.1	9.9	<2.0
Hungary	..	0.1	2[x]	0[x]	2[x]	3[x]	99	100	98	17.3	..	..	<2.0
Kazakhstan	22	3.5	4	0	2	10	91	98	82	34.6	30.0	39.0	1.5
Kyrgyzstan	7	0.4	11	2	3	25	77	98	66	64.1	49.0	69.7	2.0
Latvia	6	0.2	..	..	..	..	..	..	..	..	..	..	<2.0
Lithuania	3	0.0	..	..	..	..	..	..	..	..	..	..	<2.0
Macedonia, TFYR	10	0.2	6	1	4	7	..	..	..	..	..	..	<2.0
Moldova	12	0.5	3	..	3	10	92	97	88	23.3	..	26.7	22.0
Poland	..	0.3	..	..	..	..	..	..	..	23.8	..	..	<2.0
Romania	..	0.2	6[x]	1[x]	3[x]	8[x]	58	91	16	21.5	20.4	27.9	2.1
Russia	4	6.2	3	1	4	13	99	100	96	30.9	..	..	6.1
Slovakia	5	0.2	..	..	..	..	100	100	100	..	..	..	<2.0
Slovenia	..	0.0	..	..	..	..	100	100	100	..	..	..	<2.0
Tajikistan	71	4.3	..	..	..	..	60	93	47	..	..	..	10.3
Turkmenistan	7	0.3	12	2	6	22	..	..	..	..	..	..	12.1
Ukraine	4	2.0	3	1	6	15	98	100	94	31.7	..	..	2.9
Uzbekistan	26	6.4	19	5	12	31	85	94	79	..	..	..	19.1
Serbia and Montenegro (former Yugoslavia)	9	0.9	2	0	4	5	98	99	97	..	..	..	..
Industrial Countries	**..**	**..**	**..**	**..**	**..**	**..**	**100**	**100**	**100**	**..**	**..**	**..**	**..**
Australia	..	..	..	..	..	..	100	100	100	..	..	..	..
Austria	..	..	..	..	..	..	100	100	100	..	..	..	..
Belgium	..	..	..	..	..	..	..	..	..	..	..	..	..
Canada	..	..	..	..	..	..	100	100	99	..	..	..	..
Denmark	..	..	..	..	..	..	100	100	100	..	..	..	..
Finland	..	..	..	..	..	..	100	100	100	..	..	..	..
France	..	..	..	..	..	..	..	..	..	..	..	..	..
Germany	..	..	..	..	..	..	..	..	..	..	..	..	..
Greece	..	..	..	..	..	..	..	..	..	..	..	..	..
Ireland	..	..	..	..	..	..	..	..	..	..	..	..	..
Israel	..	..	..	..	..	..	..	..	..	..	..	..	..
Italy	..	..	..	..	..	..	..	..	..	..	..	..	..
Japan	..	..	..	..	..	..	..	..	..	..	..	..	..
Luxembourg	..	..	..	..	..	..	..	..	..	..	..	..	..
Netherlands	..	..	..	..	..	..	100	100	100	..	..	..	..

Table 3: Hunger, Malnutrition and Poverty

	Undernourished population		% under-5 (1995-2001[p]) suffering from:				% Population using improved drinking water sources 2000			Population in Poverty (%)			
	Proportion of the population undernourished (%) 1999-2001	Number of undernourished people (millions) 1999-2001	Underweight		Wasting	Stunting	Total	Urban	Rural	Below national poverty line 1984-2002[p]			Below international poverty line $1 a day 1984-2002[pq]
			Moderate & severe	Severe	Moderate & severe	Moderate & severe				National	Urban	Rural	
New Zealand	..	..	..	..	..	..	..	100	..	..	..	..	..
Norway	..	..	..	..	100	100	100	..	..	..	..	..	..
Portugal	..	..	..	..	..	..	..	..	..	..	..	..	<2.0
Spain	..	..	..	..	..	..	..	..	..	..	..	..	..
Sweden	..	..	..	..	..	..	100	100	100	..	..	..	..
Switzerland	..	..	..	..	..	..	100	100	100	..	..	..	..
United Kingdom	..	..	..	..	..	..	100	100	100	..	..	..	..
United States	..	..	1[x]	0[x]	1[x]	2[x]	100	100	100	..	..	..	..
World	..	..	27	10	8	32	82	95	71	..	..	..	..

..   Data not available.

a   Special Administrative Region, data exclude China.

b   Central and Eastern European countries and the newly independent states of the former Soviet Union.

c   Estimates used are for 1998-2000, 1999-2001 estimates unavailable.

h   Data include São Tomé and Principe and Seychelles. Data exclude Djibouti and Sudan.

i   Data include the Cook Islands, Kiribati, Marshall Islands, Micronesia, Nauru, Niue, Palau, Samoa, Tonga, Tuvalu and Vanuatu. Data exclude Hong Kong.

j   Data include Antigua and Barbuda, Bahamas, Barbados and Dominica.

k   Data include Bahamas, Barbados, Dominica, St. Kitts and Nevis, St. Lucia, and St. Vincent and the Grenadines.

m   Data include Djibouti and Sudan. Data exclude Turkey or West Bank and Gaza.

n   Data include Turkey.

p   Data refer to the most recent year available during the period specified in the column heading.

q   Measured in 1993 international prices and adjusted to local currency using purchasing power parities. Poverty rates comparable across countries, but revisions in PPP exchange rates prevents comparing this data to previous rates reported.

x   Indicates data that refer to years or periods other than those specified in the column heading, differ from the standard definition or refer to only part of a country.

y   Data exclude Afghanistan.

z   Data include Afghanistan.

    The number '0' (zero) means zero or less than half the unit of measure.

Table 4: Economic and Development Indicators

	GNP per capita US$ 2001	GNP per capita Purchasing Power Parity (PPP) ($) 2001	GDP per capita % growth 2000-2001	Human Development Index (HDI) rank 2001	Distribution of income or consumption by quintiles[k] 1983-2001[t] Lowest 20%	Second quintile	Third quintile	Fourth quintile	Highest 20%	Ratio of highest 20% to lowest 20%[e]	Total central government expenditure (% of GDP) 2000	Public education expenditure (% of GNP) 1998-2000[t]	Military expenditure (% of GDP) 2001	Per capita energy consumption (kg. of oil equivalent) 2000	Average annual deforestation[m] (% of total forest) 1990-2000
Developing Countries	..	..	..	..	..	..	..	..	..	..	..	..	..	..	..
Africa (sub-Saharan)	460[p]	1,750[p]	0.7	..	..	..	..	..	..	..	25.9	..	..	669[p]	0.8
Angola	500	1,690[c]	0.3	164	..	..	..	..	..	..	..	2.7	3.1	584	0.2
Benin	380	970	2.3	159	..	..	..	..	..	..	..	3.2[x]	..	377	2.3
Botswana	3,100	7,410	5.1	125	2.2	4.9	8.2	14.4	70.3	31.95	..	5.5[x]	3.5	..	0.9
Burkina Faso	220	1,120[c]	3.1	173	4.5	7.4	10.6	16.7	60.7	13.49	..	..	1.6	..	0.2
Burundi	100	680[c]	1.3	171	5.1	10.3	15.1	21.5	48.0	9.41	26.1	3.4	8.1	..	9.0
Cameroon	580	1,580	3.1	142	4.6	8.3	13.0	21.0	53.0	11.52	15.5	3.7	1.4	427	0.9
Cape Verde	..	..	..	103	..	..	..	..	..	..	4.4[x]	0.8	..	..	..
Central African Republic	260	1,300[c]	0.1	168	2.0	4.9	9.6	18.5	65.0	32.50	..	1.9	..	..	0.1
Chad	200	1,060	5.5	165	..	..	..	..	..	..	..	2.0[x]	1.5	..	0.6
Comoros	..	..	..	134	..	..	..	..	..	..	..	3.8	..	..	..
Congo, Dem. Rep.	80	630	−7.1	167	..	..	..	..	..	..	0.1	..	..	292	0.4
Congo, Republic	640	680	0.1	140	..	..	..	..	..	..	25.5	4.2	..	296	0.1
Côte d'Ivoire	630	1,400	−3.3	161	7.1	11.2	15.6	21.9	44.3	6.24	17.9	4.6	..	433	3.1
Djibouti	..	..	..	153	..	..	..	..	..	..	..	3.5[x]	..	..	..
Equatorial Guinea	..	..	..	116	..	..	..	..	..	..	..	0.6	..	..	..
Eritrea	160	1,030	6.9	155	..	..	..	..	..	..	..	4.8	27.5[cc]	..	0.3
Ethiopia	100	800	5.2	169	2.4	6.1	11.1	19.6	60.8	25.33	26.8	4.8	6.2	291	0.8
Gabon	3,160	5,190	0.0	118	..	..	..	..	..	..	..	3.9[x]	..	1,271	0.0
Gambia	320	2,010[c]	3.0	151	4.0	7.6	12.3	20.8	55.2	13.80	..	2.7[x]	1.0	..	−1.0
Ghana	290	2,170[c]	1.9	129	5.6	10.1	14.9	22.8	46.6	8.32	..	4.1[x]	0.6	400	1.7
Guinea	410	1,900	1.3	157	6.4	10.4	14.8	21.2	47.2	7.38	21.0	1.9[x]	1.7	..	0.5
Guinea-Bissau	160	890	−2.0	166	5.2	8.8	13.1	19.4	53.4	10.27	..	2.1	3.1	..	0.9
Kenya	350	970	−1.0	146	5.6	9.3	13.6	20.2	51.2	9.14	26.0	6.4	1.8	515	0.5
Lesotho	530	2,980[c]	2.6	137	1.4	3.7	7.7	16.5	70.7	50.50	49.7	10.1	3.1[dd]	..	..
Liberia	140	..	2.6	..	..	..	..	..	..	..	..	..	..	..	2.0
Madagascar	260	820	3.0	149	6.4	10.7	15.5	22.7	44.8	7.00	17.1	3.2	1.2[dd]	..	0.9
Malawi	160	560	−3.5	162	4.9	8.5	12.3	18.3	56.1	11.45	..	4.1[x]	0.8	..	2.4
Mali	230	770	−0.9	172	4.6	8.0	11.9	19.3	56.2	12.22	..	2.8[x]	2.0	..	0.7
Mauritania	360	1,940	1.4	154	6.4	11.2	16.0	22.4	44.1	6.89	..	3.0[x]	2.1[cc]	..	2.7
Mauritius	3,830	9,860	6.0	62	..	..	..	..	..	..	24.0	3.5	0.2	..	0.6
Mozambique	210	1,050[c]	11.5	170	6.5	10.8	15.1	21.1	46.5	7.15	..	2.4[x]	2.3	403	0.2
Namibia	1,960	7,410[c]	0.7	124	1.4	3.0	5.4	11.5	78.7	56.21	36.2	8.1	2.8	587	0.9
Niger	180	880[c]	4.2	174	2.6	7.1	13.9	23.1	53.3	20.50	..	2.7[x]	1.1[dd]	..	3.7
Nigeria	290	790	1.5	152	4.4	8.2	12.5	19.3	55.7	12.66	..	..	1.1	710	2.6
Rwanda	220	1,240	4.5	158	9.7	13.2	16.5	21.6	39.1	4.03	..	2.8[x]	3.9	..	3.9
Senegal	490	1,480	3.2	156	6.4	10.3	14.5	20.6	48.2	7.53	20.6	3.2[x]	1.5	324	0.7
Sierra Leone	140	460	3.3	175	1.1	2.0	9.8	23.7	63.4	57.64	20.9	1.0	3.6[dd]	..	2.9
Somalia	..	..	..	..	..	..	..	..	..	..	..	..	..	..	1.0
South Africa	2,820	10,910[c]	1.2	111	2.0	4.3	8.3	18.9	66.5	33.25	29.1	5.5	1.6	2,514	0.1
Sudan	340	1,750	4.9	138	..	..	..	..	..	..	8.7	..	3.0[dd]	521	1.4
Swaziland	1,300	4,430	−0.6	133	2.7	5.8	10.0	17.1	64.4	23.85	30.0	1.5	1.5	..	−1.2
Tanzania	270[f]	520	3.4	160	6.8	11.0	15.1	21.6	45.5	6.69	..	2.1[x]	1.3[cc]	457	0.2
Togo	270	1,620	−0.1	141	..	..	..	..	..	..	..	4.8	..	338	3.4
Uganda	260	1,460[c]	2.0	147	7.1	11.1	15.4	21.5	44.9	6.32	20.4	2.3[x]	2.1	..	2.0
Zambia	320	750	2.9	163	3.3	7.6	12.5	20.0	56.6	17.15	..	2.3	0.6[dd]	619	2.4
Zimbabwe	480	2,220	−9.8	145	4.6	8.1	12.2	19.3	55.7	12.11	..	10.4[x]	3.2	809	1.5
South Asia	450	2,570	3.1	..	..	..	..	..	..	..	17.9	..	..	453	0.1
Afghanistan	..	..	..	..	..	..	..	..	..	..	..	..	..	..	0.0
Bangladesh	360	1,600	3.5	139	9.0	12.5	15.9	21.2	41.3	4.59	12.7	2.5	1.3	142	−1.3
Bhutan	..	..	..	136	..	..	..	..	..	..	..	5.2	..	..	..
India	460	2,820	3.7	127	8.1	11.6	15.0	19.3	46.1	5.69	16.7	4.1[x]	2.5	494	−0.1
Maldives	..	..	..	86	..	..	..	..	..	..	..	3.9[x]	..	..	..
Nepal	250	1,360	2.4	143	7.6	11.5	15.1	21.0	44.8	5.89	16.0	3.7	1.1	343	1.8
Pakistan	420	1,860	0.3	144	8.8	12.5	15.9	20.6	42.3	4.81	23.1	1.8[x]	4.5	463	1.1
Sri Lanka	880	3,260	−2.8	99	8.0	11.8	15.8	21.5	42.8	5.35	25.7	3.1	3.9	437	1.6

Table 4: Economic and Development Indicators

	GNP per capita US$ 2001	GNP per capita Purchasing Power Parity (PPP) ($) 2001	GDP per capita % growth 2000-2001	Human Development Index (HDI rank) 2001	Distribution of income or consumption by quintiles[k] 1983-2001[t] Lowest 20%	Second quintile	Third quintile	Fourth quintile	Highest 20%	Ratio of highest 20% to lowest 20%[e]	Total central government expenditure (% of GDP) 2000	Public education expenditure (% of GNP) 1998-2000[t]	Military expenditure (% of GDP) 2001	Per capita energy consumption (kg. of oil equivalent) 2000	Average annual deforestation[m] (% of total forest) 1990-2000
East Asia and the Pacific	**1,160[q]**	**3,790[q]**	**4.5[q]**	..	..	..	..	..	..	..	**15.0**	..	..	**871[q]**	**0.2**
Brunei	..	..	..	31	..	..	..	..	..	..	..	4.8	6.1[dd]	..	..
Cambodia	270	1,790	4.2	130	6.9	10.7	14.7	20.1	47.6	6.90	..	1.9	3.0	..	0.6
China	890	3,950	6.5	104	5.9	10.2	15.1	22.2	46.6	7.90	10.9	2.1	2.3	905	−0.9
Hong Kong[a]	25,330	25,560	−0.7	26	5.3	9.4	13.9	20.7	50.7	9.57	..	..	..	2,319	..
Fiji	..	..	..	81	..	..	..	..	..	..	..	5.2[x]	2.2	..	..
Indonesia	690	2,830	2.0	112	8.4	11.9	15.4	21.0	43.3	5.15	20.5	..	1.1	706	1.2
Korea, DPR (North)	..	..	..	..	..	..	..	..	..	..	..	..	..	2,071	0.0
Korea, Rep. (South)	9,460	15,060	2.3	30	7.9	13.6	18.0	23.1	37.5	4.75	..	3.8[x]	2.8	4,119	0.1
Lao, PDR	300	1,540[c]	3.3	135	7.6	11.4	15.3	20.8	45.0	5.92	..	2.3	2.1	..	0.4
Malaysia	3,330	7,910	−1.9	58	4.4	8.1	12.9	20.3	54.3	12.34	..	6.2[x]	2.2	2,126	1.2
Mongolia	400	1,710	0.4	117	5.6	10.0	13.8	19.4	51.2	9.14	29.3	2.3	2.3	..	0.5
Myanmar (Burma)	..	..	..	131	..	..	..	..	..	..	8.7	0.5	2.3[dd]	262	1.4
Papua New Guinea	580	2,450[c]	−5.8	132	4.5	7.9	11.9	19.2	56.5	12.56	31.4	2.3	0.8[dd]	..	0.4
Philippines	1,030	4,070	1.2	85	5.4	8.8	13.1	20.5	52.3	9.69	19.6	4.2[x]	1.0	554	1.4
Singapore	21,500	22,850	−4.7	28	5.0	9.4	14.6	22.0	49.0	9.80	18.8	3.7	5.0	6,120	0.0
Solomon Islands	..	..	..	123	..	..	..	..	..	..	..	3.6[x]	..	..	..
Thailand	1,940	6,230	1.0	74	6.1	9.5	13.5	20.9	50.0	8.20	18.0	5.4[x]	1.4	1,212	0.7
Vietnam	410	2,070	5.5	109	8.0	11.4	15.2	20.9	44.5	5.56	23.4	..	..	471	−0.5
Latin America and the Caribbean	**3,580**	**6,900**	**−1.1**	..	..	..	..	..	..	..	**21.9**	..	..	**1,181**	**0.5**
Argentina	6,940	10,980	−5.6	34	..	..	..	..	..	..	17.0	4.0[x]	1.4	1,660	0.8
Belize	..	..	..	67	..	..	..	..	..	..	..	6.2	..	..	..
Bolivia	950	2,240	−1.0	114	4.0	9.2	14.8	22.9	49.1	12.28	23.8	5.5	1.6	592	0.3
Brazil	3,070	7,070	0.2	65	2.0	5.7	10.0	18.0	64.4	32.20	26.8	4.7	1.5	1,077	0.4
Chile	4,590	8,840	1.5	43	3.2	6.7	10.7	18.1	61.3	19.16	21.9	4.2[x]	2.9	1,604	0.1
Colombia	1,890	6,790	−0.3	64	1.4	6.1	10.6	18.2	63.8	45.57	19.1	..	3.8	681	0.4
Costa Rica	4,060	9,260	−0.7	42	2.6	8.0	13.2	21.4	54.8	21.08	22.3	4.4	0.0	861	0.8
Cuba	..	..	..	52	..	..	..	..	..	..	..	8.5	..	1,180	−1.3
Dominican Republic	2,230	6,650	1.1	94	5.1	8.6	13.0	20.0	53.3	10.45	16.0	2.5	..	932	0.0
Ecuador	1,080	2,960	3.7	97	3.3	7.5	11.7	19.4	58.0	17.58	..	1.6	2.1[cc]	647	1.2
El Salvador	2,040	5,160	−0.1	105	3.3	7.3	12.4	20.7	56.4	17.09	17.0	2.3[x]	0.8	651	4.6
Guatemala	1,680	4,380	−0.5	119	2.6	5.9	9.8	17.6	64.1	24.65	..	1.7	1.0	628	1.7
Guyana	..	..	..	92	4.5	9.9	14.5	21.4	49.7	11.04	..	4.1[x]	..	..	..
Haiti	480	1,870[c]	−3.8	150	..	..	..	..	..	..	10.5	1.1[x]	..	256	5.7
Honduras	900	2,760	0.0	115	2.0	6.2	11.3	19.5	61.0	30.50	..	4.0[x]	..	469	1.0
Jamaica	2,800	3,490	1.1	78	6.7	10.7	15.0	21.8	46.0	6.87	37.3	6.3[x]	..	1,524	1.5
Mexico	5,530	8,240	−1.8	55	3.4	7.4	12.1	19.5	57.6	16.94	16.0	4.4[x]	0.5	1,567	1.1
Nicaragua	..	..	..	121	2.3	5.9	10.4	17.9	63.6	27.65	35.9	5.0	1.1	542	3.0
Panama	3,260	5,440[c]	−1.2	59	3.6	8.1	13.6	21.9	52.8	14.67	28.0	5.9	1.2[cc]	892	1.6
Paraguay	1,350	5,180[c]	0.2	84	1.9	6.0	11.4	20.1	60.7	31.95	19.4	5.0	0.9	715	0.5
Peru	1,980	4,470	−1.3	82	4.4	9.1	14.1	21.3	51.2	11.64	19.3	3.3[x]	1.7	489	0.4
Suriname	..	..	..	77	..	..	..	..	..	..	..	..	..	..	..
Trinidad and Tobago	5,960	8,620	4.3	54	5.5	10.3	15.5	22.7	45.9	8.35	..	4.0[x]	..	6,660	0.8
Uruguay	5,710	8,250	−3.8	40	4.5	9.2	14.2	21.7	50.4	11.20	31.5	2.8[x]	1.3	923	−5.0
Venezuela	4,760	5,590	0.7	69	3.0	8.4	13.7	21.6	53.4	17.80	21.7	..	1.5	2,452	0.4
Middle East and North Africa	**2,220[r]**	**5,430[r]**	**1.0[r]**	..	..	..	..	..	..	..	..	..	..	**1,368[r]**	**−0.1**
Algeria	1,650	5,910[c]	0.6	107	7.0	11.6	16.1	22.7	42.6	6.09	29.3	..	3.5[dd]	956	−1.3
Bahrain	..	..	..	37	..	..	..	..	..	..	..	3.0	4.1	..	..
Cyprus	..	..	..	25	..	..	..	..	..	..	..	5.4[v]	3.1	..	..
Egypt	1,530	3,560	1.0	120	8.6	12.1	15.4	20.4	43.6	5.07	..	..	2.6	726	−3.4
Iran	1,680	5,940	3.4	106	5.1	9.4	14.1	21.5	49.9	9.78	21.9	4.4	4.8	1,771	0.0
Iraq	..	..	..	..	..	..	..	..	..	..	..	..	..	1,190	0.0
Jordan	1,750	3,880	1.2	90	7.6	11.4	15.5	21.1	44.4	5.84	31.2	5.0[x]	8.6	1,061	0.0
Kuwait	18,270	21,530	−3.9	46	..	..	..	..	..	..	44.2	..	11.3	10,529	−5.2
Lebanon	4,010	4,400	0.0	83	..	..	..	..	..	..	35.7	3.0	5.5	1,169	0.3
Libya	..	..	..	61	..	..	..	..	..	..	..	..	..	3,107	−1.4

Table 4: Economic and Development Indicators

	GNP per capita		GDP per capita	Human Development	Distribution of income or consumption by quintiles[k] 1983-2001[l]						Total central government	Public education	Military	Per capita energy	Average annual
	US$ 2001	Purchasing Power Parity (PPP) ($) 2001	% growth 2000-2001	Index (HDI) rank 2001	Lowest 20%	Second quintile	Third quintile	Fourth quintile	Highest 20%	Ratio of highest 20% to lowest 20%[e]	expenditure (% of GDP) 2000	expenditure (% of GNP) 1998-2000[f]	expenditure (% of GDP) 2001	consumption (kg. of oil equivalent) 2000	deforestation[m] (% of total forest) 1990-2000
Morocco	1,190	3,500	4.8	126	6.5	10.6	14.8	21.3	46.6	7.17	32.5	5.5[x]	4.1	359	0.0
Oman	..	..	..	79	..	..	..	..	..	..	28.6	3.9	12.2	4,046	0.0
Qatar	..	..	..	44	..	..	..	..	..	..	..	3.6	..	..	..
Saudi Arabia	8,460	13,290	−2	73	..	..	..	..	..	..	..	9.5	11.3	5,081	0.0
Syria	1,040	3,160	0.3	110	..	..	..	..	..	..	23.2	4.1	6.2	1,137	0.0
Tunisia	2,070	6,090	3.7	91	5.7	9.9	14.7	21.8	47.9	8.40	32.0	6.8[x]	1.6	825	−0.2
Turkey	2,530	5,830	−8.7	96	6.1	10.6	14.9	21.8	46.7	7.66	39.4	3.5[x]	4.9	1,181	−0.2
United Arab Emirates	..	..	..	48	..	..	..	..	..	..	11.2	1.9	2.5	10,175	−2.8
Yemen	450	730	0.0	148	7.4	12.2	16.7	22.5	41.2	5.57	26.7	10.0	6.1	201	1.8
Countries in Transition[b]	..	..	..	..	..	..	..	..	..	..	..	..	..	..	..
Albania	1,340	3,810	5.5	95	..	..	..	..	..	..	29.8	..	1.2	521	0.8
Armenia	570	2,730	9.4	100	6.7	11.3	15.4	21.6	45.1	6.73	..	2.9	3.1	542	−1.3
Azerbaijan	650	2,890	9	89	7.4	11.5	15.3	21.2	44.5	6.01	22.6	4.2	2.6	1,454	−1.3
Belarus	1,290	7,630	4.5	53	8.4	13.0	17.0	22.5	39.1	4.65	28.9	6.0	1.4	2,432	−3.2
Bosnia and Herzegovina	1,240	6,250	3.8	66	..	..	..	..	..	..	..	..	9.5	1,096	0.0
Bulgaria	1,650	6,740	5.9	57	6.7	13.1	17.9	23.4	38.9	5.81	35.3	3.4	2.7	2,299	−0.6
Croatia	4,550	8,930	4.1	47	8.3	12.8	16.8	22.6	39.6	4.77	46.5	4.2[x]	2.6	1,775	−0.1
Czech Republic	5,310	14,320	3.8	32	10.3	14.5	17.7	21.7	35.9	3.49	36.8	4.4	2.1	3,931	0.0
Estonia	3,870	9,650	5.5	41	7.0	11.0	15.3	21.6	45.1	6.44	31.4	7.5	1.7	3,303	−0.6
Georgia	590	2,580	6.2	88	6.0	10.8	15.6	22.4	45.2	7.53	12.4	..	0.7	533	0.0
Hungary	4,830	11,990	3.1	38	10.0	14.7	18.3	22.7	34.4	3.44	40.2	5.0[x]	1.8	2,448	−0.4
Kazakhstan	1,350	6,150	14.4	76	8.2	12.5	16.8	22.9	39.6	4.83	14.3	..	1.0	2,594	−2.2
Kyrgyzstan	280	2,630	4.5	102	9.1	13.2	16.9	22.5	38.3	4.21	18.0	5.4	1.7	497	−2.6
Latvia	3,230	7,760	8.2	50	7.6	12.9	17.1	22.1	40.3	5.30	31.6	5.9	1.2	1,541	−0.4
Lithuania	3,350	8,350	6.6	45	7.9	12.7	16.9	22.6	40.0	5.06	27.6	6.4	1.8	2,032	−0.2
Macedonia, FYR	1,690	6,040	−4.7	60	8.4	14.0	17.7	23.1	36.7	4.37	..	..	7.0	..	0.0
Moldova	400	2,300	6.3	108	7.1	11.5	15.8	22.0	43.7	6.15	29.6	4.0	0.4	671	−0.2
Poland	4,230	9,370	1.0	35	7.8	12.8	17.1	22.6	39.7	5.09	34.6	5.0[x]	1.9	2,328	−0.1
Romania	1,720	5,780	5.4	72	8.2	13.1	17.4	22.9	38.4	4.68	34.2	3.5[x]	2.5	1,619	−0.2
Russian Federation	1,750	6,880	5.6	63	4.9	9.5	14.1	20.3	51.3	10.47	22.9	4.4	3.8	4,218	0.0
Slovakia	3,760	11,780	3.2	39	8.8	14.9	18.7	22.8	34.8	3.95	40.5	4.2[x]	1.9	3,234	−0.3
Slovenia	9,760	17,060	2.8	29	9.1	13.4	17.3	22.5	37.7	4.14	40.2	..	1.4	3,288	−0.2
Tajikistan	180	1,140	9.3	113	8.0	12.9	17.0	22.1	40.0	5.00	11.3	2.1	1.2	470	−0.5
Turkmenistan	950	4,240	17.2	87	6.1	10.2	14.7	21.5	47.5	7.79	..	..	3.8[dd]	2,627	0.0
Ukraine	720	4,270	10.0	75	8.8	13.3	17.4	22.7	37.8	4.30	28.3	4.4	2.7	2,820	−0.3
Uzbekistan	550	2,410	3.2	101	9.2	14.1	17.9	22.6	36.3	3.95	..	..	1.1	2,027	−0.2
Yugoslavia, FR	930	..	..	..	..	..	..	..	..	..	..	..	..	1,289	0.0
Industrial Countries	..	..	..	..	..	..	..	..	..	..	..	..	..	..	..
Australia	19,900	24,630	2.8	4	5.9	12.0	17.2	23.6	41.3	7.00	23.5	4.7[x]	1.7	5,744	0.0
Austria	23,940	26,380	0.8	16	7.0	13.2	17.9	24.0	37.9	5.41	40.4	5.8[x]	0.8	3,524	−0.2
Belgium	23,850	26,150	0.7	6	8.3	14.1	17.7	22.7	37.3	4.49	45.6	5.9[x]	1.3	5,776	..
Canada	21,930	26,530[c]	0.4	8	7.3	12.9	17.4	23.1	39.3	5.38	20.3	5.5[x]	1.2	8,156	0.0
Denmark	30,600	28,490	0.6	11	8.3	14.7	18.2	22.9	35.8	4.31	34.9	8.2[x]	1.6	3,643	−0.2
Finland	23,780	24,030	0.4	14	10.1	14.7	17.9	22.3	35.0	3.47	33.4	6.1	1.2	6,409	0.0
France	22,730[z]	24,080	1.3	17	7.2	12.6	17.2	22.8	40.2	5.58	..	5.8[x]	2.5	4,366	−0.4
Germany	23,560	25,240	0.4	18	5.7	10.5	15.7	23.4	44.7	7.84	32.7	4.6	1.5	4,131	0.0
Greece	11,430	17,520	3.8	24	7.1	11.4	15.8	22.0	43.6	6.14	30.7	3.8	4.6	2,635	−0.9
Ireland	22,850	27,170	4.6	12	6.7	11.6	16.4	22.4	42.9	6.40	..	4.4	0.7	3,854	−3.0
Israel	16,750	19,630	−2.9	22	6.9	11.4	16.3	22.9	44.3	6.42	46.3	7.3	7.7	3,241	−4.9
Italy	19,390	24,530	1.3	21	6.0	12.0	16.8	22.6	42.6	7.10	41.9	4.5[x]	2.0	2,974	−0.3
Japan	35,610	25,550	−0.7	9	10.6	14.2	17.6	22.0	35.7	3.37	..	3.5[x]	1.0	4,136	0.0
Luxembourg	..	..	..	15	8.0	12.8	16.9	22.5	39.7	4.96	..	3.7[x]	0.8	..	..
Netherlands	24,330	27,390	0.4	5	7.3	12.7	17.2	22.8	40.1	5.49	..	4.8[x]	1.6	4,762	−0.3

Table 4: Economic and Development Indicators

| | GNP per capita | | GDP per capita | Human Development | Distribution of income or consumption by quintiles[k] 1983-2001[t] | | | | | | Total central government expenditure | Public education expenditure | Military expenditure | Per capita energy consumption | Average annual deforestation[m] |
	US$ 2001	Purchasing Power Parity (PPP) ($) 2001	% growth 2000-2001	Index (HDI) rank 2001	Lowest 20%	Second quintile	Third quintile	Fourth quintile	Highest 20%	Ratio of highest 20% to lowest 20%[e]	(% of GDP) 2000	(% of GNP) 1998-2000[t]	(% of GDP) 2001	(kg. of oil equivalent) 2000	(% of total forest) 1990-2000
New Zealand	13,250	18,250	2.7	20	6.4	11.4	15.8	22.6	43.8	6.84	30.8	6.1[x]	1.2	4,864	−0.5
Norway	35,630	29,340	0.9	1	9.7	14.3	17.9	22.2	35.8	3.69	36.5	6.8[x]	1.8	5,704	−0.4
Portugal	10,900	17,710	1.5	23	5.8	11.0	15.5	21.9	45.9	7.91	38.5	5.8[x]	2.1	2,459	−1.7
Spain	14,300	19,860	1.2	19	7.5	12.6	17.0	22.6	40.3	5.37	..	4.5[x]	1.2	3,084	−0.6
Sweden	25,400	23,800	0.9	3	9.1	14.5	18.4	23.4	34.5	3.79	39.3	7.8[x]	2.0	5,354	0.0
Switzerland	38,330	30,970	0.6	10	6.9	12.7	17.3	22.9	40.3	5.84	26.7	5.5[x]	1.1	3,704	−0.4
United Kingdom	25,120	24,340	2.1	13	6.1	11.7	16.3	22.7	43.2	7.08	36.0	4.5[x]	2.5	3,962	−0.8
United States	34,280	34,280	−0.8	7	5.2	10.5	15.6	22.4	46.4	8.92	19.2	4.8[x]	3.1	8,148	−0.2
World	**5,120**	**7,370**	**−0.2**	..	..	..	..	..	..	..	**25.8**	..	..	**1,694**	**0.2**

..   Data not available.

a   Special Administrative Region, data exclude China.

b   Central and Eastern European countries and the newly independent states of former Soviet Union.

c   Estimate based on regression; others are extrapolated from the latest International Comparison Program benchmark estimates.

e   Bread For the World Institute estimate.

f   Data refer to mainland Tanzania only.

k   Income shares by percentiles of population, ranked by per capita income, except as noted.

m   Positive data indicate loss of forest; negative data indicate gain in forest.

p   Data include São Tomé and Principe and Seychelles. Data exclude Djibouti.

q   Data exclude Hong Kong, Sinapore and Brunei.

r   Data include West Bank and Gaza. Data exclude Kuwait, Qatar, Turkey and United Arab Emirates.

t   Data refer to most recent year available during the period specified in the column heading.

u   Data refer to the Flemmish community only.

v   Data refer to Office of Greek Education only.

w   Not including expenditure on tertiary education.

x   UNIESCO Institute for Statistics estimate.

y   Data refer to the central government only.

z   Data include French Guiana, Guadeloupe, Martinique and Reunion.

aa   Included under lower-middle-income economies in calculating the aggregates based on earlier data.

cc   Data refer to 1999.

dd   Data refer to 2000.

     The number '0' (zero) means zero or less than half the unit of measure.

Table 5: Economic Globalization

	Trade 2001						Investment 2001						Debt 2001	
	Exports of goods and services (% of GDP)		Manufactured exports (% of merchandise exports)	Food Trade		Imports of goods and services (% of GDP)	Gross capital formation (% of GDP)	Net private capital flows[c] ($ millions)	Foreign direct investment ($ millions)	Aid (% of gross capital formation)	Foreign direct investment (% of gross capital formation)	Foreign direct investment, gross (% of PPP GDP)	Total external debt (US $ millions)	Debt service (% of exports of goods and services)
				Food exports (% of merchandise exports)	Food imports (% of merchandise imports)									
	1990	2001												
Developing Countries	..	..	..	..	..	..	..	..	..	..	..	..	..	..
Africa (sub-Saharan)	**27**	**31**	**33**	**16**	**11**	**32**	**18**	**11,670**	**12,788**	**23.4**	**21.7**	**8.1**	**202,976**	**9**
Angola	39	74	..	..	..	62	34	897	1,119	8.3	34.8	9.9	9,600	26
Benin	14	15	6	23	20	28	19	131	131	60.1	28.8	0.0	1,665	10.0[m]
Botswana	55	51	..	..	..	35	22	55	222	2.5	5.0	1.4	370	1.7
Burkina Faso	13	10	..	..	..	26	25	26	26	61.7	4.0	..	1,490	11.0[m]
Burundi	8	6	0	91	23	18	7	0	0	274.3	0.0	1.7	1,065	36.3
Cameroon	20	32	5	17	15	29	18	−16	75	26.3	5.0	..	8,338	9.9[m]
Cape Verde	..	..	..	..	..	..	..	..	..	..	..	..	..	..
Central African Republic	15	12	..	..	..	15	14	8	8	56.0	5.7	..	822	11.5
Chad	13	14	..	..	..	53	42	80	80	26.9	12.0	..	1,104	10.0[m]
Comoros	..	..	..	..	..	..	..	..	..	..	..	..	..	..
Congo, Dem. Rep.	30	18	..	..	..	17	5	32	32	95.4	12.1	..	11,392	0
Congo, Republic	54	84	..	..	..	50	27	59	59	10.0	7.9	..	4,496	3.3
Côte d'Ivoire	32	39	14	50	17	32	10	137	246	18.2	23.9	2.5	11,582	8.1
Djibouti	..	..	..	..	..	..	..	..	..	..	..	..	..	..
Equatorial Guinea	..	..	..	..	..	..	..	..	..	..	..	..	..	..
Eritrea	20	21	..	..	..	76	35	34	34	115.2	14.1	..	410	4.5
Ethiopia	8	15	10	71	7	31	18	10	20	96.0	1.7	..	5,697	20.6[m]
Gabon	46	60	2	1	18	41	31	170	200	0.6	15.1	14.5	3,409	13.6
Gambia	60	54	17	81	35	71	18	36	36	72.8	50.8	..	489	13.8[m]
Ghana	17	52	16	49	18	70	24	244	89	51.2	7.0	2.2	6,759	8.9[m]
Guinea	31	28	28	2	23	29	22	1	2	41.3	0.2	0.1	3,254	9.2[m]
Guinea-Bissau	10	41	..	..	..	74	22	30	30	135.6	69.7	..	668	0.7[m]
Kenya	26	26	21	59	14	35	13	−37	5	31.1	0.4	0.0	5,833	11.4
Lesotho	17	34	..	..	..	86	37	113	117	18.4	39.9	14.7	592	12.4
Liberia	..	..	..	..	..	..	..	13	13	..	..	..	1,987	0.6
Madagascar	17	29	50	36	14	32	16	9	11	49.6	1.6	0.2	4,160	3.4[m]
Malawi	24	26	..	..	..	38	11	58	58	210.2	30.6	..	2,602	15.5[m]
Mali	17	31	..	..	..	42	21	103	103	62.7	18.4	..	2,890	4.5[m]
Mauritania	46	38	..	..	..	51	27	27	30	97.4	11.2	..	2,164	16.5[m]
Mauritius	65	64	74	24	16	63	24	−75	−48	2.0	−4.3	1.1	1,724	4.7
Mozambique	8	22	8	23	14	44	42	450	480	62.3	32.0	13.3	4,466	2.7[m]
Namibia	47	54	..	..	..	66	24	..	..	14.4	..	..	..	..
Niger	15	17	3	38	44	25	11	7	13	111.0	5.9	..	1,555	6.6[m]
Nigeria	43	48	0	0	20	49	28	920	1,104	1.6	9.7	2.9	31,119	11.5
Rwanda	6	9	..	..	..	26	18	5	5	92.7	1.5	0.3	1,283	7.6
Senegal	25	30	29	46	27	38	20	167	126	45.0	13.5	4.0	3,461	9.3[m]
Sierra Leone	24	17	..	..	..	37	8	4	4	563.9	6.8	..	1,188	74.3[m]
Somalia	10	..	..	..	..	..	..	0	0	..	..	..	2,532	..
South Africa	24	28	59[d]	8[d]	5[d]	25	15	6,627	7,162	2.5	42.2	10.9	24,050	6.8
Sudan	..	13	..	..	..	16	18	574	574	7.8	25.9	4.6	15,348	3.2
Swaziland	76	69	..	..	..	81	19	35	21	12.5	8.9	3.6	308	2.5
Tanzania	13	16[e]	15	70	16	24[e]	17[e]	197	224	77.7	14.1	2.1	6,676	7.3[e,m]
Togo	33	33	50	18	23	50	21	67	67	17.9	25.7	5.7	1,406	5.9
Uganda	7	12	7	69	12	26	20	147	145	68.9	12.7	2.5	3,733	9.7[m]
Zambia	36	27	13	10	8	37	20	126	72	51.2	9.9	3.8	5,671	13.4[m]
Zimbabwe	23	22	28	47	9	21	8	−28	5	22.5	0.8	..	3,780	3.4
South Asia	**9**	**15**	**78**	**12**	**7**	**17**	**22**	**3,798**	**4,066**	**4.4**	**3.1**	**0.6**	**161,657**	**12.9**
Afghanistan	..	..	..	..	..	..	..	..	..	..	..	..	..	..
Bangladesh	6	15	..	7	..	22	23	304	78	9.5	0.7	0.2	15,216	9
Bhutan	..	..	..	..	..	..	..	..	..	..	..	..	..	..
India	7	14	77	13	5	15	23	3,534	3,403	1.6	3.2	0.6	97,071	12.6
Maldives	..	..	..	..	..	..	..	..	..	..	..	..	..	..
Nepal	11	22	67	10	13	32	24	19	19	28.8	1.4	0.0	2,700	6.2
Pakistan	16	18	85	11	12	19	16	−308	383	20.7	4.1	0.7	31,019	21.3
Sri Lanka	29	37	77	21	14	44	22	243	172	9.4	4.9	1.1	8,529	9.2

Table 5: Economic Globalization

	Trade 2001						Investment 2001						Debt 2001	
	Exports of goods and services (% of GDP)		Manufactured exports (% of merchandise exports)	Food Trade		Imports of goods and services (% of GDP)	Gross capital formation (% of GDP)	Net private capital flows[c] ($ millions)	Foreign direct investment ($ millions)	Aid (% of gross capital formation)	Foreign direct investment (% of gross capital formation)	Foreign direct investment, gross (% of PPP GDP)	Total external debt (US $ millions)	Debt service (% of exports of goods and services)
				Food exports (% of merchandise exports)	Food imports (% of merchandise imports)									
	1990	2001												
East Asia and the Pacific	**26[g]**	**41[g]**	**80[g]**	**8[g]**	**6[g]**	**36[g]**	**31[g]**	**36,817[g]**	**48,913[g]**	**1.3**	**9.0[g]**	**4.6[g]**	**504,125[g]**	**6.1[g]**
Brunei	..	..	..	..	..	..	..	..	..	..	..	..	..	..
Cambodia	6	53	..	..	..	61	18	113	113	67.1	18.6	3.3	2,704	1.1
China	18	26	89	5	4	23	38	43,238	44,241	0.3	10.1	4.9	170,110	4.2
Hong Kong[a]	134	144	95	2	4	139	26	..	22,834	0.0	54.7	28.8		..
Fiji	..	..	..	..	..	..	..	..	..	..	..	..	..	..
Indonesia	25	41	56	9	10	33	17	−7,312	−3,278	6.1	−13.2	3.2	135,704	13.8
Korea, DPR (North)	..	..	..	..	..	..	..	..	..	..	..	..	..	..
Korea, Rep. (South)	29	43	91	2	6	41	27	9,279	3,198	−0.1	2.8	1.5	110,109	7.1
Lao, PDR	..	..	..	..	..	..	..	24	24	62.5	6.1	1.4	2,495	9
Malaysia	75	116	80	6	5	98	29	855	554	0.1	2.2	5.7	43,351	3.6
Mongolia	24	64	26	4	17	80	30	62	63	67.5	20.0	6.0	885	7.9
Myanmar (Burma)	3	0	..	2	..	0	13	145	208	..	..	..	5,670	2.8
Papua New Guinea	41	47	2	15	18	43	19	2	63	..	46.3	2.2	2,521	7.1
Philippines	28	49	91	6	9	47	18	2,076	1,792	4.5	13.9	2.7	52,356	13.3
Singapore	202	174	85[l]	2[l]	4	152	24	..	8,609	0.0	41.4	22.0	..	..
Solomon Islands	..	..	..	..	..	..	..	..	..	..	..	..	..	..
Thailand	34	66	74	15	5	60	24	−3,052	3,820	1.0	13.9	3.5	67,384	7.9
Vietnam	26	55	..	..	..	57	31	710	1,300	14.2	12.9	4.0	12,578	6.5
Latin America and the Caribbean	**14**	**19**	**49**	**22**	**8**	**20**	**20**	**72,067**	**69,309**	**1.6**	**18.9**	**4.4**	**765,395**	**19.4**
Argentina	10	11	33	44	6	10	14	−3,897	3,214	0.4	8.5	2.2	136,709	48.6
Belize	..	..	..	..	..	..	..	..	..	..	..	..	..	..
Bolivia	23	18	22	31	15	24	13	637	662	70.5	64.1	8.3	4,682	16.1[m]
Brazil	8	13	54	28	6	14	21	23,336	22,636	0.3	21.5	5.1	226,362	28.6
Chile	35	35	18	26	7	33	21	5,727	4,476	0.4	32.6	9.2	38,360	5.2
Colombia	21	19	39	18	12	19	15	3,597	2,328	3.1	18.9	2.9	36,699	28.1
Costa Rica	35	43	62	32	8	45	18	630	454	0.1	15.5	4.2	4,586	8.2
Cuba	..	16	..	..	..	18	10	..	..	..	..	..	..	..
Dominican Republic	34	24	..	..	..	32	23	1,729	1,198	2.1	24.2	5.7	5,093	6.6
Ecuador	33	31	12	42	8	34	25	1,444	1,330	3.8	29.6	7.4	13,910	22
El Salvador	19	29	55	35	17	43	16	674	268	10.7	12.2	2.0	4,683	7.4
Guatemala	21	19	38	51	14	28	15	403	456	7.1	14.4	12.0	5,037	8.5
Guyana	..	..	..	..	..	..	..	..	..	..	..	..	..	..
Haiti	16	13	..	..	..	33	31	3	3	14.4	0.3	..	1,250	4.5
Honduras	36	38	27	64	18	55	31	126	195	34.7	10.0	3.1	5,051	5.7[m]
Jamaica	52	41	73	23	15	56	30	1,385	614	2.3	26.2	9.0	4,956	16.8
Mexico	19	28	85	5	5	30	21	28,079	24,731	0.1	19.3	4.6	158,290	14.1
Nicaragua	25	..	13	82	16	..	..	13	132	..	..	..	6,391	22.2[m]
Panama	38	33	13	77	12	35	28	1,799	513	1.0	4.1	6.0	8,245	11.2
Paraguay	33	23	16	69	14	38	24	−14	79	3.6	4.6	2.3	2,817	8.3
Peru	16	16	22	31	13	17	18	1,400	1,064	4.5	10.7	2.2	27,512	20.8
Suriname	..	..	..	..	..	..	..	..	..	..	..	..	..	..
Trinidad and Tobago	45	55	46	5	9	43	19	830	835	−0.1	49.4	..	2,422	3.8
Uruguay	24	19	42	45	11	20	13	796	318	0.6	12.7	1.7	9,706	30.3
Venezuela	39	23	11	2	11	18	19	2,644	3,448	0.2	14.7	3.1	34,660	20.9
Middle East and North Africa	**33[h]**	**34[h]**	**14[h]**	**3[h]**	**18[h]**	**27[h]**	**22[h]**	**7,462[h]**	**5,460[h]**	**3.2[h]**	**4.5[h]**	**1.3[h]**	**200,641[h]**	**11.3**
Algeria	23	37	2	0	28	21	26	243	1,196	1.3	8.2	..	22,503	19.5
Bahrain	..	..	..	..	..	..	..	..	..	..	..	..	..	..
Cyprus	..	..	..	..	..	..	..	..	..	..	..	..	..	..
Egypt	20	18	33	10	26	23	15	2,068	510	8.2	3.3	0.5	29,234	8.8
Iran	22	28	10	4	16	21	29	1,049	33	0.3	0.1	0.0	7,483	4.1
Iraq	..	..	..	..	..	..	..	..	..	..	..	..	..	..
Jordan	62	44	66	15	18	69	26	−114	100	18.9	4.4	1.2	7,479	14.7
Kuwait	45	55	20	0	17	37	9	..	−39	0.1	−1.4	1.1	..	..
Lebanon	18	12	69	19	18	42	19	2,757	249	7.7	8.0	..	12,450	40.5

Table 5: Economic Globalization

	Trade 2001						Investment 2001						Debt 2001	
	Exports of goods and services (% of GDP)		Food Trade			Imports of goods and services (% of GDP)	Gross capital formation (% of GDP)	Net private capital flows[c] ($ millions)	Foreign direct investment ($ millions)	Aid (% of gross capital formation)	Foreign direct investment (% of gross capital formation)	Foreign direct investment, gross (% of PPP GDP)	Total external debt (US $ millions)	Debt service (% of exports of goods and services)
			Manufactured exports (% of merchandise exports)	Food exports (% of merchandise exports)	Food imports (% of merchandise imports)									
	1990	2001												
Libya	..	36	..	..	..	15	13	..	..	..	..	1.2	..	..
Morocco	26	30	64	21	14	36	25	2,633	2,658	6.1	31.6	8.5	16,962	21.9
Oman	53	..	12	6	22	..	..	−867	42	..	..	0.4	6,025	6.8
Qatar	..	..	..	..	..	..	..	..	..	..	..	..	..	..
Saudi Arabia	46	42	9	1	16	24	19	..	..	0.1	..[k]	0.0	..	..
Syria	28	38	8	9	19	31	21	204	205	3.7	5.0	1.5	21,305	2.1
Tunisia	44	48	77	9	8	52	28	1,108	457	6.9	8.3	2.3	10,884	13.4
Turkey	13	34	82	13	4	31	16	906	3,266	0.7	13.4	2.5	115,118	24.6
United Arab Emirates	65	..	..	..	..	..	..	..	..	..	..	..	..	..
Yemen	14	38	1	..	..	37	20	−210	−205	22.5	−10.8	2.2	4,954	6.3
Countries in Transition[b]	..	..	..	..	..	..	..	..	..	..	..	..	..	..
Albania	15	19	84	6	19	42	19	203	207	33.6	25.9	5.0	1,094	3.1
Armenia	35	26	43	14	25	46	19	74	70	53.8	17.7	3.3	1,001	8.1
Azerbaijan	..	42	4	2	16	38	21	216	227	19.3	19.4	25.3	1,219	4.7
Belarus	46	68	69	8	12	71	22	83	96	1.4	3.5	0.8	869	2.7
Bosnia and Herzegovina	..	27	..	..	..	60	21	226	222	..	18.9	..	2,226	18.3
Bulgaria	33	56	57	10	5	63	20	1,043	692	12.5	25.1	5.2	9,615	15.5
Croatia	78	47	73	10	9	53	24	2,236	1,512	2.3	31.4	8.2	10,742	13.7
Czech Republic	45	71	89	4	5	74	30	5,194	4,924	1.8	28.9	8.8	21,691	4.4
Estonia	60	91	75	10	11	94	28	624	539	4.5	35.2	15.4	2,852	0.9
Georgia	40	22	..	..	..	38	19	173	160	49.2	27.1	4.4	1,714	8.1
Hungary	31	60	85	8	3	63	27	3,952	2,440	3.0	17.2	5.8	30,289	8.5
Kazakhstan	74	46	20	7	9	49	26	4,947	2,763	2.6	47.9	12.4	14,372	4.7
Kyrgyzstan	29	37	20	16	14	37	16	−73	5	75.2	2.0	3.5	1,717	12
Latvia	48	46	59	9	12	54	28	880	177	5.1	8.4	7.2	5,710	2.9
Lithuania	52	50	58	12	9	56	22	521	446	5.0	17.3	3.8	5,248	5.9
Macedonia, FYR	26	40	70	16	14	56	17	466	443	43.3	77.5	13.0	1,423	10.3
Moldova	49	50	34	63	14	74	20	70	94	40.2	31.5	10.1	1,214	15.3
Poland	29	29	79	8	6	33	22	9,611	5,713	2.5	15.0	4.5	62,393	11.5
Romania	17	34	81	4	8	42	22	2,633	1,157	7.6	13.7	3.0	11,653	13.7
Russian Federation	18	37	22	1	20	24	22	1,488	2,469	1.6	3.6	1.6	152,649	12
Slovakia	27	74	84	4	6	82	32	303	1,475	2.5	22.6	11.8	11,121	6.2
Slovenia	84	59	90	4	6	63	28	..	503	..	2.7	3.8	..	..
Tajikistan	28	83	..	..	..	87	12	39	22	..	19.2	..	1,086	6.3
Turkmenistan	..	47	7	0	12	47	37	..	..	3.3	6.8	..	..	14.4
Ukraine	28	56	..	..	..	54	20	426	792	6.8	10.3	2.2	12,811	6.5
Uzbekistan	29	28	..	..	..	28	19	46	71	7.0	3.2	..	4,627	20.6
Yugoslavia, FR	..	25	59	17	9	48	13	10	0	89.2	0.0	..	11,740[f]	2
Industrial Countries	..	..	..	..	..	..	..	..	..	..	..	..	..	..
Australia	17	23	28	21	5	23	21	..	4,394	n/a	14.0	4.8	..	..
Austria	40	52	82	5	6	53	23	..	5,898	n/a	13.6	5.0	..	..
Belgium	71	84	79[j]	9[j]	9[j]	81	21	..	73,635[j]	n/a	18.2	9.6	..	..
Canada	26	44	62	7	6	39	20	..	27,438	n/a	20.2	9.6	..	..
Denmark	36	46	65	20	12	39	21	..	7,238	n/a	21.2	10.4	..	..
Finland	23	40	86	2	6	32	20	..	3,739	n/a	15.4	14.6	..	..
France	21	28	82	11	8	26	20	..	52,504	n/a	19.9	10.4	..	..
Germany	29	35	86	4	7	33	20	..	31,526	n/a	8.5	5.4	..	..
Greece	18	25	52	24	12	33	23	..	1,585	n/a	4.3	1.9	..	..
Ireland	57	95	88	7	7	80	24	..	9,865	n/a	99.9	27.0	..	..

Table 5: Economic Globalization

	Trade 2001						Investment 2001						Debt 2001	
	Exports of goods and services (% of GDP)		Manufactured exports (% of merchandise exports)	Food Trade		Imports of goods and services (% of GDP)	Gross capital formation (% of GDP)	Net private capital flows[c] ($ millions)	Foreign direct investment ($ millions)	Aid (% of gross capital formation)	Foreign direct investment (% of gross capital formation)	Foreign direct investment, gross (% of PPP GDP)	Total external debt (US $ millions)	Debt service (% of exports of goods and services)
				Food exports (% of merchandise exports)	Food imports (% of merchandise imports)									
	1990	2001												
Israel	35	40	94	3	5	47	19	..	3,224	..	21.2	4.0	..	..
Italy	20	28	88	6	9	27	20	..	14,874	n/a	6.9	3.6	..	..
Japan	10	10	93	1	13	10	25	..	6,191	n/a	0.6	1.1	..	..
Luxembourg	..	..	..	..	..	..	..	..	..	n/a	..	..	..	..
Netherlands	59	65	70	16	10	60	22	..	51,239	n/a	61.8	26.0	..	..
New Zealand	28	37	29	47	9	35	20	..	1,731	n/a	32.7	8.5	..	..
Norway	41	47	21	6	7	30	22	..	2,166	n/a	16.2	3.6	..	..
Portugal	33	32	85	7	11	41	28	..	5,945	n/a	19.2	12.9	..	..
Spain	16	30	78	15	10	31	25	..	21,540	n/a	14.5	8.7	..	..
Sweden	30	46	84	3	7	41	18	..	13,085	n/a	35.4	9.6	..	..
Switzerland	36	45	92	3	5	41	22	..	8,628	n/a	16.2	8.9	..	..
United Kingdom	24	27	80	5	8	29	17	..	63,109	n/a	25.8	12.7	..	..
United States	10	11	82	8	4	15	21	..	130,800	n/a	15.1	3.1	..	..
World	**20**	**30**	**78**	**7**	**7**	**28**	**22**	..	**746,470**	**0.9**	**17.6**	**5.1**	..	..

.. Data not available.

a Special Administrative Region, data exclude China.

b Central and Eastern European countries and the newly independent states of the former Soviet Union.

c Net private capital flows consist of private debt flows (commercial bank lending, bonds and other private credits) and nondebt private flows (foreign direct investment and portfolio equity investment).

d Data on export commodity shares refer to the South African Customs Union, which comprises Botswana, Lesotho, Namibia and South Africa.

e Mainland Tanzania only.

f World Bank estimate.

g Data exclude Hong Kong and Singapore.

h Data exclude Kuwait, Turkey and United Arab Emirates.

i Data include Iceland. Data exclude Israel.

j Data include Luxembourg.

k Foreigners are barred from investing directly in the Saudi stock market, but they may invest indirectly through mutual funds.

l Data include re-exports.

m Data are from debt sustainability analyses undertaken as part of the Debt Initiative for Heavily Indebted Poor Countries (HIPCs). Present value estimates for these countries are for public and publicly guaranteed debt only.

n/a Not applicable.

The number '0' (zero) means zero or less than half the unit of measure.

Table 6: United States – National Hunger and Poverty Trends

	1970	1980	1990	1995	2000	2001	2002
Total population (millions)	**205.1**	**227.8**	**249.4**	**262.9**	**282.2[d]**	**285.1[d]**	**288.0[d]**
Food insecurity prevalence estimates							
All U.S. households—food insecure (%)	..	..	..	10.3	10.5	10.7	11.1
Without hunger	..	..	..	6.4	7.3	7.4	7.6
With hunger	..	..	..	3.9	3.1	3.3	3.5
Adult members (total)—food insecure (%)	..	..	..	9.5	10.1	10.2	10.5
Without hunger	..	..	..	6.1	7.3	7.3	7.5
With hunger	..	..	..	3.4	2.8	3.0	3.0
Child members (total)—food insecure (%)	..	..	..	17.4	18.0	17.6	18.1
Without hunger	..	..	..	11.6	13.9	16.9	17.3
With hunger	..	..	..	5.8	4.1	0.6	0.8
Percent of federal budget spent on food assistance[a]	**0.5**	**2.4**	**1.9**	**2.48**	**1.83[e,f]**	**1.83[e,f]**	
Total infant mortality rate (per 1,000 live births)	**20.0**	**12.6**	**9.1**	**7.6**	**6.9**	**6.8**	**..**
White	17.8	11.0	7.7	6.3	5.7	5.7	..
White, non-Hispanic	..	..	..	..	5.7[c]	..	..
African American	32.6	21.4	17.0	15.1	14.1	14.0	..
Hispanic	..	..	7.8	..	5.6[c]	..	..
American Indian	..	..	..	..	7.4[c]	..	..
Asian or Pacific Islander	..	..	..	..	4.1[c]	..	..
Total poverty rate (%)	**12.6**	**13.0**	**13.5**	**13.8**	**11.3**	**11.7**	**12.1**
Northeast	..	..	10.2	12.5	10.3	10.7	10.9
Midwest	..	..	11.9	11.0	9.5	9.4	10.3
South	..	..	15.9	15.7	12.5	13.5	13.8
West	..	..	11.6	14.9	11.9	12.1	12.4
White	9.9	10.2	10.7	11.2	9.4	9.9	10.2
Non-Hispanic	..	..	..	..	7.5	7.8	8.0
African American	33.5	32.5	31.9	29.3	22.1	22.7	24.1
Hispanic	..	25.7	28.1	30.3	21.2	21.4	21.8
American Indian/Alaskan Native[b]	..	..	..	..	25.9	..	..
Asian and Pacific Islander	..	..	..	..	10.8	10.2	10.2
Elderly (65 years and older)	24.6	15.7	12.2	10.5	10.2	10.1	10.4
Female-headed households	38.1	36.7	33.4	32.4	24.7	26.4	26.5
Total child poverty rate (%) (18 years and under)	**15.1**	**18.3**	**20.6**	**20.8**	**16.2**	**16.3**	**16.7**
White	..	13.9	15.9	16.2	13.0	13.4	13.6
Non-Hispanic	..	..	..	..	9.4	9.5	9.4
African American	..	42.3	44.8	41.9	30.9	30.2	32.3
Hispanic	..	33.2	38.4	40.0	28.0	28.0	28.6
Asian and Pacific Islander	..	..	17.6	19.5	14.5	11.5	11.7[g]
Unemployment rate (%)	**4.9**	**7.1**	**5.6**	**5.6**	**4.0**	**4.8**	**5.8**
White	4.5	6.3	4.8	4.9	3.5	4.2	5.1
African American	..	14.3	11.4	10.4	7.6	8.7	10.2
Hispanic	..	10.1	8.2	9.3	5.7	6.6	7.5

Table 6: United States – National Hunger and Poverty Trends

	1970	1980	1990	1995	2000	2001	2002
Household income distribution (per quintile in %)							
All races							
Lowest 20 percent	4.1	4.2	3.9	3.7	3.6	3.5	3.5
Second quintile	10.8	10.2	9.6	9.1	8.9	8.7	8.8
Third quintile	17.4	16.8	15.9	15.2	14.8	14.6	14.8
Fourth quintile	24.5	24.8	24.0	23.3	23.0	23.0	23.3
Highest 20 percent	43.3	44.1	46.6	48.7	49.6	50.1	49.7
Ratio of highest 20 percent to lowest 20 percent[e]	10.6	10.5	11.9	13.2	13.8	14.3	14.2
White							
Lowest 20 percent	4.2	4.4	4.2	4.0	3.7	3.7	..
Second quintile	11.1	10.5	10.0	9.3	9.0	8.9	..
Third quintile	17.5	17.0	16.0	15.3	14.9	14.7	..
Fourth quintile	24.3	24.6	23.9	23.3	22.9	22.9	..
Highest 20 percent	42.9	43.5	46.0	48.1	49.4	49.8	..
Ratio of highest 20 percent to lowest 20 percent[e]	10.2	9.9	11.0	12.0	13.4	13.5	..
African American							
Lowest 20 percent	3.7	3.7	3.1	3.2	3.2	3.0	..
Second quintile	9.3	8.7	7.9	8.2	8.6	8.6	..
Third quintile	16.3	15.3	15.0	14.8	15.2	15.0	..
Fourth quintile	25.2	25.2	25.1	24.2	23.8	24.2	..
Highest 20 percent	45.5	47.1	49.0	49.6	49.3	49.2	..
Ratio of highest 20 percent to lowest 20 percent[e]	12.3	12.7	15.8	15.5	15.4	16.4	..
Hispanic origin							
Lowest 20 percent	..	4.3	4.0	3.8	4.3	4.0	..
Second quintile	..	10.1	9.5	8.9	9.8	9.4	..
Third quintile	..	16.4	15.9	14.8	15.7	15.2	..
Fourth quintile	..	24.8	24.3	23.3	23.8	23.2	..
Highest 20 percent	..	44.5	46.3	49.3	46.4	48.3	..
Ratio of highest 20 percent to lowest 20 percent[e]	..	10.3	11.6	13.0	10.8	12.1	..

.. Data not available.

a Data refer to fiscal year.

b 3-year average, 1998, 1999 and 2000.

c Preliminary.

d U.S. Census annual population estimates, July of each year.

e Bread for the World Institute estimate.

f "Food Assistance" includes the following programs: Food stamp-related, Child nutrition, Supplemental food (including WIC), Food donations, Nutrition for the elderly, and Administrative costs.

g Data for 2002 is "Asian alone," or "people who reported Asian and did not report any other race category." (U.S. Census Bureau, Poverty in the United States: 2002, 32).

Table 7: United States – State Hunger and Poverty Statistics

	Total population (millions) July 2002	Food insecure (% of households) 2000-2002	Food insecure with hunger (% of households) 2000-2002	Infant mortality rate (per 1,000 live births) 1999-2001			% population in poverty 2001-2002	Unemployment rate (%) 2002
				All races	White	African American		
Alabama	4.48	12.5	3.7	9.5	6.8	15.3	15.2	5.9
Alaska	0.64	11.8	4.3	7.0	5.6	..	8.7	7.7
Arizona	5.44	12.5	3.7	6.8	6.3	16.6	14.1	6.2
Arkansas	2.70	14.6	4.4	8.2	7.2	12.3	18.8	5.4
California	35.00	11.7	3.5	5.4	5.0	11.5	12.8	6.7
Colorado	4.50	9.2	2.8	6.2	5.8	12.7	9.2	5.7
Connecticut	3.46	7.6	2.8	6.2	5.3	13.1	7.8	4.3
Delaware	0.81	6.8	1.9	9.2	7.0	16.1	7.9	4.2
District of Columbia	0.57	9.3	2.3	13.0	5.3	16.9	17.6	6.4
Florida	16.69	11.8	3.7	7.1	5.5	12.7	12.6	5.5
Georgia	8.54	12.9	3.5	8.4	5.9	13.4	12.1	5.1
Hawaii	1.24	11.9	3.6	7.1	6.8	..	11.4	4.2
Idaho	1.34	13.7	4.3	6.9	6.8	..	11.4	5.8
Illinois	12.59	8.6	2.7	8.2	6.3	16.4	11.5	6.5
Indiana	6.16	8.9	2.8	7.8	7.0	14.4	8.8	5.1
Iowa	2.94	9.1	2.8	5.9	5.6	15.8	8.3	4.0
Kansas	2.71	11.7	3.9	7.1	6.6	14.1	10.1	5.1
Kentucky	4.09	10.8	2.9	6.8	6.5	10.4	13.4	5.6
Louisiana	4.48	13.1	2.9	9.4	6.4	13.7	16.9	6.1
Maine	1.29	9.0	2.8	5.3	5.3	..	11.9	4.4
Maryland	5.45	8.2	2.9	8.0	5.2	13.6	7.3	4.4
Massachusetts	6.42	6.4	2.1	4.9	4.4	9.9	9.5	5.3
Michigan	10.04	9.2	3.0	8.1	6.2	16.7	10.5	6.2
Minnesota	5.02	7.1	2.2	5.7	5.1	11.7	6.9	4.4
Mississippi	2.87	14.8	4.5	10.4	6.9	14.7	18.9	6.8
Missouri	5.67	9.9	3.3	7.4	5.9	16.0	9.8	5.5
Montana	0.91	12.8	4.1	6.6	5.9	..	13.4	4.6
Nebraska	1.73	10.7	3.1	6.9	6.3	13.0	10.0	3.6
Nevada	2.17	9.3	3.3	6.2	5.6	11.7	8.0	5.5
New Hampshire	1.27	6.7	2.1	5.2	5.1	..	6.1	4.7
New Jersey	8.58	8.5	2.7	6.4	5.0	13.5	8.0	5.8
New Mexico	1.85	14.3	3.8	6.6	6.5	14.6	17.9	5.4
New York	19.13	9.4	2.9	6.2	5.1	10.9	14.1	6.1
North Carolina	8.31	12.3	3.7	8.7	6.6	15.1	13.4	6.7
North Dakota	0.63	8.1	2.0	8.0	7.3	..	12.7	4.0
Ohio	11.41	9.8	3.3	7.8	6.6	15.1	10.1	5.7
Oklahoma	3.49	14.3	5.1	8.1	7.4	14.3	14.6	4.5
Oregon	3.52	13.7	5.0	5.5	5.5	7.3	11.3	7.5
Pennsylvania	12.33	9.4	2.7	7.2	6.0	15.1	9.5	5.7
Rhode Island	1.07	10.1	3.4	6.3	5.5	12.8	10.3	5.1
South Carolina	4.10	12.3	4.3	9.3	6.2	15.2	14.7	6.0
South Dakota	0.76	8.0	2.2	7.1	6.2	..	10.0	3.1
Tennessee	5.79	11.3	3.3	8.5	6.5	16.0	14.5	5.1
Texas	21.74	14.8	4.1	5.9	5.3	10.9	15.3	6.3
Utah	2.32	15.2	4.6	5.0	5.0	..	10.2	6.1
Vermont	0.62	9.0	2.4	5.9	5.9	..	9.8	3.7
Virginia	7.29	7.3	1.8	7.2	5.5	13.0	8.9	4.1
Washington	6.07	12.3	4.4	5.3	5.0	10.8	10.8	7.3
West Virginia	1.80	9.4	2.7	7.4	7.3	9.9	16.6	6.1
Wisconsin	5.44	8.1	3.3	6.8	5.7	16.8	8.2	5.5
Wyoming	0.50	10.7	4.3	6.6	6.7	..	8.8	4.2
Puerto Rico	3.86	..	..	9.7	9.7	10.2	..	..
United States	**287.97**	**10.8**	**3.3**	**6.9**	**5.7**	**13.6**	**11.9**	**5.8**

.. Data not available.

Table 8: United States – Nutrition and Assistance Programs

	Food Stamp Participation: Monthly Average by State							
	1995[e]	1996[e]	1997[e]	1998[e]	1999[e]	2000[e]	2001[e]	2002[e]
Alabama	524,522	509,214	469,268	426,819	405,273	396,057	411,292	443,547
Alaska	45,448	46,233	45,234	42,451	41,262	37,524	37,897	46,165
Arizona	480,195	427,481	363,779	295,703	257,362	259,006	291,372	378,722
Arkansas	272,174	273,900	265,854	255,710	252,957	246,572	256,441	283,909
California	3,174,651	3,143,390	2,814,761	2,259,069	2,027,089	1,831,697	1,668,351	1,710,306
Colorado	251,880	243,692	216,748	191,015	173,497	155,948	153,952	178,490
Connecticut	226,061	222,758	209,529	195,866	178,168	165,059	157,031	168,591
Delaware	57,090	57,836	53,655	45,581	38,571	32,218	31,886	39,628
District of Columbia	93,993	92,751	90,391	85,396	84,082	80,803	73,494	74,271
Florida	1,395,296	1,371,352	1,191,664	990,571	933,435	882,341	887,256	985,130
Georgia	815,920	792,502	698,323	631,720	616,600	559,468	573,537	645,633
Hawaii	124,575	130,344	126,901	122,027	125,155	118,041	108,313	106,370
Idaho	80,255	79,855	70,413	62,393	57,201	58,191	59,667	69,998
Illinois	1,151,035	1,105,160	1,019,600	922,927	820,034	779,420	825,295	886,344
Indiana	469,647	389,537	347,772	313,116	298,213	300,314	346,551	410,884
Iowa	184,025	177,283	161,184	141,067	128,790	123,322	126,494	140,729
Kansas	184,241	171,831	148,734	119,218	114,875	116,596	124,285	140,403
Kentucky	520,088	485,628	444,422	412,028	396,440	403,479	412,680	450,102
Louisiana	710,597	670,034	575,411	536,834	516,285	599,851	518,384	588,458
Maine	131,955	130,872	123,767	115,099	108,749	101,598	104,383	111,147
Maryland	398,727	374,512	354,436	322,653	264,393	219,180	208,426	228,329
Massachusetts	409,870	373,599	339,505	292,997	261,021	231,829	219,223	242,542
Michigan	970,760	935,416	838,917	771,580	682,680	602,857	641,269	750,037
Minnesota	308,206	294,825	260,476	219,744	208,062	196,050	197,727	216,960
Mississippi	479,934	457,106	399,062	329,058	288,057	275,856	297,805	324,852
Missouri	575,882	553,930	477,703	410,966	408,331	419,959	454,427	515,006
Montana	70,873	70,754	66,605	62,328	60,898	59,466	61,957	63,347
Nebraska	105,133	101,625	97,176	94,944	92,404	82,414	80,652	88,459
Nevada	98,538	96,712	82,419	71,531	61,673	60,905	69,396	97,035
New Hampshire	58,353	52,809	46,000	39,578	37,438	36,266	35,554	41,053
New Jersey	550,628	540,452	491,337	424,738	384,888	344,677	317,579	319,799
New Mexico	238,854	235,060	204,644	174,699	178,439	169,354	163,245	170,457
New York	2,183,101	2,098,561	1,913,548	1,627,170	1,540,784	1,438,568	1,353,542	1,346,644
North Carolina	613,502	631,061	586,415	527,790	505,410	488,247	493,672	574,369
North Dakota	41,401	39,825	37,688	33,801	33,442	31,895	37,755	36,781
Ohio	1,155,490	1,045,066	873,562	733,565	639,786	609,717	640,503	734,679
Oklahoma	374,893	353,790	321,894	287,577	271,351	523,287	271,001	316,684
Oregon	288,687	287,607	258,615	238,446	223,978	234,387	283,705	359,138
Pennsylvania	1,173,420	1,123,541	1,008,864	906,735	834,898	777,112	748,074	766,615
Rhode Island	93,434	90,873	84,627	72,301	76,394	74,256	71,272	71,933
South Carolina	363,822	358,341	349,137	333,017	308,570	295,335	315,718	379,310
South Dakota	50,158	48,843	46,901	45,173	44,065	42,962	44,594	47,663
Tennessee	662,014	637,773	585,889	538,467	510,828	496,031	521,510	598,012
Texas	2,557,693	2,371,958	2,033,750	1,636,175	1,400,526	1,332,785	1,360,642	1,554,428
Utah	118,836	110,011	98,338	91,764	88,163	81,945	79,716	89,899
Vermont	59,292	56,459	53,005	45,702	44,287	40,831	38,874	39,914
Virginia	545,829	537,531	476,088	396,581	361,581	336,080	332,312	352,172
Washington	476,019	476,391	444,800	364,418	306,654	295,061	308,589	350,373
West Virginia	308,505	299,719	287,035	269,140	247,249	226,897	221,361	235,736
Wisconsin	320,142	283,255	232,103	192,887	182,206	193,021	215,786	262,310
Wyoming	35,579	33,013	28,584	25,452	23,477	22,459	22,539	23,530
Guam	..	..	17,783	25,249	19,758	22,234	22,723	24,457
Puerto Rico	n/a	n/a	n/a	n/a	n/a	n/a	..	..
United States	**26,618,773**	**25,540,331**	**22,854,273**	**19,788,115**	**18,182,595**	**17,155,093**	**17,312,974[g]**	**19,093,798[h]**

Table 8: United States – Nutrition and Assistance Programs

	WICª Annual Participation by State							
	1995ᵉ	1996ᵉ	1997ᵉ	1998ᵉ	1999ᵉ	2000ᵉ	2001ᵉ	2002ᵉ
Alabama	121,979	118,163	118,899	117,319	115,172	103,930	111,049	118,616
Alaska	19,235	22,410	23,537	23,829	26,131	24,395	23,628	25,094
Arizona	122,179	141,466	145,849	142,000	142,488	145,544	147,285	151,186
Arkansas	87,362	90,662	87,310	82,939	82,882	82,131	79,826	84,153
California	1,003,611	1,141,598	1,224,224	1,216,253	1,229,495	1,219,430	1,243,509	1,266,542
Colorado	70,617	70,523	75,068	74,679	74,801	71,967	72,124	77,501
Connecticut	63,625	62,520	59,368	60,267	58,299	50,867	49,252	51,329
Delaware	15,444	15,831	15,581	15,635	15,274	15,844	16,568	17,241
District of Columbia	17,368	16,116	16,747	16,593	16,406	15,060	15,204	15,117
Florida	317,095	332,130	354,971	345,150	337,559	296,298	316,758	340,954
Georgia	217,207	223,746	230,153	232,258	224,069	216,319	226,365	237,124
Hawaii	25,410	27,466	30,807	34,098	34,137	32,080	32,467	32,986
Idaho	31,120	31,085	31,475	31,678	31,543	31,286	32,641	33,448
Illinois	244,661	244,223	236,068	237,262	241,016	243,655	251,329	260,080
Indiana	132,621	132,532	132,700	131,099	128,269	120,648	117,880	124,162
Iowa	65,260	66,020	66,293	65,885	63,996	60,793	60,664	63,010
Kansas	55,890	54,377	54,754	52,896	52,345	52,773	53,260	57,898
Kentucky	118,198	119,457	122,948	122,910	122,056	112,182	111,004	113,112
Louisiana	133,992	139,603	139,223	136,866	135,430	130,042	125,916	129,200
Maine	26,905	26,300	26,663	25,786	24,646	22,073	20,962	21,470
Maryland	86,349	87,961	91,412	92,744	93,338	94,194	93,829	96,153
Massachusetts	113,605	115,942	118,818	117,681	115,042	113,842	112,623	113,176
Michigan	209,272	212,270	218,371	217,924	215,138	213,049	214,951	215,989
Minnesota	90,979	93,971	94,807	95,101	90,101	90,093	96,192	102,008
Mississippi	102,718	102,532	100,124	99,097	96,863	95,836	98,874	102,272
Missouri	127,005	129,245	131,638	128,176	126,640	123,738	125,144	128,029
Montana	20,889	22,155	21,679	21,428	21,346	21,288	21,413	21,402
Nebraska	35,715	36,101	33,041	31,770	33,047	32,793	34,427	37,074
Nevada	31,053	36,310	37,324	37,972	37,415	38,781	40,646	41,297
New Hampshire	19,423	19,342	19,179	18,678	18,100	17,049	16,507	16,894
New Jersey	141,962	137,988	141,514	140,732	129,603	127,013	128,577	133,946
New Mexico	53,816	56,131	54,040	56,183	56,494	57,802	59,464	59,914
New York	452,997	466,185	478,980	482,882	476,563	466,818	460,252	454,577
North Carolina	182,264	188,828	194,566	197,954	196,389	190,258	200,678	208,377
North Dakota	17,754	17,484	16,868	15,810	14,930	14,303	14,053	13,823
Ohio	259,121	258,400	254,668	250,815	245,994	242,921	247,092	253,923
Oklahoma	95,964	103,373	108,348	109,581	108,485	108,375	105,907	109,391
Oregon	82,212	86,048	89,299	31,341	92,831	86,061	93,246	97,058
Pennsylvania	260,544	262,111	257,018	246,337	235,526	230,914	226,434	222,879
Rhode Island	21,450	22,382	22,596	22,768	22,454	21,783	21,925	22,451
South Carolina	124,252	123,669	118,966	118,556	110,850	108,204	111,408	109,575
South Dakota	22,397	22,439	21,945	20,507	20,445	20,409	20,505	20,278
Tennessee	137,280	144,174	150,289	148,692	148,824	148,662	149,490	153,212
Texas	637,229	641,150	683,583	691,292	707,872	737,206	750,122	786,530
Utah	53,287	54,893	57,511	57,391	59,592	57,549	58,928	61,445
Vermont	16,140	16,061	16,133	16,308	16,051	16,401	15,966	15,903
Virginia	126,882	126,760	129,520	132,317	131,304	128,163	130,094	129,103
Washington	112,915	129,256	145,147	144,052	141,089	145,850	150,138	152,055
West Virginia	51,890	54,173	55,065	53,962	52,335	50,996	50,064	50,265
Wisconsin	109,151	109,712	108,886	108,352	104,041	100,574	100,128	102,776
Wyoming	11,745	11,965	12,447	11,789	11,583	10,907	11,103	11,353
Guam	..	..	..	..	..	..	..	6,208
Puerto Rico	182,795	204,717	211,454	206,968	205,228	214,651	219,620	209,442
United States	**6,894,413**	**7,187,831**	**7,406,866**	**7,367,397**	**7,311,206**	**7,192,604**	**7,305,577**	**7,490,841**ʰ,ᴵ

Table 8: United States – Nutrition and Assistance Programs

	TANF[b] Individual Recipients: Monthly Average by State[f]							
	1995[e]	1996[e]	1997[e]	1998[e]	1999[e]	2000[e]	2001[e]	2002[e]
Alabama	113,971	101,772	77,096	54,164	49,470	55,858	49,100	42,706
Alaska	36,257	36,532	34,434	29,599	25,221	22,425	16,997	17,623
Arizona	185,282	166,865	140,161	100,216	88,665	84,458	82,595	94,279
Arkansas	61,631	57,231	49,156	32,633	29,023	28,704	27,751	27,731
California	2,674,971	2,592,547	2,318,036	1,997,709	1,661,769	1,283,356	1,228,605	1,160,882
Colorado	105,921	95,858	71,088	53,089	35,207	27,880	27,132	31,491
Connecticut	169,358	159,736	151,801	115,941	77,947	63,903	59,566	53,102
Delaware	24,097	23,314	21,139	10,547	16,613	15,338	12,355	12,357
District of Columbia	71,950	69,668	64,663	55,949	50,035	45,748	43,425	42,159
Florida	606,490	540,667	403,838	252,257	184,486	143,078	124,586	123,247
Georgia	377,630	338,830	254,243	182,274	147,581	137,782	120,501	128,177
Hawaii	65,963	66,375	60,593	46,724	44,069	42,306	40,645	30,466
Idaho	23,967	22,173	12,277	4,059	2,545	2,333	2,246	2,374
Illinois	684,438	642,465	563,129	474,976	335,395	246,469	182,673	133,708
Indiana	176,939	140,514	119,429	109,114	107,688	101,380	115,519	138,885
Iowa	97,331	86,311	75,864	66,212	57,539	52,363	51,392	53,434
Kansas	77,030	65,201	49,463	34,718	33,912	35,300	32,967	35,808
Kentucky	184,482	172,003	150,900	119,161	95,488	86,501	81,750	77,658
Louisiana	250,865	229,097	166,395	134,370	101,257	82,934	65,504	60,704
Maine	58,746	54,801	46,944	39,537	33,757	27,506	26,134	26,039
Maryland	220,148	195,287	153,367	115,728	81,736	71,326	68,221	65,565
Massachusetts	262,646	229,777	199,403	167,315	121,784	98,144	95,057	108,068
Michigan	578,463	510,409	428,622	332,240	243,818	199,185	195,369	201,695
Minnesota	178,260	168,672	151,907	139,993	120,788	123,838	112,688	94,584
Mississippi	140,454	124,248	92,211	52,667	36,191	34,013	35,710	40,434
Missouri	249,254	224,880	186,396	147,035	128,703	124,535	121,364	118,753
Montana	33,376	30,214	24,326	17,727	13,618	14,230	15,401	16,440
Nebraska	41,496	38,966	37,439	35,657	31,838	27,183	23,802	25,500
Nevada	40,808	35,444	28,787	25,472	18,203	16,438	19,461	27,640
New Hampshire	26,859	23,306	19,248	16,045	15,203	13,739	13,501	14,499
New Jersey	309,556	279,515	242,285	189,418	155,753	125,050	113,481	102,657
New Mexico	103,051	99,119	71,573	75,237	79,183	68,986	56,105	47,338
New York	1,240,825	1,157,503	1,017,878	908,776	793,366	694,950	613,353	412,530
North Carolina	305,240	269,841	230,819	172,813	124,004	97,053	91,526	91,084
North Dakota	14,149	13,071	10,633	8,682	8,123	8,646	8,881	8,344
Ohio	591,659	538,597	466,524	340,179	262,806	236,976	199,352	190,998
Oklahoma	120,196	99,035	80,294	69,316	49,715	32,281	33,895	36,923
Oregon	100,680	80,946	57,672	46,395	46,761	41,072	41,976	40,916
Pennsylvania	582,160	527,214	437,898	357,684	278,036	231,983	215,175	210,595
Rhode Island	60,375	57,429	55,286	53,369	49,020	44,246	41,628	38,957
South Carolina	126,534	114,709	81,944	60,110	41,029	40,179	40,266	50,866
South Dakota	16,797	15,759	12,550	9,609	7,680	6,656	6,365	6,603
Tennessee	270,805	248,310	166,582	149,440	153,286	147,902	155,094	164,823
Texas	729,525	661,975	530,281	370,857	310,698	346,753	349,279	331,363
Utah	44,077	39,096	32,067	28,934	28,151	23,188	21,815	19,982
Vermont	26,777	24,764	21,086	19,644	17,585	15,626	15,060	13,407
Virginia	178,679	155,249	122,766	100,358	85,933	69,315	65,051	67,262
Washington	282,658	271,270	246,202	202,573	166,100	148,444	141,397	137,755
West Virginia	102,303	88,437	82,899	44,179	30,150	33,470	39,037	41,643
Wisconsin	202,448	158,581	98,732	41,651	41,984	38,186	40,030	45,231
Wyoming	14,120	12,180	5,679	2,586	1,576	1,118	987	826
Guam	..	..	..	..	..	..	9,729	10,783
Puerto Rico	164,317	152,242	140,344	121,402	102,806	87,354	75,114	67,413
United States	**13,418,386**	**12,320,970**	**10,376,224**	**8,347,041**	**6,836,093**	**5,821,857**	**5,469,184[g]**	**5,146,132**

a   Special Supplemental Nutrition Program for Women, Infants and Children.
b   Temporary Assistance for Needy Families.
d   Preliminary data, subject to change.
e   Data refer to fiscal year.
f   Data refer to calendar year.
g   Data include Guam.
h   Data include Virgin Islands.
i   Data include American Samoa.
n/a   Not Applicable.

Sources for Tables

Table 1: Global Hunger – Life and Death Indicators

Total population, projected population, projected growth rate, life expectancy: The Population Reference Bureau, *2003 World Population Data Sheet,* data posted at http://www.prb.org.

Population under age 15: Statistics and Population Division of the U.N. Secretariat, "Indicators of Youth and Elderly Populations," data posted at http://www.un.org/Depts/unsd/social/youth.htm.

Total fertility rate, urban population, infant mortality, low birth-weight infants, children immunized, under-5 mortality rate, maternal mortality rate: U.N. Children's Fund, *The State of the World's Children, 2003 (SWC)* (New York: UNICEF, 2003).

Refugees: U.S. Committee for Refugees, *World Refugees Survey, 2003* (Washington, D.C.: Immigration and Refugee Services of America, 2003) data posted at http://www.refugees.org.

Table 2: Global Food, Nutrition and Education

Per capita dietary energy supply, food production per capita: Food and Agriculture Organization of the United Nations (FAO) database, http://apps.fao.org/default.jsp.

Vitamin A supplementation coverage, gender-related primary school enrollment: *SWC, 2003.*

Total adult literacy rate, gender-based adult literacy rate, total net primary school enrollment, combined educational enrollment: U.N. Development Program, *Human Development Report, 2003 (HDR)* (New York: Oxford University Press, 2003).

Table 3: Hunger, Malnutrition and Poverty

Undernourished population: FAO, *The State of Food Insecurity in the World, 2003* (Rome: FAO, 2003).

Underweight, wasting, stunting, safe water: *SWC, 2003.*

Population in poverty: World Bank, *World Development Indicators, 2003 (WDI).*

Table 4: Economic and Development Indicators

GNP data, PPP data, distribution of income or consumption, central government expenditures, per capita energy consumption, annual deforestation: *WDI, 2003.*

Human Development Indicators rank, public education expenditures, military expenditures: *HDR, 2003.*

Table 5: Economic Globalization

Exports, imports, net private capital flows, gross capital formation, investment, aid, debt: *WDI, 2003.*

Table 6: United States – National Hunger and Poverty Trends

Total population: U.S. Census Bureau, data posted at http://eire.census.gov/popest/data/national.php.

Food insecurity prevalence: U.S. Department of Agriculture (USDA), *Household Food Security in the United States, 2002.* Food Assistance and Research Nutrition Service, Report No. 35 (FANRR-35). October, 2003. Report posted at http://www.ers.usda.gov/publications/fanrr35/.

Infant mortality: Centers for Disease Control and Prevention, National Center for Health Statistics, *Births, Marriages, Divorces, and Deaths: Provisional Data for 2001,* data posted at http://www.cdc.gov/nchs/products/pubs/pubd/nvsr/50/50-16.htm.

National poverty rate, poverty rates by race, region and age: U.S. Census Bureau, *Poverty in the United States: 2002.* September 2003. Report posted at http://www.census.gov/hhes/www/poverty02.html.

Unemployment by race: U.S. Department of Labor, Bureau of Labor Statistics, data posted at http://www.bls.gov/cps/#charunem.

Income: U.S. Census Bureau, *Income in the United States: 2002.* September 2003. Historical Income Tables-Household, data posted at http://www.census.gov/hhes/www/income02.html.

Table 7: United States – State Hunger and Poverty Trends

Total population: U.S. Census Bureau, data posted at http://www.census.gov.

Food insecurity prevalence: USDA, *Household Food Security in the United States, 2002.* Food Assistance and Research Nutrition Service, Report No. 35 (FANRR-35). Report posted at http://www.ers.usda.gov/publications/fanrr35/.

Infant mortality: Centers for Disease Control and Prevention, National Vital Statistics Report, Volume 52, Number 2. *Infant Mortality Statistics.* September 2003, 18, http://www.cdc.gov/nchs/data/nvsr/nvsr52/nvsr52_02.pdf.

Poverty: U.S. Census Bureau, *Poverty in the United States: 2002,* data posted at http://www.census.gov/hhes/www/poverty01.html.

Unemployment by state: U.S. Department of Labor, Bureau of Labor Statistics, data posted at http://www.bls.gov/lau/lastrk02.htm.

Table 8: United States – Nutrition and Assistance Programs

Food stamp participation: USDA, Food and Nutrition Service Program Data, http://www.fns.usda.gov/pd/fsfypart.htm.

Special Supplemental Nutrition Program for Women, Infants and Children (WIC) participation: USDA, Food and Nutrition Service Program data, http://www.fns.usda.gov/pd/wifypart.htm.

Temporary Assistance for Needy Families (TANF): U.S. Department of Health and Human Services, Administration for Children and Families, data posted at http://www.acf.dhhs.gov/news/stats/2002tanfrecipients.htm.

Acronyms

CIDA Canadian International Development Agency

CIS Commonwealth of Independent States (former Soviet Union)

CPS Current Population Survey

DES Dietary Energy Supply

EITC Earned Income Tax Credit

ERS Economic Research Service of the U.S. Department of Agriculture

FAO Food and Agriculture Organization of the United Nations

FDI Foreign Direct Investment

G-8 Group of Eight (United States, Great Britain, Germany, France, Canada, Japan, Italy and Russia)

GAO U.S. Government Accounting Office

GDI Gross Domestic Investment

GDP Gross Domestic Product

GNP Gross National Product

HDI Human Development Index

HIPC Highly Indebted Poor Country

HUD U.S. Department of Housing and Urban Development

IFAD International Fund for Agricultural Development

IFIs International Financial Institutions

IFPRI International Food Policy Research Institute

IMF International Monetary Fund

IMR Infant Mortality Rate

LDCs Least Developed Countries

MCA Millennium Challenge Account

MDGs Millennium Development Goals

NAHO National Anti-Hunger Organizations

NGO Nongovernmental Organization

ODA Official Development Assistance

OECD Organization for Economic Cooperation and Development

PPP Purchasing Power Parity

PRSP Poverty Reduction Strategy Paper

TANF Temporary Assistance for Needy Families

TEFAP The Emergency Food Assistance Program

UNCTAD U.N. Conference on Trade and Development

UNDP U.N. Development Program

UNICEF U.N. Children's Fund

USAID U.S. Agency for International Development

USDA U.S. Department of Agriculture

WFP World Food Program

WIC Special Supplemental Nutrition Program for Women, Infants and Children

WHO World Health Organization

WTO World Trade Organization

Glossary

24-hour recall – A dietary assessment tool used to measure undernourishment. A group of subjects recount amounts and types of foods eaten over a 24-hour period. Data analysts then determine consumption rates or nutrient deficiency levels of the group.

Alliance to End Hunger – A coalition of anti-hunger activists that includes religious bodies, businesses, universities, civil rights groups, labor unions and others. The mission of the Alliance to End Hunger is to engage diverse institutions more deeply in an effort to win the shifts in U.S. public opinion, institutions and policy that could dramatically reduce hunger in the United States and internationally.

Anemia – A condition in which the hemoglobin concentration (the number of red blood cells) is lower than normal due to disease or as a result of a deficiency of one or more essential nutrients such as iron.

Anthropometrical measures – Comparative measurements of the human body. Anthropometric measurements – including height, weight and head circumference – are commonly used as indices of growth and development for infants and children. Since stunting and wasting are telltale signs of undernourishment, anthrometric measurements can be used to gauge levels and severity of hunger.

Assets – Legal property of material value, such as land title. Under most developed legal systems, assets can be borrowed against or converted to cash, increasing solvency (the ability to meet one's needs).

Block grants – Federal government lump-sum payments to the states, which then have wide discretion over the use of these funds.

Child mortality rate – The annual number of deaths of children between ages 1 and 5 per 1,000 live births.

Chronic hunger – A prolonged, consistent lack of food and nutrition that slowly erodes one's health and well-being.

Civil society – The sphere of civic action outside of the government comprised of citizens' groups, nongovernmental organizations, religious congregations, labor unions and foundations.

Civil society organizations – Voluntary popular organizations and associations through which individuals work together to pursue interests, values and ideas for their perceptions of the common good.

Community food security – Refers to the level of availability, access to and use of food in a community.

Cretinism – Physical and mental retardation due to iodine deficiency.

Current Population Survey (CPS) – A monthly survey of households conducted by the U.S. Census Bureau to collect statistics on the national labor force. Since 1995, the CPS has been accompanied by a Food Security Supplement (CPS-FSS), employed by the U.S. Department of Agriculture to assess rates of food insecurity in the United States.

Daily calorie requirement – The average number of calories needed to sustain normal levels of activity and health, taking into account age, sex, body weight and climate; on average, about 2,350 calories per person per day.

Debt relief – Measures to reduce the debt owed by developing country governments to either private lenders (commercial banks like Citibank), governments (like Germany or the United States) or international financial institutions (like the International Monetary Fund or World Bank).

Debt service – The sum of repayments of principal and payments of interest on debt.

Democratization – The process by which political systems move toward democratic principles and practices, such as open multiparty regime with regular and fair elections, universal suffrage, freedom of the press and other civil liberties.

Developed countries – Also called "industrial countries" or "the North," these are high-income countries, which the World Bank defines as having a gross national income per capita in 1999 of $9,266 or more. Most developed countries have an industrial economy, and most people living in these countries have a high economic standard of living, though significant populations also may live in poverty. Currently, about 50 countries in the world are considered high income, and their combined population is about 0.9 billion, less than one-sixth of the world's population.

Developing countries – Low- and middle-income countries in which most people have a lower standard of living with access to fewer goods and services than do most people in high-income countries. Also known as the "Third World," "the South" and the "less-developed" countries. Currently, about 125 countries are considered developing countries and home to approximately 5 billion people.

Dietary diversity (as a measure of undernourishment) – The number of different foods or food groups consumed by an individual or household over a given period of time. This measurement can serve as an indicator of food access.

Dietary energy supply (DES) – The total daily food supply, expressed in calories, available within a country for human consumption.

Earned Income Tax Credit (EITC) – A U.S. federal government program that reduces or eliminates taxes for many low-income working people and, in some cases of very low incomes, provides funds.

Empowerment – Measures that expand poor people's ability and access to participate in, negotiate with, influence, control and hold accountable institutions that affect their lives. Broadly, it is the expansion of freedom of choice and action. It is a participatory process that places decision-making responsibility and the resources to act into the hands of those who will benefit.

Fair market value – For housing, a standard of measure set by the U.S. Department of Housing and Urban Development that "fair market rent" does not exceed 30 percent of a family's income.

Famine – An extreme collapse in local availability and access to food that causes a widespread rise in deaths from outright starvation or hunger-related illnesses.

Fertility rate – The average number of children born by women during their lifetimes, used as a measure of long-term population changes.

Food access – The ability to physically acquire food. Poor people's access to food is often limited by lack of money, lack of transportation and illness in a family.

Food and Agriculture Organization of the United Nations (FAO) – U.N. agency specializing in agriculture, forestry, fisheries and rural development. FAO was founded with a mandate to raise levels of nutrition and standards of living, improve agricultural productivity and better the condition of rural populations.

Food availability – The existence of sufficient food in an area, country or community, either through local agricultural production or importation, to feed its inhabitants. Drought is one cause of insufficient food availability and can result in famine.

Food use – An aspect of food security that considers how food is prepared and used by the body. For example, a sick person may have access to food available in his or her community, yet his or her body will be unable to absorb the nutrients from the food due to illness.

Food insecurity – A condition of uncertain availability of or ability to acquire safe, nutritious food in a socially acceptable way.

Food security – For every person, assured access to enough nutritious food to sustain an active and healthy life with dignity. Includes food availability, food access and appropriate food use.

Food self-reliance – A strategy where countries strive to boost harvests and diversify agricultural production to increase exports and food availability for domestic consumption.

Food self-sufficiency – A strategy whereby countries, communities or regions rely exclusively on their own food production.

Food sovereignty – The right of each nation to maintain and develop its own capacity to produce its basic foods, respecting cultural and productive diversity.

Food stamps – Credit for low-income people to buy food in retail stores. Previously issued in the form of coupons and now issued electronically with debit cards.

Foreign aid: See *Official development assistance.*

Foreign direct investment (FDI) – Investment from abroad into ownership and control of productive activities in a country, as opposed to more passive stock and bond investment.

Globalization – In economic terms, it is the process of increasing integration of national economies at the global level. In social terms, the increasing interconnectedness of peoples and cultures and the increasing exchange of ideas.

Goiter – Enlargement of the thyroid gland (causing a swelling in the front of the neck) due to iodine deficiency.

Green Revolution – Modification of agriculture in the 1960s and 1970s to improve agricultural production through the use of new technologies, including new machines, fertilizer, pesticides, irrigation and cultivation methods, and high-yielding varieties of grains, such as rice, wheat and corn. This revolution was meant to make India and other Asian countries self-sufficient in food production.

Gross domestic investment (GDI) – Total investment in new facilities or productive capacity, usually expressed as a proportion of gross domestic product.

Gross domestic product (GDP) – The value of all goods and services produced within a nation during a specified period, usually a year.

Gross national product (GNP) – The value of all goods and services produced by a country's citizens, wherever they are located.

Group of 8 – The wealthiest industrial countries: Canada, France, Germany, Italy, Japan, Russia, United Kingdom and United States (formerly the Group of 7, excluding Russia).

Heavily Indebted Poor Countries (HIPC) – Adopted in 1996, this initiative provides assistance to eligible countries to reduce external debt burdens to sustainable levels, enabling them to service their external debt without the need for further debt relief and without compromising economic growth. Assistance under this initiative is limited to countries that have established a strong track record of policy implementation to ensure that debt relief is used effectively.

Human Development Index (HDI) – As used by the U. N. Development Program, a measure of well-being based on economic growth, educational attainment and health.

Human rights – The basic rights and freedoms afforded all human beings, including the right to food and other basic necessities, the right to life and liberty, freedom of thought and expression, and equality before the law. A summary list can be found in the U. N. Universal Declaration of Human Rights.

Hunger – A condition in which people do not get enough food to provide the nutrients (carbohydrate, fat, protein, vitamins, minerals and water) for fully productive, active and healthy lives.

Hunger season – The seasonality of agricultural harvests leave many poor people hungry during certain months of the year because they rely on agriculture for both food supply and income. During this time, food availability and food access are limited.

Industrial countries – Countries in which most people have a high economic standard of living (though there are often significant poverty populations). Also called the "developed countries" or "the North."

Infant mortality rate (IMR) – The annual number of deaths of infants under age 1 per 1,000 live births.

Inflation – An increase in overall prices, which leads to a decrease in purchasing power.

Informal sector – Economic activities beyond the effective reach of taxing or regulatory authorities, also known as "underground," "hidden," "gray" or "shadow" market activities.

Infrastructure – The basic facilities, services and installations needed for the functioning of a community or society such as transportation, communications, financial, educational and health care systems.

Input – The resources that are used in farm production, such as chemicals, equipment, feed, seed and energy.

Intellectual property rights – Guarantees to individuals, businesses or organizations of exclusive rights to the intangible creations, such as an invention, an industrial process or an artistic work. Includes patents, copyrights, trademarks and legally protected trade secrets.

International financial institutions (IFIs) – Intergovernmental agencies, including the International Monetary Fund and the World Bank, which make loans to governments.

International Monetary Fund (IMF) – An international organization that makes loans to countries with short-term foreign exchange and monetary problems. These loans are conditioned upon the borrowing country's willingness to adopt IMF-approved economic policies.

Jubilee 2000 – A worldwide movement calling for cancellation of the unpayable foreign debt of heavily indebted poor countries by 2000.

Jubilee 2000 USA – A movement in the United States, working in collaboration with Jubilee 2000, calling for cancellation of poor-country debt. That cancellation includes acknowledgement of responsibility by lenders and borrowers, as well as mechanisms to prevent recurrence of such debts.

Least developed countries (LDCs) – According to the United Nations, LDCs are low-income countries that suffer from long-term handicaps to economic growth, in particular low levels of human resource development and/or severe structural weakness.

Livelihood security – The ability of a household to meet its basic needs for food, shelter, water, sanitation, health care and education.

Living wage – The wage level a person must earn to live at an adequate standard of living.

Low birth-weight infants – Babies born weighing 2,500 grams (5 pounds, 8 ounces) or less who are especially vulnerable to illness and death during the first months of life.

Macroeconomic policies – Policies related to general levels of production and income, and the relationship among economic sectors. "Microeconomics" deals with individual units of activity, such as a firm, household or prices for a specific product.

Malnutrition – A condition resulting from inadequate consumption (undernutrition) or excessive consumption of a nutrient, which can impair physical and mental health, and can be the cause or result of infectious diseases.

Market economy – An economy in which prices for goods and services are set primarily by private markets rather than by government planning or regulation.

Market liberalization – The degree to which a market is hampered by outside influence, such as tariffs or barriers. The less impediments, the more liberalized a market is said to be.

Millennium Challenge Account (MCA) – The MCA was designed to absorb increased development assistance funding from the U.S. government and to channel those funds to poor countries in the form of grants. Countries will qualify for MCA funding if their leaders govern responsibly, plan to implement development initiatives and operate with economic transparency.

Millennium Development Goals (MDGs) – The MDGs are a set of objectives for the betterment of quality of life for all people first laid out in a series of international conferences in the 1990s, then officially adopted by the United Nations in 2000 with the Millennium Declaration. The goals serve as a road map for development to be achieved by 2015.

Microcredit – Small, short-term loans to low-income people, who are too poor to borrow from commercial banks to help them start their own businesses, generate income and raise their standard of living.

Microenterprises – A business with five or fewer employees and little working capital.

Micronutrients – Vitamins, major minerals and trace elements needed for a healthy, balanced diet. Micronutrient deficiencies also are called "hidden hunger." "Macronutrients" are protein, carbohydrates and fat.

Glossary

Minimum caloric requirement – See *Daily calorie requirement*.

Morbidity – The proportion of sickness or of a specific disease in a geographic locality.

Multilateral aid – Financial or material assistance channeled to developing countries via international organizations such as the World Bank, the European Union or U.N. agencies (as distinguished from bilateral aid).

National Anti-Hunger Organizations (NAHO) – A coalition of organizations, formerly known as the Medford Group, working together to end hunger in the United States. Members include: America's Second Harvest, Bread for the World, Center on Hunger and Poverty, Congressional Hunger Center, End Hunger Network, Food Research and Action Center (FRAC), Interfaith Hunger Coordinators, MAZON: A Jewish Response to Hunger, RESULTS and Share Our Strength.

Nongovernmental organizations (NGOs) – Groups and institutions that are entirely or largely independent of government and that have primarily humanitarian or cooperative rather than commercial objectives. They include private agencies in industrial countries that support international development; organized indigenous groups; member-groups in villages; charitable and religious associations; independent cooperatives; community associations; water-user societies; women's groups; and pastoral associations. Citizen groups that raise awareness and influence policy also are NGOs.

North-South – Pertaining to relations between the rich countries of the North and the poor countries of the South.

Obesity – A form of malnutrition resulting in severe overweight in which one consumes too many calories over a period of time. Obesity is marked specifically by an excessive amount of body fat in relation to lean body mass.

Official development assistance (ODA) – The term used by the Organization for Economic Cooperation and Development for grants and loans to developing countries undertaken by governments to pursue economic development at concessional financial terms.

Organization for Economic Cooperation and Development (OECD) – A group of 30 industrialized countries that pursue economic development while fostering good governance in the public sector and in corporate activity. Members include: Australia, Austria, Belgium, Canada, Czech Republic, Denmark, Finland, France, Germany, Greece, Hungary, Iceland, Ireland, Italy, Japan, Korea, Luxembourg, Mexico, Netherlands, New Zealand, Norway, Poland, Portugal, Slovak Republic, Spain, Sweden, Switzerland, Turkey, United Kingdom and United States. The Commission of the European Union also takes part in the OECD's work.

Political will – Impetus or motivation by political leaders to pass legislation or measures that create change or political movement on an issue.

Poverty – The lack of sufficient money or resources to provide the basic needs of survival for oneself and one's family.

Poverty line – An official measure of poverty defined by national governments. In the United States, it is calculated as three times the cost of the USDA's Thrifty Food Plan, which provides a less-than-adequate diet. In 2003 the poverty line was $15,260 for a family of three, $18,400 for a family of four. Poverty also can be measured internationally, by determining the percentage of per capita income levels under $1 or $2 per day for a population. Income levels are adjusted for purchasing power parity so that they are comparable from country to country.

Private investment – Commitment of funds by private individuals or corporations.

Privatization – The transfer of ownership of companies and delivery of services from government to private firms or agencies.

Protein-energy malnutrition – Inadequate protein and/or energy intake that occurs due to macronutrient and micronutrient deficiencies of an inadequate diet. Protein-energy malnutrition results in loss of energy and affects many people in developing countries.

Public investment – Investment of funds by governments and intergovernmental organizations.

Public policy advocacy – Political action taken by citizens focused on the policies, programs and practices of governments, international financial institutions and corporations.

Purchasing power parity (PPP) – An estimate of the amount of money required to purchase comparable goods in different countries, usually expressed in U.S. dollars.

Recession – A period in which a country's gross domestic product declines in two or more consecutive three-month periods; a period of reduced economic activity that is less severe than a full-fledged economic crisis or "depression."

Repatriation – The return of persons who have been involuntarily displaced by war, famine, persecution or other extreme circumstances to their country of origin.

Right to Food Resolution – Legislation enacted by the U.S. Congress in 1976 declaring "the right of every person in the country and throughout the world to food and a nutritionally adequate diet."

Rule of law – Law by government that is fair and enforceable.

Social safety nets – Government policies and charitable programs designed to ensure basic needs are met among low-income, disabled and other vulnerable social groups. Safety nets may also provide protection against risks, such as lost income, limited access to credit or devastation from natural disaster.

Sovereignty – Supreme independent political authority, generally residing in national governments.

Starvation – Suffering or death from extreme or prolonged lack of food.

Stunting – Failure to grow to normal height caused by chronic undernutrition during the formative years of childhood.

Subsidy – A direct or indirect benefit granted by a government for the production or distribution (including export) of a good or to supplement other services.

Sustainability – Society's ability to shape its economic and social systems so as to maintain both natural resources and human life.

Sustainable agriculture – Agriculture that is practiced in a way that does not deplete the earth of natural resources, does not harm the surrounding ecological equilibrium and allows for continued farming on the same land year after year.

Sustainable development – The reduction of hunger and poverty in environmentally sound ways. It includes: meeting basic human needs, expanding economic opportunities, protecting and enhancing the environment, and promoting pluralism and democratic participation.

Temporary hunger – Food insecurity that occurs for a defined period of time and does not recur. Crisis situations such as hurricanes often cause temporary hunger.

Transition economies – Former communist states in Eastern Europe and Central Asia.

U.N. Millennium Project Task Force on Hunger – One of 10 expert-led task forces set up to recommend the best strategies for achieving the Millennium Development Goals. The hunger task force will submit a recommended plan of implementation for the world to cut the number of hungry people in half by 2015.

Under-5 mortality rate – The annual number of deaths of children younger than 5 per 1,000 live births. A high rate correlates closely with hunger and malnutrition.

Underemployment – Partial or inadequate employment of an individual or the labor force as a whole.

Undernutrition – A condition resulting from inadequate consumption of calories, protein and/or nutrients to meet the basic physical requirements for an active and healthy life. Measured by the Food and Agricultural Organization of the United Nations by country as the number of people and the percentage of the population consuming less than 1,800 calories per day.

Underweight – A condition in which a person is below the average, expected or healthy weight for her or his age and height.

Unemployment – The state of being without work, usually applied to those not working involuntarily.

Uprooted people – People displaced against their will from their communities, including refugees who flee homelands, people displaced within their own countries, and people living in "refugee-like" circumstances who are not legally recognized as refugees.

Vulnerability to hunger – A condition of individuals, households, communities or nations who have enough to eat most of the time, but whose poverty makes them especially susceptible to hunger due to changes in the economy, climate, political conditions or personal circumstances.

Wasting – A condition in which a person is seriously below the normal weight for his or her height due to acute undernutrition or a medical condition.

Welfare – Financial and other assistance provided by government and private charitable organizations to people in need in the areas of nutrition, education, health care and employment.

World Bank – An intergovernmental agency that makes long-term loans to the governments of developing nations. Formally called the International Bank for Reconstruction and Development.

World Health Organization (WHO) – The U.N. special agency for health that strives to attain the highest possible level of health for all people.

World Trade Organization (WTO) – An international organization, headquartered in Geneva, established in 1995 to enforce the Uruguay Round global trade agreement.

Acknowledgments

We are deeply grateful for the valuable insights provided by sponsors and colleagues who contributed to this report.

A special thanks to Mark Nord, sociologist for the Food Assistance Branch of the Economic Research Service, U.S. Department of Agriculture, and John Staatz, professor and co-director of the Food Security Cooperative Agreement, Department of Agricultural Economics at Michigan State University, who presented on issues related to U.S. and African food security at the April 2003 consultation for the report.

The following sponsors and colleagues participated in the expert consultation and/or reviewed a draft manuscript of the report.

Issac Akinyele, Michael Altamura, Fran Beckar, Lynn Brantly, John Cook, Ed Cooney, Stacy Dean, Lisa Dreier, Bill Ewing, Rafael Flor, Bill Guyton, Janine Jones, Anne Kim, Michael Laracy, Judith Lewis, Jo Anne Lyon, Hilary Marston, Anthony Matthews, Milla McLachlan, Courtney Miller, John Monahan, Mark Nord, Lynn Parker, Charles Riemenschneider, Andy Rivas, Dottie Rosenbaum, Barry Sackin, John Sauer, Gerhard Schmalbruch, Alex de Sherbinin, Abigail Spring, John Staatz, Erinn Staley, Jim Sundholm, Betty Voskuil, Vera Weill-Halle, William Widman, Margaret Ziegler.

The following colleagues assisted with research trips to Louisiana, Mississippi, Montana, Oregon and Texas and/or met with report staff to discuss issues related to U.S. and international food security.

Betsy Alexander, John Alvord, Julie Brewer, Linda Cage, Judy Carter, Elizabeth Coleman, Evelyn Knolle, Nettie Fields, Julie Fleck, Tom Freedman, Cassandra Garrison, Cheryl Goers, Dorothy Grady, Mike Hanback, Lew Hille, Nan Johnson, Richard King, Mark Prell, Dan Pruett, Mark Ragan, Charles Riemenschneider, Cathy and Felipe Salinas, Fr. Mike Seifert, Emily Elliott Shaw, Eric Schockman, Kim Thomas, Barb Weaver, Zelinda Welch, Richard Whitwer, Patti Whitney Wise.

Daniel Martin and Christopher Rhodes assisted in early research and editorial discussions of the report.

We also extend our gratitude to Bread for the World/Bread for the World Institute staff who provided comments, guidance and support in the research, writing and production of the report.

Sponsors

Associate Publisher (Gifts of $25,000 or more)

International Fund for Agricultural Development (IFAD) is an international financial institution and specialized agency of the United Nations headquartered in Rome. Established as a result of the 1974 World Food Conference, IFAD has an exclusive mission: to work with the poorest populations in rural areas of developing countries to eliminate hunger and poverty, enhance food security, raise productivity and incomes, and improve the quality of lives. IFAD adopts and advocates a targeted, community-based approach that emphasizes empowering rural poor people and promoting their access to productive resources.

Via del Serafico, 107
00142 Rome, Italy
Phone: 39 6 54591
Fax: 39 6 5043463
E-mail: ifad@ifad.org

1775 K Street NW, Suite 410
Washington, DC 20006 USA
Phone: (202) 331-9099
Fax: (202) 331-9366
Web site: www.ifad.org

Benefactor (Gifts of $10,000 or more)

Christian Children's Fund (CCF) is a global force for children, helping the world's poorest and most vulnerable children survive and thrive to reach their full potential. One of the world's oldest and most respected international child development organizations, CCF works in approximately 30 countries and assists approximately 4.6 million children and families worldwide, regardless of race, creed or origin.

CCF is a member of CCF International, a network of affiliated worldwide organizations, working for the well-being of children in 51 countries. CCF International supports locally led initiatives that strengthen families and communities, helping them overcome poverty and protect the rights of their children. CCF programs seek to be holistic and comprehensive, incorporating health, education, nutrition and livelihood interventions to protect, nurture and develop children in a sustainable way. CCF works in any environment where poverty, conflict and disaster threaten the well-being of children.

2821 Emerywood Parkway
Richmond, VA 23294
Phone: (800) 776-6767
Web site: www.christianchildrensfund.org

The Community of Christ World Hunger Committee seeks to engage the church and others in a response to the needs of hungry people throughout the world. Its primary purpose is to support programs of food production, storage and distribution; fund projects to provide potable water; supply farm animals; instruct in food preparation and nutrition; and educate in marketing strategies for produce. It also seeks to advocate for the hungry and educate about the causes and alleviation of hunger in the world.

The majority of proposals reviewed by the committee originate with Outreach International and World Accord, agencies recognized by the church as engaged in participatory human development that is global in scope. Direct grants to Community of Christ jurisdictions for community hunger projects, as well as disaster relief, also are considered.

1001 W. Walnut
Independence, MO 64050-3562 USA
Phone: (816) 833-1000, ext. 3073
Fax: (816) 521-3096
Web site: www.CofChrist.org/hunger

Covenant World Relief is the relief and development arm of The Evangelical Covenant Church. Covenant World Relief was formed in response to the Covenant's historic commitment to being actively involved in Christ's mission to respond to the spiritual and physical needs of others.

5101 N. Francisco Avenue
Chicago, IL 60625-3611 USA
Phone: (773) 784-3000
Fax: (773) 784-4366
Web site: www.covchurch.org

Episcopal Relief & Development is a compassionate response of the Episcopal Church to human suffering in the world. For over 60 years, ERD has assisted people in more than 100 countries. Working with the Anglican Communion as well as ecumenical partners, it provides emergency assistance in times of disaster, rebuilds devastated communities after the immediate crisis is over, and offers long-term solutions to help people sustain safer, healthier and more productive lives.

815 Second Avenue
New York, NY 10017 USA
Phone: (800) 334-7626, ext. 5129
Fax: (212) 983-6377
E-mail: er-d@er-d.org
Web site: www.er-d.org

Evangelical Lutheran Church in America World Hunger Program is a 30-year-old ministry that confronts hunger and poverty through emergency relief, long-term sustainable development and organizing, education, advocacy and stewardship of financial resources. Seventy-two percent of the program works internationally and 28 percent works within the United States. Lutheran World Relief (Baltimore) and Lutheran World Federation (Geneva) are key implementing partners in international relief and development throughout the world.

8765 W. Higgins Road
Chicago, IL 60631-4190 USA
Phone: (800) 638-3522, ext. 2709
Fax: (773) 380-2707

The Independent Presbyterian Church Foundation is a public charity established in 1973 by the congregation of the Independent Presbyterian Church. It holds and administers all endowment funds received by the church. Composed primarily of congregational gifts and bequests, these endowments represent an added dimension of Christian stewardship that complements rather than supplants strong congregational giving. Each endowment fund is governed by terms established by the donors or by various church-related governing bodies. The purposes of funds held and managed by the Foundation are administered to support the mission and ministry of the Independent Presbyterian Church as that mission and ministry is defined by the session of the church. The Foundation distributes funds to support internal programs and ministries as well as external organizations doing the work of Christ in the world.

> 3100 Highland Avenue
> Birmingham, AL 35205 USA
> Phone: (205) 933-1830
> Fax: (205) 933-1836
> Web site: www.ipc-usa.org

The Lutheran Church Missouri Synod World Relief/ Human Care provides emergency relief and sustainable development funding for domestic and international projects. LCMS World Relief provides grants for Lutheran congregations and social ministry organizations in the United States as well as other groups with Lutheran involvement that are engaged in ministries of human care. Domestic support also is provided to Lutheran Disaster Response and Lutheran Immigration and Refugee Service. International relief and development assistance is channeled through the Synod's mission stations and partner churches as well as through Lutheran World Relief.

> 1333 S. Kirkwood Road
> St. Louis, MO 63122-7295 USA
> Phone: (800) 248-1930
> Fax: (314) 996-1128
> E-mail: lcms.worldrelief@lcms.org

For 35 years, the **Presbyterian Hunger Program** has provided a channel for congregations to respond to hunger in the United States and around the world. With a commitment to the ecumenical sharing of human and financial resources, the program provides support for direct food relief efforts, sustainable development and public policy advocacy. A network of 100 Hunger Action Enablers leads the Presbyterian Church (USA) in the study of hunger issues, engagement with communities of need, advocacy for just public policies, and the movement toward simpler corporate and personal lifestyles.

> 100 Witherspoon Street
> Louisville, KY 40202-1396 USA
> Phone: (502) 569-5816
> Fax: (502) 569-8963
> Web site: www.pcusa.org/hunger

Share Our Strength (SOS) works toward ending hunger and poverty in the United States and abroad by supporting food assistance, treating malnutrition and other consequences of hunger, and promoting economic independence among people in need. SOS meets immediate demands for food while investing in long-term solutions to hunger and poverty by mobilizing both industry and individuals in such efforts as Operation Frontline, a food and nutrition education program that trains culinary professionals and financial planners who volunteer

to teach six-week cooking, nutrition, food budgeting and financial planning classes to low-income individuals; Taste of the Nation, the nation's largest culinary benefit to fight hunger; and Writers Harvest: The National Reading, the nation's largest literary benefit.

> 733 15th Street NW, Suite 640
> Washington, DC 20005 USA
> Phone: (202) 393-2925
> Fax: (202) 347-5868
> E-mail: info@strength.org
> Web site: www.strength.org

The U.N. Development Program (UNDP) is the United Nation's global development network, advocating for change and connecting countries to knowledge, experience and resources to help people build a better life. UNDP is on the ground in 166 countries, working with them on their own solutions to global and national development challenges. As they develop local capacity, they draw on the people of UNDP and its wide range of partners.

> 1 U.N. Plaza, 20th Floor
> New York, NY 10017 USA
> Web site: www.undp.org

The U.N. World Food Program (WFP) is the food-aid arm of the United Nations and the primary U.N. agency fighting to eradicate world hunger. WFP strives to provide "food for life" to sustain victims of man-made and natural disasters; "food for growth" aims to improve the nutrition and quality of life of the most vulnerable people at critical times in their lives; and "food for work" seeks to help build assets and promote the self-reliance of poor people and communities, particularly through labor-intensive work programs. WFP provides commodities to least developed and low-income food-deficit countries, with a focus on feeding the most vulnerable people: women, children and the elderly. WFP envisions a world in which every woman, man and child has access, at all times, to the food needed for an active and healthy life.

> Via Cesare Giulio Viola, 68
> Parco dei Medici
> 00148 Rome, Italy
> Phone: (39-06) 6513-1
> Fax: (39-06) 6590-632/637
> Web site: www.wfp.org

The United Methodist Committee on Relief (UMCOR) was formed in 1940 in response to the suffering of people during World War II. It was a "voice of conscience" expressing the concern of the church for the disrupted and devastated lives churned out by the war. UMCOR has expanded its ministry to more than 70 countries by ministering with compassion to "persons in need, through programs and services which provide immediate relief and long-term attention to the root causes of their need." Focusing on refugee, hunger and disaster ministries, the work of UMCOR, a program department of the General Board of Global Ministries of the United Methodist Church, is carried out through direct services and a worldwide network of national and international church agencies that cooperate in the task of alleviating human suffering.

> 475 Riverside Drive, Room 330
> New York, NY 10115 USA
> Phone: (212) 870-3816
> Hotline: (800) 841-1235
> Fax: (212) 870-3624
> E-mail: umcor@gbgm-umc.org

The World Cocoa Foundation is a comprehensive program which "takes science into the field," improving production efficiency, increasing farmer yields and using cocoa to promote production reforestation of degraded tropical lands – all in a sustainable, environmentally responsible manner. The Foundation is supported by worldwide chocolate industry (manufacturers and processors).

Today the world consumes about 3 million tons of cocoa beans annually. And the worldwide demand for chocolate, the high quality product made from cacao beans, continues to increase. Unfortunately, an estimated one-third of the world's cocoa crop is lost to pests and diseases every year. Much of Brazil's cocoa crop already has been destroyed, and Indonesian cocoa is at risk. If serious cocoa diseases reach West Africa, where 70 percent of the world's cocoa is grown, the result could be devastating for cocoa farmers who count on cocoa for much needed income.

> 8320 Old Courthouse Road, Suite 300
> Vienna, VA 22182
> Phone: (703) 790-5011
> Fax: (703) 790-5752
> Web site: www.worldcocoafoundation.org

Sponsors (Gifts of $5,000 or more)

The Adventist Development and Relief Agency (ADRA) International is an independent humanitarian agency established in 1984 for the specific purpose of providing individual and community development and disaster relief. Committed to improving quality of human life, ADRA serves people in need without regard to their ethnic, political or religious association.

ADRA's development and relief work is divided among five core activities: food security, economic development, primary health, disaster preparedness and response, and basic education. In addition to feeding the hungry, ADRA works to prevent hunger through long-term development programs. Struggling families and individuals learn how to support and feed themselves by using agricultural methods that do not hurt the environment. ADRA also helps improve access to food and ensures equitable distribution of food among community members.

> 12501 Old Columbia Pike
> Silver Spring, MD 20904 USA
> Phone: (800) 937-2372
> Web site: www.adra.org

America's Second Harvest is the nation's largest domestic hunger relief organization. Through a network of more than 200 food banks and food-rescue programs, America's Second Harvest provides emergency food assistance to more than 23 million hungry Americans each year, 9 million of whom are children. Last year, America's Second Harvest distributed 1.8 billion pounds of food to needy Americans, serving all 50 states and Puerto Rico. Its goal is to end hunger in America.

> 35 E. Wacker Drive, Suite 2000
> Chicago, IL 60601
> Phone: (312) 263-2303
> Fax: (312) 263-5626
> E-mail: feedback@secondharvest.org
> Web site: www.secondharvest.org

Baptist World Aid (BWAid) works through Baptist communities around the world, mitigating suffering and providing long-range help for persons in need, regardless of religion, nationality, tribe or class. BWAid also helps poor people avoid situations of famine and malnourishment and improves their capacity for self-help and wage earning.

> 405 N. Washington Street
> Falls Church, VA 22046 USA
> Phone: (703) 790-8980
> Fax: (703) 790-5719
> E-mail: bwaid@bwanet.org
> Web site: www.bwanet.org

Canadian Foodgrains Bank is a specialized food-program agency established in 1982 and now operated by 13 church-related relief and development organizations. It collects substantial amounts of food grain donations directly from Canadian farmers and more than 200 community groups that collectively grow crops for donation to the Canadian Foodgrains Bank. The approximately $3.9 million per year in grain and cash donations, combined with matching support from the Canadian International Development Agency, are used to provide food assistance and food security support to food-deficit countries and communities around the world to meet immediate food needs and support the longer-term ability of communities and households to feed themselves. In addition, the Canadian Foodgrains Bank engages in focused public policy research and advocacy in the areas of agricultural trade policy, Canadian aid policy and the application of a human rights approach to reducing hunger.

> Box 767, 400-280 Smith Street
> Winnipeg Manitoba
> Canada R3C 2L4
> Phone: (204) 944-1993
> Fax: (204) 943-2597
> E-mail: cfgb@foodgrainsbank.ca
> Web site: www.foodgrainsbank.ca

Catholic Relief Services (CRS) is the overseas relief and development agency of the U.S. Catholic community. Founded in 1943, CRS provides more than $300 million in development and relief assistance in more than 80 nations worldwide. Working in partnership with the Catholic church and other local institu-

Sponsors

tions in each country, CRS works to alleviate poverty, hunger and suffering, and supports peace-building and reconciliation initiatives. Assistance is given solely on the basis of need. Even while responding to emergencies, CRS supports more than 2,000 development projects designed to build local self-sufficiency. CRS works in conjunction with Caritas Internationalis and CIDSE, worldwide associations of Catholic relief and development agencies. Together, these groups build the capacity of local nonprofit organizations to provide long-term solutions. In the United States, CRS seeks to educate and build awareness on issues of world poverty and hunger and serves as an advocate for public policy changes in the interest of poor people overseas.

209 W. Fayette Street
Baltimore, MD 21201-3443 USA
Phone: (410) 625-2220
Fax: (410) 685-1635
E-mail: webmaster@catholicrelief.org
Web site: www.catholicrelief.org

Church World Service (CWS) is the global relief, development and refugee-assistance ministry of Protestant, Orthodox and Anglican denominations. Founded in 1946, CWS works in partnership with local organizations worldwide to support sustainable self-help development, meet emergency needs and address the root causes of poverty and powerlessness.

475 Riverside Drive, Suite 700
New York, NY 10115-0050 USA
Phone: (800) 297-1516
Fax: (212) 870-3523
Web site: www.churchworldservice.org

Founded in 1980, **EuronAid** is an operational European network of nongovernmental organizations (NGOs) active in the field of food aid and food security. EuronAid facilitates the implementation of NGO programs funded by the European Commission (EC), undertakes capacity development activities by providing information and training on relevant issues, and promotes critical dialogue between NGOs and the EC on policies related to food aid and food security. EuronAid's professional services include the procurement and logistics of food, agricultural implements and other aid commodities; a door-to-door transport system; access to global and regional suppliers of relevant commodities; and international tendering facilities. EuronAid has 40 active members and partnerships with more than 100 NGOs, including civil society organizations from developing countries. Committed to food security and sustainable development, EuronAid promotes the local and regional purchase of relief goods to stimulate local agricultural production and markets.

P.O. Box 12
NL-2501 CA
The Hague, The Netherlands
Phone: 31 70 3305757
Fax: 31 70 3641701
E-mail: euronaid@euronaid.nl
Web site: www.euronaid.nl

Foods Resource Bank is a Christian response to world hunger. Its goal is for hungry people to know the dignity and pride of feeding themselves by making it possible for them, through sustainable agricultural programs, to produce food for their families with extra to share, barter or sell. Foods Resource Bank endeavors to twin rural and urban communities in "growing projects" in the United States, allowing participants to give a gift only they can give. These volunteers grow crops, sell them in the United States and the resulting money is used by implementing members (many of the mainline denominations) to establish food security programs abroad. Foods Resource Bank creates solidarity between America's bounty and the needs of the world's hungry.

2141 Parkview
Kalamazoo, MI 49008 USA
Phone: (269) 349-3467
Web site: www.FoodsResourceBank.org

Heifer International is a nonprofit charitable organization working to end world hunger by giving cows, goats and other kinds of livestock, along with appropriate training to impoverished, undernourished families around the globe. In turn, these people give to others their animals' offspring, multiplying the benefits of each donated animal. "Passing the gift" is fundamental to Heifer's approach to sustainable development. As people share their animals' offspring with others along with their knowledge and resources, an ever-expanding network of hope, dignity and self-reliance is created that expands the globe.

Since it began in 1944, Heifer has worked directly with millions of families in 128 countries and 38 U.S. states, and has affected the lives of millions more through an average of six pass-on animals for each animal it provides. Each year Heifer's message of hope reaches still others through the media and through its own publications, such as its quarterly *World Ark* magazine. Heifer's three learning centers in Arkansas, California and Massachusetts offer hands-on educational experiences with seminars, service learning projects and hunger immersion experiences.

1015 Louisiana Street
Little Rock, AR 72202 USA
Phone: (501) 907-2600
Fax: (501) 907-2602
Web site: www.heifer.org

Lutheran World Relief (LWR) acts on behalf of U.S. Lutherans in response to natural disasters, humanitarian crises and chronic poverty in some 50 countries in Africa, Asia, Latin America and the Middle East. In partnership with local organizations, LWR supports more than 150 community projects to improve food production, health care, environment and employment, with special emphasis on training and gender equality. LWR monitors legislation on foreign aid and development, and advocates for public policies that address the root causes of hunger and poverty. LWR values the God-given gifts that each person can bring to the task of promoting peace, justice and human dignity. LWR began its work in 1945.

Lutheran World Relief	LWR Office of Public Policy
700 Light Street	122 C Street NW, Suite 125
Baltimore, MD 21230-3850	Washington, DC 20001
USA	USA
Phone: (410) 230-2700	Phone: (202) 783-6887
or (800) LWR-LWR-2	Fax: (202) 783-5328
E-mail: lwr@lwr.org	Web site: www.lwr.org

Mennonite Central Committee (MCC), founded in 1920 by the Mennonite and Brethren in Christ churches in North America, seeks to demonstrate God's love by working among people suffering from poverty, conflict, oppression and natural disaster. MCC serves as a channel of interchange by building relationships that are mutually transformative. MCC strives for peace, justice and dignity of all people by sharing our experiences, resources and faith in Jesus Christ. MCC's priorities include disaster relief, capacity building (including Ten Thousand Villages), peace building and connecting people.

21 S. 12th Street, Box 500
Akron, PA 17501 USA
Phone: (717) 859-1151
Fax: (717) 859-2171
E-mail: mailbox@mcc.org
Web site: www.mcc.org

The mission of **Physicians Against World Hunger** is to alleviate chronic hunger by supporting programs that implement microlending and education to break the hunger cycle. As part of this educational service, beginning in 2003, Physicians Against World Hunger also will make available a speaker to societies and organizations that wish to know more about world hunger.

2 Stowe Road, Suite 13
Peekskill, NY 10566 USA
Phone: (914) 737-8570
Fax: (914) 737-6016
Web site: www.pawh.org

Friends (Gifts under $5,000)

Academy for Educational Development
Board of World Mission of the Moravian Church
Catholic Charities
Christian Reformed World Relief Committee
Church of God
Food for the Hungry
Freedom from Hunger
Islamic Society of North America
MAZON: A Jewish Response to Hunger
Nazarene Compassionate Ministries International
Oxfam America Inc.
Reformed Church in America
Save the Children
United Church of Christ: Justice and Witness Ministries; Wider Church Ministries
U.S. Fund for UNICEF
World Hope International
World Relief

Index